CONCEPTS OF ISLAM SIMPLIFIED

for
Parents, Young Muslims,
New Muslims and Curious Minds

Abu Mustafa Zakariya

Cover design: Hassen Rasool

In the Name of Allah, the Most Kind, the Most Compassionate.

All praise and all gratitude are due to Allah alone, the Lord and Master of all creation.

May Allah's peace and blessings be upon Muhammad, His last and final Messenger, and his family.

For my parents, my wife and my children.

Acknowledgements

I am humbly grateful to Allah, the Almighty, and Extremely Kind. All praises and thanks go to Allah who provided me the opportunity, the means, the ability and the inspiration to undertake this work.

They say 'necessity is the mother of invention', so I start by thanking my dear children, especially my elder two (BJ and CP). Trying, along with my wife, to teach them Islam, forced me to break down the concepts of Islam which can be quite abstract, into something simple enough that little children could understand them. This book is the outcome of that process of digesting and simplifying.

I am indebted to my wonderful mother, who has been blessed with tremendous faith and piety. She taught my siblings and me all about Allah, the Prophet Muhammad (peace be upon him) and Islam from our earliest days. She planted the seeds and nurtured us, and receives all the reward of any good we do. Alongside her, my father has truly been the rock upon whose shoulders we stand. This book would not have been possible without them, and all they have done, and continue to do, for us.

My biggest supporter has been my wife. A beautiful soul who has encouraged me tirelessly even when I wavered along the way. In raising our children we have brainstormed many topics and issues together. She has been my sounding board and biggest reviewer. Without her encouragement, I may well have shied away from publishing.

I owe a great debt of gratitude to those who kindly read and reviewed this book: Faraz, Brother Dawood, Brother Khalid, Brother Omar, and my dear Hana. They took time out of their busy lives and their input has been truly invaluable. I am grateful to Hassen Rasool who kindly designed the book cover. Finally, a special thank you to Ayesha, who kindly edited my book.

Note on Quranic Translations Used

This book contains many Quranic verses (*ayats*) rendered in English. I have always been conscious that English translations of the Quran, despite the best efforts of translators, sometimes struggled to produce prose that native English speakers would regard as natural, or have used archaic English. I have therefore selected from a variety of well-known English translations: Sahih International, Yusuf Ali, Muhammad Sarwar, Mohsin Khan, and M.H. Shakir. Where the English does not seem contemporary from any of them for today's age, I have selected the most suitable version and adjusted to allow a better flow, whilst maintaining the original meaning.

Note on Hadith References

Where hadiths (the teachings or sayings of the Prophet Muhammad, peace be upon him) are quoted, I have referenced the esteemed authors who compiled them.

Note on Mentioning Prophet Muhammad

It is Muslim tradition that whenever Prophet Muhammad is mentioned, the benediction (prayer asking for divine blessings) of 'May Allah's peace and blessings be upon him,' is added. To keep the simple style and flow of this book, this benediction has not been written out, but the Muslim reader is reminded to please add this in their reading.

CONTENTS

Contents

Contents

Contents

Contents

Contents

Introduction

Islam was sent by Allah the Creator, as guidance to mankind. This guidance serves to explain not only who He is, why we are here, where we are going, but also as the instructions and rules for how to live our lives on this earth. Traditional teaching of Islam gives basic and important tenets of belief. However in the modern world this can seem somewhat abstract, and my own experience has been that it does not translate easily to applicability with daily life. Moreover, in the practical aspects of practising Islam, it is easy to get bogged down in the dogma of what is allowed (*halal*) and what is prohibited (*haram*). The essence of Islam, along with simple questions that we all ponder, can be obscured in the vast amount of knowledge within the framework of Islam.

The idea for this book was conceived when my wife and I started teaching Islam to our children. It became evident that clarity and simplicity was needed, especially living in modern times when there are challenges to faith at every corner. Abstract concepts needed to be broken down to something children could grasp. The ideas were crystallised further when I moved on to teaching children in the community, running discussion forums for them. It dawned on me that similar clarity was needed for several groups of people:

- Muslim parents now teaching their children and encountering questions for which they never received clear answers, or modern topics that have not been addressed in a simple manner
- those who are already Muslim (by virtue of being born into a Muslim family), but had never really studied and understood their faith – a group where Islam has been more a cultural identity rather than true faith, and now they have questions
- young Muslim adults pondering life, now with questions of their own that need answering
- those who are new (converts) to Islam, and are trying to comprehend the wealth of information and guidance in Islam

- those who are looking for answers about life and are curious about Islam's position

This was coupled with questions that I myself had experienced, but found the answers were not readily 'out there' or were not given clearly in mainstream Islamic teachings. I have also been frustrated reading the works of erudite and sincere scholars which convey deep knowledge but are written in difficult and technical language, requiring numerous sentences to be reread multiple times to grasp the point. Their work is not accessible to the lay public. I am not a scholar, but a Muslim student of knowledge. In the course of my journey, I have learnt, what I would say, is *basic and essential* Islamic knowledge through the good fortune of studying with authentic teachers, who are highly learned and respected scholars.[1] I have collated and distilled this, along with my own reflections, into a summary that is hopefully highly simplified and easy to understand.

The book is divided into four parts. After giving some general principles of Islam (Part I), I cover guidance on behaviour i.e. moral conduct (Part II), then concepts of belief and worship (Part III) and finally some further advanced Islamic principles (Part IV). Breaking with traditional approaches which start with belief, I have covered guidance on moral conduct first. This is not to underplay belief at all, but to emphasise how important our moral conduct is in the scheme of Islam. Unfortunately, this often appears to get relegated to second place in more classical style teachings, which although not the intention of the esteemed scholars, is more than likely how the reader takes the message. This has been confirmed by asking numerous children, 'What is Islam?' and finding they only equate Islam with the 'five pillars'.[2] Moral conduct and other essentials of belief have completely failed to enter their understanding about what Islam really is. Unfortunately there is a real risk that this lack

---

[1] With authentic lineage of knowledge as discussed later in *Knowledge*.
[2] Shahadah (testimony of faith), salat (ritual prayer), zakat (obligatory charity), fasting the month of Ramadan, Hajj (obligatory pilgrimage).

of understanding remains until adulthood and continues throughout their life.

The book deliberately simplifies Islamic *concepts* and tries to present them in an easily understandable and relatable style. There are other possible answers and perspectives, which some scholars or more learned Muslims may prefer. These may be valid as well, and the book does not seek to present the only and exclusive interpretation. Indeed some difference of opinion is healthy and is actually part of Islam, in order to allow flexibility. When asked why Allah tells us to do something or why is it so in Islam, Muslims who are further along their journey, having built up a greater degree of faith (called Iman in Islam), tend to be genuinely comfortable with the answer 'because it is the command of Allah'. Whilst this is true, it is intellectually unsatisfactory and unappealing to those at an earlier stage in their journey, who need a substantial answer. In particular, the Muslim youth have questions. There *are* answers for all the questions out there, and it is incumbent on the Muslim body to make sure these are readily available, especially for the Muslim youth. This book is the humble endeavour on my part.

It is essential when seeking answers that there is sincerity of heart to find the truth. If the heart is harbouring bias or one is not genuine in one's search, the answers or arguments presented, no matter how sound, will be rejected. For the reader I would urge a little reflection, at the outset, on what their true intention is in reading this book. One needs to be honest that they are seeking the truth no matter what that amounts to.

As this is a book of concepts, it does not go into the specifics of 'How to', e.g. how to perform the ritual prayer, how to do ablution, how to perform Hajj, etc. The reader can find a multitude of such books, and I have given some suggestions in *Further Reading*. As the knowledge here is basic but essential for Muslims, I would advise readers to continue their journey of learning by studying with authentic scholars or teachers.

It is also important that lay readers do not try to derive their own legal rulings from this book. If someone does find themselves in a real-life quandary, they should seek expert advice from the people of knowledge (muftis, scholars or reliable imams).

Finally, Allah knows best. Anything good I have said is from Allah and anything wrong is from my own shortcomings, for which I seek forgiveness from Allah and my fellow people.

PART I
A FEW GENERAL
PRINCIPLES

Islam as a Journey: Slow and Steady Wins the Race

Allah (God) has provided a complete way of life. New Muslims, or those looking to increase their practice of Islam, can become overwhelmed the more they learn of Islam. This is unfortunately compounded by well-intentioned but over-exuberant members of the Muslim community, who feel it is their job to bring a lifelong journey to the poor rookie in a matter of just days. They enthusiastically encourage learning the Arabic prayers, Arabic being a difficult language for Western minds to pronounce as well as grasp; the rules and method of ablution (ritual cleansing); the multitude of rulings of the permissible (*halal*) and the prohibited (*haram*); etiquettes and character that one should develop; growing a beard for a man, and taking on a *hijab* (head covering) for a woman. Recommendation even includes changing one's name to a Muslim one (which is not necessary). In addition, they bombard and batter the poor newbie daily with social media messages and videos, to help their Islamic 'growth'.

Gradualism, making changes slowly over time, is a bedrock of Islam. The Quran was revealed over 23 years for a reason. Simple examples such as the prohibition of alcohol embodied this concept. Intoxicants such as alcohol were targeted in three stages, being discouraged initially but fully outlawed only with the last injunction. This gradual aspect of development is lost by the over-enthusiastic community members, who sadly risk driving out the fledglings in faith.

Allah asks us to make effort. However, the outcome and results are from Him alone. The natural rule Allah has made is that the more effort you make, the more likely you are to succeed, *but* what you actually achieve is Allah's Will. Think of the supreme elite athlete 'certain' for that Olympic Gold medal, only to tear a muscle or sprain a joint during the heats, or to trip at a key moment in a key race. Our job is to try our best. This means we are not in competition with anyone else. We are competing with only ourselves. Each person's starting point in belief and moral conduct will be different, as will be their abilities and skills. It follows therefore that everyone's journey will be different. Unlike the human paradigm where success is measured according to the actual result achieved, success in Allah's Eyes is how much *effort* we made. We need to be *effort-centric*, not result-centric. Two students sitting an exam may get the same grade, but the truly successful one is the one who worked hard for it, not the one who coasted along and did well because they were 'smart'. Had the latter applied themselves properly, they could have achieved an even higher grade.

The key is to endeavour to improve with time, *however incremental*. This is why the Prophet explained that Allah loves more a tiny deed that is done consistently, rather than a wonderous big deed done as a one-off. [3] Knowing what is required of us and how to do that necessitates gaining knowledge. Seeking knowledge, with a will to implement it, is therefore integral to personal improvement.

Newly practising Muslims may also find themselves drawn to old habits and 'sins'. It can be deeply troubling to engage in lifestyles that Islam forbids, yet try to remain Muslim. Alcohol, for instance, is a big part of life for many before they become Muslim. The resolution to such a discord can unfortunately culminate in conceding to the lifestyle and dropping Islam. Similarly, non-Muslims deeply inclined to Islam may resist what truly appeals to their soul, because they enjoy a particular habit they know will be condemned in Islam – 'I know I can never give that up, so I had better leave off becoming Muslim'. It is vitally important to remember three things:

1. Being Muslim[4] is a necessity to gain Paradise. A Muslim who sins is still ultimately destined for Paradise. A non-Muslim[5] can never gain Paradise.

---

[3] Sahih Bukhari
[4] Muslim is one who believes that there is only one God, and Muhammad was His final messenger.
[5] One who rejected Islam.

2. We are human and have been created imperfect – which is not by accident but by Allah's design. We will all make mistakes and that is part of the journey.
   But know that Allah is the All-Forgiving, who loves to forgive.

3. Allah created man *so that* He can forgive him and show mercy to him. Repentance is a great gift from the Almighty. Sincere repentance is *always* met with forgiveness.

Just because we struggle to give up a particular habit is not a reason to lose hope, and abandon faith. Instead, it is better that we first reconcile ourselves to the fact that we *do* have shortcomings and weaknesses. This is true for every person, no matter what level of faith they have. Then we need to make a firm resolve to overcome these. Finally, we need to continue to strive and make effort. Where we fall back, we repent and resolve again to overcome the weakness. We keep these weaknesses private - there is no rejoicing in them. Most certainly one does not twist interpretations of the Quran or teachings of the Prophet (hadith) to try to justify them – this is a very serious transgression.

And we do not despair. We must keep hope that we will eventually overcome these, though we may slip, perhaps repeatedly, along the way. This approach is necessary for that unshakeable habit, and is the right way, rather than to ditch Islam entirely. So, better to accept the truth and get on the journey of Islam, even if you cannot immediately leave that habit.

For new Muslims, discomfort at abandoning the social norms of their non-Muslim family and community increases the pressure on them to return to their old ways. Guidance is the greatest gift our Creator bestows on any soul. Reaffirm with certitude, repeatedly, why Islam is the Truth. This is necessary from time to time, no matter how strong one's faith is. It is human nature to pause and just wonder. Seek the help of sensible and knowledgeable Muslims, who explain aspects of Islam in a way that leaves no room for doubt whatsoever. Treat non-Muslim family and community with kindness and politeness. Change is always met with resistance. Change in faith poses an unwelcome challenge to the identity of one's family and community. Be confident and happy to share your story of finding Islam with them, and hope it will inspire them too. In the worst-case scenario, one should keep one's faith discreet, to allow them time to accept it. *Your Islam should lead you to become a better person.* When parents, spouse and siblings see the improvement in your character, and the way you deal with them, with time there will be an acceptance. Having found your way to the Truth, cling to it for dear, dear life.

Bottom line:

• One should go slow and steady (gradualism).

• Do not become overwhelmed.

• Do what you can manage. Do not bite off more than you can chew.

• Over exuberant community members should politely be told to give some space (leave social media groups that overdo it).

• Unshakeable lifestyles and habits may need time to change – accept that but keep up hope and resolve to improve.

• Treat non-Muslim family and community with kindness and politeness, but remain firm in your faith.

• Allah measures us by our effort, not by our results. Be effort-centric, not result-centric.

Prioritisation in Islam

In any exam, there are some questions that carry big marks, whilst there are many other questions that carry just a few. The best exam strategy is to ensure that time spent on the question is appropriate to its marks. In other words, make sure more time is spent on the big questions.

Islam is no different when it comes to the test of this world. Our responsibilities, and what Allah asks of us, can be divided into two broad categories:

- Our responsibility to the Creator i.e. to Allah Himself (in Arabic called *huqooq ul Allah*)
- Our responsibility to His Creation i.e. to fellow people, animals, environment (called *huqooq ul ibaad*)

In both groups, there are some serious and heavy priorities that far outweigh the rest. These are obligatory acts. For the rights of Allah, the obligatory acts of worship overshadow the voluntary ones. So, the obligatory five daily prayers exceed all voluntary extra prayers, no matter what their quantity. The obligatory fasts of the holy month of Ramadan are considerably superior to any additional voluntary fasts.

Similarly, in our responsibility to our fellow creation (essentially our moral conduct), obedience and respect to our parents is an obligation and the absolute pinnacle of our behaviour. Love and respect for our spouse, children, and siblings follow.

Why are the obligatory so favoured by Allah? With the voluntary extra acts, whether they are worship or service to our fellow man, we undertake these out of our own choice. When and where we want, how much we want. The obligations on the other hand, are by Allah's choice. The when, the where, the how many, is all His Will, and our fulfilling His Command, is therefore a superior act of obedience.

The concept of prioritisation is extremely important. Allah is the Supremely Kind and He has created countless opportunities to earn His Pleasure. As one increases in one's knowledge of Islam, one finds there are a great many such good deeds. However, not all deeds are equal. It is surprisingly easy to become focused on deeds that are indeed good, but are not obligatory, and therefore not of paramount importance. The risk is the compromising of the big deeds with not only *the loss of the reward* of the big deed(s) but also *incurring sin* for failing in the obligation. For instance, setting up a charitable service to help look after elderly members in the community. A great initiative, but if, in the midst of one's preoccupation, one's own elderly parents are being neglected and struggling with their daily life, then there has been a catastrophic miscalculation, and failure to realise the priorities. The point is not to discourage wonderful acts of conduct or worship, but to make sure the obligatory ones are taken care of first and are not compromised in any way.

Bottom line:

• Prioritisation in both worship and moral conduct is extremely important.

• It is critical to ensure the big tasks are taken care of well, before taking on lesser tasks.

• Obligatory acts far outweigh voluntary ones.

The Prophet as the Best Role Model and the Spirit of Islam

The Quran was revealed over a period of 23 years. One of the key reasons for this was to allow people to see guidance and revelation put into practice, through the conduct of the Prophet Muhammad. Allah states that the Prophet is the best role model for every human:

Indeed in the Messenger of Allah you have a good example to follow, for him who hopes in (the Meeting with) Allah and the Last Day and remembers Allah much. {Quran 33: 21}

Emulating him in every aspect of life is the key to success. How he behaved with his family, friends, the community around him both Muslim and non-Muslim, his enemies, how he handled money, governed society etc. Revelation from God in fact comprised two forms:

1. the Quran, which is the Speech of God

2. the teachings and behaviour of the Prophet (called the Sunnah).

Allah makes this second aspect clear when He says about the Prophet:

He does not speak out of his own desires.

It is no less than Revelation revealed to him. {Quran 53: 3-4}

Through the character of the Prophet one can learn to appreciate the *spirit* of Islam. This is exceedingly important. Following the death of the Prophet, generations of scholars who were pious and wise, formulated rulings of what was permissible (*halal*) and prohibited (*haram*) in both worship and worldly dealings, a branch of Islamic study known as '*fiqh*'. These derivations are useful and important, as they allow a framework for basic practices. However, people unfortunately get bogged down with technical discussions and legalities, and lose sight of the *spirit* of Islam. The obsession with these rulings, therefore, can become counter-productive.

Good examples are the rights and obligations the husband and wife have towards each other in marriage. From a legal (*fiqh*) perspective, the husband must provide accommodation and living expenses for the home as well as for his wife. From a legal viewpoint, he is not obligated to listen to her, nor to actually love her. The wife needs to ensure she takes responsibility for the upbringing of the children, but is not obligated to be kind to, or love her husband. If the legal rulings alone were used to guide the marriage, it is clear marriage would be a disaster. The Prophet however, emphatically preached, and *demonstrated himself*, love and mercy to all, especially one's spouse. In one such teaching he advised:

> *The best among you is the best towards his wife (i.e. spouse) and I am the best of you to my wives {Ibn Majah}.*

He personified the *spirit* of Islam, and is explaining here that people should emulate him in having the best conduct towards their spouse. Marriage needs love and compassion at its foundation, not legal rulings, rights and obligations. In fact, even in secular society no one would look to the law for how to run their marriage. Similarly, the *spirit* of Islam, derived from the Prophet, shows us how to conduct our marriage.

Another example is the wiping over socks (called *khuffs* in Arabic), as part of ablution, which is ritual cleansing (*wudu*). *Wudu* is essential before one undertakes ritual prayer, and comprises several steps, including washing the face, arms, wiping the head, and washing the feet. The mainstay for ablution of the feet is washing them, but there is a legal ruling that socks can be wiped over with wet hands, based on the fact that the Prophet did do this *on occasions*. This has resulted in many people wiping over their socks as a norm for performing ablution, all year round (figuratively speaking).[6] Note, I am not referring to the scholarly debate[7] over what constitutes *khuffs*, whether these comprise leather socks, or thick socks, or any type of socks, etc. Wiping over leather socks is universally agreed upon, and some wear these specifically to be able to wipe over them to perform *wudu*, rather than wash the feet. Legally this is sound, but this is certainly not the Sunnah (the regular practice of the Prophet) and not the *spirit* he fostered, which was to wash his feet. Wiping over *khuffs* was done as an exception, such as when travelling. The point to take is that legal rulings for exceptions was exactly for that, *for exceptions*. Some Muslims take the permissibility for an exception and turn it into the norm. Muslims should seek to follow the mainstay practice of the Prophet and maintain the *spirit* of Islam he taught.

Bottom line:

• God's Revelation comprised two parts:

1. Quran - the Speech of Allah

2. Sunnah – the practices and teachings of the Prophet.

• The Prophet is the greatest role model for all of humanity.

• The *spirit* of Islam embodied by the Prophet's own behaviour needs to be at the heart of our conduct.

---

[6] To be clear here – a guy may shower in the morning, including washing his feet, so completing his *wudu*. Then he puts on the *khuffs*. For the rest of the day the *wudu* is renewed by wiping over the *khuffs*.

[7] i.e. *Fiqh* debate

The Elevated Status of the Prophet and the Command to Pray *FOR* Him

Man is the greatest of Allah's creation, of which the prophets are the highest, and of whom Prophet Muhammad is the absolute pinnacle. Prophet Muhammad is the ultimate creation of Allah. Allah honours him such that he is mentioned as part of the testimony of faith (*shahada*, discussed later). A person cannot be Muslim unless they accept that, as well as God being One alone, Muhammad is His final Messenger. What an elevated status. This rank is not afforded to any other prophet.

Allah further honours Prophet Muhammad by commanding Muslims to pray to Allah to send His blessings upon the Prophet, as well as his family – called *salawat* in Arabic.

> *Indeed, Allah confers blessings upon the Prophet, and His angels (ask Him to do so). O you who believe, ask (Allah to confer) blessings upon him and ask (Allah to grant him) peace. {Quran 33: 56}*

The Prophet has already been guaranteed Paradise, and the very highest level in fact. So, why this command? Firstly, it is emphasising to mankind the truly elevated status that Allah has bestowed upon him. We need to do more than just recognise this. We need to have the highest level of love and respect for him. In fact, the Prophet himself explained that:

> *None of you will have faith till he loves me more than his father, his children and all mankind. {Sahih Bukhari}*

Here, having faith does not refer to being a Muslim or not. It refers to achieving perfection in faith.

Furthermore, Allah's Command also serves as a means of gratitude to Allah for sending His guidance, which included a man who was a walking and talking guide, an example for all mankind and the best teacher. Allah says about the Prophet:

And We have not sent you (i.e. Muhammad) but as a mercy to the worlds. {Quran 21: 107}

He was a mercy, because not only did he clarify and set straight correct belief about God, but he also taught mankind how to behave in the best manner.

At the same time, this command shows that despite his status, the Prophet was not a deity, but a man, and as such he is also in need of Allah's Mercy. As one of the teachings of the Prophet to the Companions demonstrates:

(The Prophet said): 'No one of you will enter Paradise by his deeds alone.' They asked, 'Not even you, O Messenger of Allah?' He said, 'Not even me, unless Allah covers me with His Grace and Mercy'. {Sahih Bukhari}.

This is extremely important. Some Muslims groups are at risk of deifying him. The line between veneration and deification of a prophet has to be observed. It also makes distinction with other faiths, such as Christianity, where a prophet is accepted as divine. Just to re-iterate, the command of Allah to send blessings upon the Prophet is for mankind to beseech Allah to send blessings on the Prophet. It is not praying to the Prophet himself.

As we shall come to see, Allah's commands are an obligation on Muslims, but fulfilling the command comes with magnanimous rewards. The Prophet explained that:

Whoever sends blessings upon me once, Allah will send blessings upon him tenfold and will erase from him ten misdeeds and raise him ten degrees in status. {Sunan Nasaa'i}

So sending blessings on the Prophet once meets with ten rewards, plus ten sins forgiven, plus elevation in rank of ten degrees. The importance of *salawat* is appreciated in the spiritual aspects of Islam which develop contentment, upliftment in character, and closeness to Allah, and where undertaking copious amounts of *salawat* play a major role.

<u>Bottom Line:</u>

• Supplicating Allah to send blessings on the Prophet (*salawat*) is a command of Allah.

• It demonstrates the elevated level of the Prophet and the degree of honour Allah confers on him.

• It is a means of thanking Allah for His guidance, of which the Prophet himself is a part of that guidance.

• It also shows that the Prophet was a man who is in need of Allah's Mercy, like the rest of mankind.

• As with all of Allah's commands, completing them brings tremendous rewards.

The Lenses of Islam

Islam teaches that man's time in this world is transitory and short. The real destination and final abode is the Hereafter. The guidance given in Islam is comprehensive for every aspect of our lives and, as such, Islam gives us Lenses through which this world is to be viewed. These Lenses of Islam give clarity and show the truth. For example, what is real success? Having a good job, spacious home, fancy car, abundant wealth? (discussed later). This also means that when evaluating any discovery or news we start with the perspective of Truth. Scientific discoveries and theories such as the Big Bang or the theory of evolution, where interpretations may be put forth suggesting that God does not exist or is redundant in the process, do not shake our faith. We simply need to look at the evidences presented using the Lenses of Islam which show us that Allah is the Creator, and the Maintainer of life and the universe. If these discoveries are correct, they are simply tools of Allah, they do not replace Him.

Allah does not make mistakes, and has not forgotten anything in His Creation. Nor has He undertaken anything unnecessarily. Everything has a purpose, though man often does not see this given his limitations. The

Quran is the Word of Allah. The words and structure are very specific and deliberate. There is nothing extra or superfluous in it. Not a single sentence, not a single word, not even a single vowel. This is very important and part of the Lenses of Islam. When attempts are made to understand the Quran, interpretations that it has parts or words that are extra (with the implication: not necessary) or that there have been omissions are simply wrong. These interpretations need to be shunned. In these cases, it is necessary to dig deeper to understand why Allah has chosen to say what He says in that particular way.

The Quran has been the guidance for mankind already for more than 1400 years, and it will continue to be so until the end of time. As society, technology and way of living change over time, it follows that its 6,236 verses cannot be a lexicon of law. Instead, they provide concepts and principles along with some direct commands and prohibitions, suitable for all times. One of the unique features of the Quran is that it often speaks directly to the reader. Some of the meaning is immediately apparent. However, the verses were revealed in the context of situations that arose, or questions that people posed to the Prophet, over a period of 23 years. The verses need to be interpreted in *that* context for deeper understanding. In other words, the life story of the Prophet (called Seerah) is very important, along with his teachings (the Sunnah) which elucidated the meaning of the Quran. Similarly the Quran does not go into specifics and fine details. These are expanded by the Sunnah. A good example is prayer. The command to pray comes repeatedly in the Quran. But the way to pray came from the example of the Prophet, who said 'Pray as you see me pray',[8] and his method has been relayed precisely through the generations.

Bottom line:

• The Muslim must view the world through the Lenses of Islam.

• The Quran is the Word of Allah and is therefore perfect. Any analysis of

---

[8] Sahih Bukhari and Sahih Muslim.

the Quran *must* start with this premise.

• The Quran must be interpreted in the *context* of when the revelations were sent. This needs knowledge of the biography of the Prophet (called Seerah) and his explanations (called hadith).

The Need for Loss

Man's nature is one of ungratefulness and taking things for granted. It is an extremely unfortunate reality of man that he does not appreciate what he has, until he has lost it. The most common reaction to loss is 'Why me?' This is not the Islamic way. The *required* Islamic response is to show patience, and thankfulness for what one did have and what one continues to have. Furthermore, it is to know that Allah is the All-wise and Most Compassionate, so that whatever happens, there is good in it for us, in some shape or form. We may see this eventually, perhaps after a long time, or maybe never.

Permanent loss, or the realisation that certain dreams or desires can never be fulfilled in this world, build a yearning for the Next Life, where there is no pain, and complete fulfilment. This could be the loss of close family members. It could be onset of disability. This is an important and necessary part of our training in this world. This is how Allah breaks our attachment from this world. They are reminders that this world is temporary and not the final destination. Whilst there are many comforts afforded here, the real life and final abode is the Next One, where one is reunited with one's family (minus all their negative traits) and all desires are met.[9]

Bottom Line:

• Loss is a necessary part of our training in this life.

---

[9] Quan 41: 31

• Allah is All Wise, and all that He does for us has good in it, though it may not be apparent to us.

• Loss is one way in which Allah trains us to break our attachment to this world.

Islam and Culture

Every nation has its own language, identity and culture. Islam was sent as guidance to all mankind for all time. As Islam spread geographically, over generations, there has inevitably been a variable concoction of pre-existing culture mixed in with its teachings. There is no harm in cultural practices that are in line with Islamic values. This was seen at the time of the Prophet, who as a boy (and therefore before Prophethood) witnessed the formation of a covenant between the tribes of Mecca, called the *Hilf al-Fudool* ('the virtuous alliance'), a pact to uphold justice for any person who was wronged, regardless of whether the victim was a Meccan or not. Up until then, tribal society only gave support and protection to those of their own clan. Visitors and travellers were unprotected and so at risk of abuse. The covenant was a milestone, giving rights to outsiders as well for the first time, and the Prophet later in life commented about the pact that 'if now after Islam I am called to honour it, I would certainly do so'.[10]

Unfortunately there are numerous cultural practices that violate Islamic principles but are widespread to the point that many Muslims believe that they are part of Islam. Examples include wedding rituals. Subcontinental 'Muslim' marriages, for example, often have a number of rituals that originate from Hindu tradition, such as a 'mehndi' (literally 'henna'), where henna is applied to the bride ceremoniously, followed by several celebratory dance routines, all in front of a mixed gathering. Girls dancing in a mixed crowd is not Islamic. Then there is the bride's family providing the dowry, which can be exorbitant, sometimes at the demand of the bridegroom's family. In contrast, Islamic marriage comprises a *nikah*,

---

[10] Sunan al-Kubra by Imam Al-Nasa'i

which are the wedding vows and wedding contract. This is followed on a subsequent day by a *walima*, which is a wedding meal celebrating the husband and wife as a couple. The dowry is not provided by the bride but actually by the bridegroom to the bride, and is something reasonable. Another example is the expectation that the newly married couple will live in the family home, as often the groom is still living at home with his parents. Islam affords the wife the right to her own space and home. Suggesting that the son moves out to his own place is taken offensively by his family who see this is the start of his wife exerting control in the family. Such culture needs to be abandoned.

Bottom line:

• A distinction must be made between Islam and culture.

• Cultural practices not compatible with Islam need to be abandoned.

• Muslims, especially new Muslims, must be careful about taking on practices from other Muslims that do not have a real Islamic basis.

PART II
GUIDANCE ON
BEHAVIOUR

Moral Conduct: 'H₃MK'

Moral conduct is of *extreme* importance in Islam. Why so? Because **spreading goodness is the absolute tenet of behaviour of a Muslim.** Just how important is this? Let's consider these counsels of the Prophet:

> *I have been sent to this world to perfect moral character.*
> *{Bukhari: al-Adab al-Mufrad}*

Here the Prophet is summarising h is mission in one line, and thus giving profound emphasis not just to good character, but the highest moral conduct. You cannot be clearer than that. Though correcting belief was central to his mission – namely that there is only one God without partners, who is to be worshipped alone and obeyed completely – this obedience is inextricably intertwined with excellence in moral conduct i.e. how we behave.

When asked about who the best of the believers are, the Prophet replied:

> *They are those who have the best character and manners.*
> *{Sunan at-Tirmidhi; Sunan Abu Dawood}*

Note that he did not say the best of the believers are those who fasted the most, or who prayed the most, though prayer and fasting is extremely beloved to Allah. In fact the Prophet also said:

> *No deed that will be placed on the scale of deeds (on the Day of Judgement) will be heavier than good character. Indeed, a person with good character will attain the rank of those with a good record of voluntary fasts and prayers. {Sunan at-Tirmidhi}*

Therefore, the most upright character actually carries the elevated status of being the best of deeds. All Muslims, and indeed all those whose faith has the concept of Afterlife, want to enter Paradise after this world. When the Prophet was asked about which act leads people to enter Paradise the most, he replied, 'Piety and good character'.[11] Again, his reply was not any of the ritual worships, important though they are. Furthermore, not only do Muslims wish to attain Paradise, they want to be in the highest level and to be neighbours of the Prophet Muhammad and his family. The Prophet said:

> *The dearest to me among you and the nearest to me on the Day of Judgement are those who have the best character. {Sunan at-Tirmidhi}*

Finally, as we covered earlier, the Prophet is the best role model for humanity. We should strive to emulate him in every aspect as best as we can. So what does Allah say about him?

> *And indeed, you (i.e. Muhammad) are of a great moral character. {Quran 68: 4}*

Can there be any doubt about the significance of moral conduct?

When a colleague calls in sick at work, do you feel a genuine sadness at their absence, or do you breathe a sigh of relief and think 'thank God, it will be a better day today'? We all have colleagues like this, but here is the thing – do we fall into this bracket ourselves? If we have to be away from home for a while, do our spouse and children genuinely miss us, or are they secretly delighted to get a break from us – 'thank God I'll get a few days off from nagging and criticising'. Do family members enjoy being on holiday with us, or do they have to put up with us? If people are happier when we are not around, that is a damning indictment on our character. It is easy to identify other people as having bad character, but we seriously need to pause and reflect on our own personal conduct and character.

Some people in positions of authority might justify their distasteful behaviour as necessary 'in order to get the job done'. Positions of

---

[11] Sunan at-Tirmidhi; Sunan Ibn Maajah

leadership do not justify poor conduct. A leader is actually more effective when people look up to them on account of their excellent conduct.

So what does Allah require in this regard? In essence, Allah tells us to be:

1. Humble

2. Helpful

3. Honest

4. Modest

5. Kind

- what I have formulated as '**H₃MK**'.

Humility

ISLAM = HUMILITY

Humility, not only in front of the Creator, but also with our fellow man, is the cornerstone of Islam. Its importance can be appreciated from the story of Creation. The angels and the jinn (another type of being with free will) were created well before man, and had worshiped Allah for countless years. When Adam, the first man, was created, Allah ordered both the angels and jinn to prostrate to him, as a mark of respect for what was Allah's finest creation. Interestingly, the angels were surprised and first enquired *respectfully* why this was so. Allah then demonstrated to them man's special qualities that raise him in rank. All the angels then prostrated, but a group from the jinn, led by Iblees (Satan) refused.[12] Iblees declared he was better than man, as he was made of fire whilst man was made of clay.[13] No doubt his feeling that his preceding countless years of worship seemed to have been relegated to second place also played an

---

[12] Quran 2: 30-35;
[13] Quran 7: 12

addition role in his disobedience – again, arrogance. He knew that Allah is All-Knowing, but these feelings overwhelmed this knowledge. True humility in front of the Creator necessitates absolute obedience. Note, respectful enquiry was allowed, as demonstrated by the angels, followed by obedience.

Thus the very first sin was that of arrogance. Iblees' arrogance was such, in fact, that he responded to this sin by blaming Allah – 'You caused me to slip!'[14] When Adam and Huwa (Eve), on the other hand, fell into sin by eating from the forbidden tree under the misguidance of Iblees, they turned to Allah with humility, immediately asking for forgiveness, which Allah accepted. The need for humility is also emphatically made in the Quran, where Allah says Hell is the place for the arrogant,[15] whilst the Prophet explained that a person whose heart carries even an atom's weight of arrogance will not be admitted to Paradise.[16] All arrogance must be shed. Both arrogance towards Allah *AND* arrogance towards our fellow man.

Why is this so? Humility before Allah affirms our slavehood to Him, and that He is our Master. Although 'slave' carries negative connotations in today's age, this is not the case with reference to Allah. There is no higher level for man than being a slave of Allah. With regards to fellow man, arrogance underlies a great deal of man's mischievous and evil behaviours. Thinking we are better than those around us or other races, breeds a sense of entitlement. This ferments into injustice and oppression of the 'lesser' mortals. Humans subjecting others or nations into slavery is one such manifestation.

Being judgemental is also a form of arrogance. We think we know better, so others who behave differently must be bad, wrong, or misguided. It is important judgement is reserved for Allah alone. The Prophet never judged anyone, and remained kind even to those who were vehement opponents.

---

[14] Quran 15: 39
[15] Quran: 16: 29; 40: 76
[16] Sahih Muslim

If we see others committing sin, we are meant to dislike the sin, not the person. Why?

1. We may be seeing the sins, but the same person may be doing some supremely noble work behind closed doors that catapults their status above ours.

2. The 'sinner' may turn over a new leaf, and repent to Allah. Repentance that is genuine is met with forgiveness from Allah, and the past sins are turned into good deeds. This again may catapult their status above ours (see *Repentance*).

3. The disbeliever may see the light, and accept Islam. This person's sins will be erased clean. Some of the most vitriolic opponents to Islam have gone on to convert to Islam, not just in the Prophet's time, but even today.

Modern examples of this last group include Arnoud van Doorn, a Dutch official who belonged to an anti-Islamic far right party. After being involved with the distribution of an Islamophobic movie, he began to conduct his own research into Islam culminating in his own conversion. He broke from his party and performed Hajj in 2014. His eldest son also went on to become Muslim.

Humility is also critical to gaining knowledge, whether of Islam or some worldly subject e.g. mathematics, science, engineering. No one can gain progress in any field unless they first acquire knowledge (even experience is acquisition of knowledge, through one's own trials and errors). One has to accept that one does not know in order to start the journey of learning. If one thinks they know everything already, or know better, then what improvement can they possibly make? Crucially, unless one is humble, one will not seek, nor take on, the guidance of Allah. We recognise that we do not know, Allah knows, and we need Him to bestow knowledge and guidance upon us, for our benefit. In the matter of Islam, limited or erroneous knowledge coupled with arrogance will breed a sense of exclusivity of the truth coupled with rigidity. This will hinder self-improvement and produce bitter argumentation with others, rather than softness and flexibility, which is what Islam actually encourages. Sadly, in the worst cases, it can lead to extremism, and unfortunately violence. We do not have exclusivity of the truth. Humility engenders that there can be other valid opinions, or that we may be wrong.

Arrogance resides in all of us. In some it is readily apparent. In others, it is hidden, perhaps even to the person themselves. A person may actively work on their own humility, but can still harbour arrogance. What we have e.g. job, education, home, family, wealth, etc, easily make us feel that we are something special. Those whom we encounter who do not have the same, are lesser people than us in our eyes, if we truly choose to reflect deeper. For example, at a community event, a high-flying professional meets a person who does not have much higher education, drives a taxi for a living, and lives in an undesirable area. The highly educated individual who enjoys a much posher neighbourhood exchanges pleasantries, but after a few minutes looks to move to somebody more their level. Later they discover the taxi driver is the bedrock for numerous volunteer community projects, putting their own little charitable endeavours to shame.

Arrogance is a poisonous trap being laid around us all the time. It can even arise in those who are humble, thinking that they are more humble than others. Those who are highly knowledgeable in Islam, such as scholars, can find themselves thinking they are better than those around them because of how much knowledge they have attained, or looking down on others as they feel they know best. Worse, they can develop a sense of exclusivity of the truth. We can do a good deed for someone and then feel proud at what we have done, or worse, feel that that person now owes us something. Conquering arrogance is therefore a constant battle. We need to retain insight that *it is buried deep within us*, and like a boat with a hole that is always taking on water, we need to keep bucketing it out. When doing a good deed for someone, it is best to keep a short term memory – quickly forget what you did so as not to let it go to your head, nor to expect the person to reciprocate in the future (so avoid the 'he owes me one now' mentality).

The need for humility is also seen in the teaching of the Prophet that the believer should take counsel from his fellow being.[17] When a friend or relative advises us or points out a fault in us, our natural response is highly defensive as we lick our wounded pride. The Prophet is counselling us to be humble, and pay heed to the friend/relative, taking their criticism as a mirror being held up to us. It is the impetus for us to reflect and improve ourselves. This approach requires humility on the part of the listener. Conversely, a believer should have concern for his fellow man. So if he sees a fault in him/her, he should seek to advise but in a considered, courteous and soft manner.

Bottom Line:

• Learning can only start with acknowledgement that one is ignorant.

• Seeking and implementing guidance in our lives requires humility.

• Humility before Allah affirms our slavehood to Him.

• Humility before fellow man saves us from judgemental, unjust and oppressive behaviour.

• Keep a short-term memory when undertaking good deeds.

• BE HUMBLE, BE HUMBLE, BE HUMBLE.

Helpfulness

The Muslim is a giver, not a taker. They are not just at the service of others, but are actually waiting to jump at opportunities to serve. There is a genuine concern for others, and the desire and proactivity to help wherever and whenever possible. Being of service is incredibly important. Why so? Spreading goodness and manifesting kindness which are obligatory on the Muslim, necessitate doing good for others. Helping others actually puts kindness into action. The Muslim cannot live life as a hermit. How can one

---

[17] Sahih Bukhari

demonstrate their kindness or spread goodness unless it is to somebody else? This is not just about helping those who need assistance, but actually actively putting oneself in a position of service. So for example, at a community event, standing behind the food counter and serving people the meals, rather than getting in line to eat. Or at its conclusion, tidying up, clearing up the rubbish and putting away the tables and chairs. And all of this is whilst one is a simple attendee at the function, not one of the organisers.

Such an attitude is clearly of benefit for the community – many hands make light work, of course. It eases the burden of others. Helping out breeds camaraderie and team spirit, which strengthens relationships and thus communities. It ensures that the group functions as efficiently and effectively as possible, as everyone pitches in. But it also directly benefits the one providing the help. Firstly, the deeds receive the Pleasure of Allah and with it His Reward. Furthermore, being of service to others nurtures humility and kindness, extremely important traits to develop to the highest level. Note that this is done completely altruistically, not to ingratiate oneself with the desperate one, which, if it were the case, would actually invalidate the deed.

The Prophet taught:

> *Whoever removes a heavy grief from a believer from amongst the sorrows of this life, Allah will remove a grief from him amongst the sorrows of the Day of Resurrection. Whoever brings ease to one in (financial) difficulty, Allah will make it easy for him in this life and the Hereafter. {Sahih Muslim}*

The message is one of serving others, especially those in need and facing hardship. The reward – on the Day of Judgement, when everyone will be desperate – is that Allah will provide relief to those who provided it to their brethren in this world. A tremendous reward. At that time, there will be nothing one can do to improve their situation. It is a time of accountability. Prayers, giving thanks, asking for forgiveness; none of these will be possible. There will be no way to increase one's account of good deeds or to reduce one's burden of sin. There will be no way to even improve one's circumstances on that Day, when the conditions will be truly unbearable. At that time, any relief given by Allah will be a lifeline.

Being of service to one's parents ranks in a league all of its own (covered below). This cannot be overstated, and is to be viewed as Priority Number One. No opportunity is to be wasted in serving them. The next priority is one's family: spouse, children, siblings, etc., followed by friends, neighbours, and everyone else. Even at work one needs to keep service at the forefront. Work for most will be about earning a living, but no chance should be missed where one can be of help. For instance, a businessman may have a very cheap transport arrangement for his goods. But he may choose to go with a slightly more expensive firm, knowing that the owner is a local community member whose business is struggling.

Everyone tends to live within their own little universe, thoroughly preoccupied by their own plans, worries, concerns and ambitions. This is especially so in the fast-paced modern era. Reflect here, that in order to aid someone, one needs to come out of their bubble to identify opportunities to help others. Note the degree of helpfulness and service being referred to. It is not about being helpful when someone asks you, but actively finding chances to help others. Furthermore, people have their dignity and will often be shy to ask for help. It is therefore a prerequisite that one has established good rapports with all those around themselves, and that one takes an active, sincere and genuine interest in their lives and their situation. Only then will they be aware if they can be of assistance. Also reflect on the fact that if people are in need of help and are willing to ask for it, they will approach someone who is approachable. The importance of good character is evident here. If one is seen as friendly and helpful, people might come forward. If one is not seen as sincere and kind, they will seek out others for advice or assistance, even if one is best placed to help.

Being helpful to others can be indirect too. For example, contributing financially to a shelter for orphans. Or removing something harmful from the path or environment. This could be something as small as picking up a piece of paper from the corridor floor, with the concern that someone could slip on it. I personally know of a case where a fit and healthy man shattered his hip bone after slipping awkwardly on something as trivial as an orange peel.

Opportunities to help others are a gift from Allah. They are a chance to demonstrate one's character, perform good deeds and earn Allah's Pleasure – they are literally pennies from Heaven. That is quite profound and worth bearing in mind. Unfortunately, people often get offended or irritated when asked to help, especially with regards to financial assistance. Someone asked to contribute to a particular charity or a project for the destitute has been given an opening to use their wealth in a rewarding way. Grab every chance to help others.

Bottom Line:

- Always serve others rather than be served.

- Be a coiled spring - jump at every possible opportunity to be of service to others.

- Helping others breeds kindness and humility.

- Helping out strengthens relationships and the community.

- Come out of your bubble frequently, to identify how to help others.

- Opportunities to help others are gifts from God.

Honesty

Honesty is unwavering. The Prophet said the following:

> *I enjoin you to be truthful, for truthfulness leads to righteousness and righteousness leads to Paradise. A man may continue to tell the truth and endeavour to be truthful until he is recorded with Allah as a speaker of truth. And beware of lying, for lying leads to*

wickedness and wickedness leads to Hell. A man may continue to tell lies and endeavour to tell lies, until he is recorded with Allah as a liar. {Sahih Bukhari, Sahih Muslim}

There are four characteristics, whoever has them all is a pure hypocrite, and whoever has one of them has one of the characteristics of hypocrisy, until he gives it up: when he is entrusted with something, he betrays that trust, when he speaks he lies, when he makes a covenant he betrays it, and when he disputes he resorts to obscene speech. {Sahih Bukhari, Sahih Muslim}

People are not perfect; they can be weak and prone to characteristics that are unbecoming. But lying is a choice and is not acceptable. A hypocrite is the worst of all types of people, and is one who pretends to be Muslim whilst actually not so at heart, and seeks to destroy the Muslim community from the inside. In the second hadith above, the Prophet made clear that lying was a trait of such people.

Honesty extends to dealings and transactions. Business is conducted scrupulously. There are numerous warnings about the seriousness of dishonesty in business. One complete chapter (called *surah*) in the Quran is in fact named after and dedicated to this topic – Chapter 86, *Al-Mutaffifeen*, 'Those who defraud others'. These people are warned of severe punishments for their deceit.

The level of this trait is seen in the character of the Prophet. There were no banks at the time of the Prophet, so people used to entrust their wealth or valuable possessions to upstanding members of the community for safe keeping. Such people had to be highly trustworthy. The Prophet was one of these entrusted individuals, his honesty being exemplary to the point that he was also known as 'Al-Ameen', the Truthful one. After declaring his Prophethood and embarking on his mission, a number of family members and most of the community refused to accept his call. Some became truly bitter and vocal enemies. However, despite their abhorrence towards the new religion, even these vitriolic enemies continued to entrust material possessions and wealth to the Prophet for safekeeping! So unwavering was the Prophet in his honesty and trustworthiness.

There are a few notable exceptions to this, where some massaging of the truth is permitted. A husband is allowed to compliment his wife even if he actually does not believe it himself at that moment, and vice versa for the wife. For instance, she makes a new dish that he finds difficult to swallow down. 'How is it?' she asks, beaming about her new endeavour. The honest answer, that even an alley cat would probably not touch it, has to be replaced with 'Mmm, lovely'. A person can also tell a white lie where it will actually aid reconciliation between two parties, without which there would be no prospect. For instance, a father and son have severed ties, which you are trying to help mend. You can tell the father that the son really does actually love him still, even if this is not the case. The father might then soften and say the same about his son, allowing you to go back to the son and report that father's feelings.

Backbiting and loose talk

Private conversations one has with others are a trust. They are not for revealing to anyone else. On the topic of conversations, backbiting is to say something unpleasant *but true*, about someone else behind their back. Were they to hear it themselves, they would not like it. This is expressly prohibited. To say something not only unpleasant but *also untrue* is slander, which is even worse. The tongue is capable of phenomenal damage, planting seeds of animosity, creating discord and wrecking relationships. The tongue has led to divorce, brawling, and war.

The importance of avoiding backbiting or worse, slander, is demonstrated in many sayings of the Prophet. For example, the one who guards his private parts (i.e. refrains from fornication) and his tongue (i.e. refrains from backbiting and slander) will be guaranteed Paradise.[18] In another saying, the Prophet took hold of his tongue and said 'Restrain this… is there anything that topples people onto their faces into Hellfire other than

---

[18] Sahih Bukhari

the work of their tongues?'[19] One complete chapter of the Quran (Chapter 104, *Surah al-Humazah*) is named 'The Slanderer' and addresses the gravity of slander. On the matter of backbiting, Allah declares the enormity of this act to be equivalent to eating the flesh of your dead brother.[20] Recall that backbiting is saying what is *true* about the person of your conversation, but they would dislike having it mentioned.

Noticeably in today's society, the vast majority of all conversations involve bad mouthing a third person behind their back. Undertake a simple exercise: one day, monitor all the social conversations you participate in, or happen to hear. Make a mental note of what portion refer to a third party in a negative light and therefore would either be backbiting, or slander. Then reflect on how those conversations have coloured your view of the people discussed. This will impact your future dealings with those people, those negative points will remain embedded in your head. Now consider how your views and subsequent interactions would be, if you had not discussed them at all, or only positive comments had been made about them.

Our conversations impregnate our heart with seeds of positivity or negativity for other people. We must be extremely mindful of them. The significance our conversations have on people's happiness and wellbeing is demonstrated in the Quran. There are numerous descriptions of Paradise, a place of eternal bliss and happiness. On several occasions, it is described as a place where there will be no vain (i.e. hurtful) talk.[21] In other words, loose talk is so damaging to our happiness that a truly happy place has no room *whatsoever* for detrimental and negative conversations or comments. The job of Muslims is to spread peace and happiness, hence the stern warnings on backbiting and slander. Where a Muslim does not have anything good to say, they keep quiet. To avoid backbiting, it is useful to think how the person being discussed would feel if they were overhearing

---

[19] Sunan at-Tirmidhi
[20] Quran 49: 12
[21] Quran 56: 25; 78: 35

the conversation? If they would get offended, then you had better not talk about them.

The power of the tongue to wreak havoc can be seen with the atrocities committed against humanity throughout history. Nations and races have been horrifically persecuted, tortured and massacred. The Jewish Holocaust of the second World War, the Bosnian genocide of the Balkans War, the Tutsi genocide in Rwanda are just a few examples. However, the seeds of all of these abominations was negative rhetoric followed by dehumanising talk, which ferments into violence and oppression. Agatha Christie, the acclaimed murder mystery writer, insightfully concludes the career and life of her famous fictional detective, Hercule Poirot, with the case of a man who effects murders not by committing the crimes himself but by instigating others to murder, through careful cunning insinuations.[22] This is the power of words.

There are exceptions to this rule. In matters of business or marriage, it is imperative to speak the truth. In these cases, harm could result to others by concealing a person's undesirable traits. For instance, a friend of yours proposes to a girl, and the girl's father approaches you to inquire about your friend's character. Here it is incumbent on you to speak honestly about his strengths and weaknesses. Similarly, if someone is considering going into business with your friend, and seeks your view, you must give an honest opinion.

Bottom Line:

• Always be scrupulously honest.

• Guard your conversations against backbiting and slander.

• If you feel you might back-bite, bite your tongue instead.

---

[22] Agatha Christie. Curtain: Poirot's Last Case.

Modesty

Allah bestows a tremendous honour upon women in that He has created *all of them* beautiful by endowing them with adornments. A woman's hair, her skin and body shape provide a great deal of her natural beauty. This is further enhanced by make-up which can be remarkably transformative, accentuating her beauty to a different level. Add a vast array of conspicuous jewellery, and multitudinous garments of different styles and patterns. To accompany this, women have an in-built desire to beautify themselves. However, not only do they like to look beautiful, but they also have a strong inclination to be appreciated. Men, on the other hand, are programmed to look at their beauty. This can be easily demonstrated. Sit down one day with a coffee on a busy street and watch people. When women are walking past, especially young ladies who have dressed themselves up, observe the men around. Almost all will turn their heads to take a look, some will even unashamedly look her up and down. And this will be regardless of the age of the man.

Allah has set a pivotal rule for this world. He has embedded humankind with natural desires and, out of obedience to Allah, they have to restrain them to within prescribed limits. And therein is the test. Some of the desires are for enjoyment provided they are kept to permitted levels whilst some are totally off limits. Allah is looking for true submission to Him. Allah gives these rules in His guidance, but alongside them is vital help to facilitate adhering to them. Along with His rules and their inherent test, there is wisdom and benefit to man, though the test may be tough.

The woman's desire to openly beautify herself and to be appreciated is a strong desire that she must curtail. This has to be limited to her husband and permitted male family members. The man's desire to look at women and admire their beauty has to be limited to his wife. This is what Allah requires as part of true submission. So those are the desires – how does Allah order them to be controlled? For a man, he needs to guard his gaze (covered below). For women, Allah orders them, when out in public, to keep their hair covered with a headscarf (called *hijab*) and their body covered with a loose wide garment (called *jilbab*) so as not to allow their body shape to be apparent.[23] In this way her beauty, a lot of which is inherent in her hair and body shape, has been shielded from the public.

So the desire and its control are a test of submission from Allah. But where is the benefit? The woman beautifying herself and displaying this beauty, coupled with the man enjoying ogling her, is the starting point that could lead to a series of mini encounters: from gazing at each other to small talk, to meeting up for a coffee and chit chat, to having a meal together, spending more time together to finally giving in to temptation and intimate relations. Fornication or adultery is a grave sin. Amongst the stern tests that Allah has placed on this earth is the strong natural attraction between the opposite genders. But Allah seeks for mankind to establish communities built from strong nuclear families. Promiscuity and illicit relationships break families and destroy communities. Broken homes will profoundly compromise the upbringing of children, with the risk of producing wayward, heedless adults who are very likely to affect the next generation, severely compromising their ability to find the right path. The natural desire between men and women requires a great deal of restraint and care to prevent it from culminating in illicit sexual relations.

> *Do not even approach adultery. It is indecent and an evil act.*
> *{Quran 17: 32}*

Note very carefully, Allah does not give the command 'Do not fornicate'; He goes way beyond that and warns clearly *do not even come close* to fornication. All the above carries two important implications. Firstly, carnal relations outside of marriage are a very serious and mighty sin, so much so that one needs to keep well clear of it. Secondly the modesty in dress and behaviour that Allah commands serves as protection by keeping at bay *even* the very initiating step of the cascade. One is careful not to

---

[23] As the purpose is modesty, obviously the garment must not be see through either.

entice others, nor become enticed oneself.

Some Muslim women question where this command to cover herself has been given. It comes in the Quran itself; Allah says:

> *And tell the believing women to lower their gaze and guard their private parts and not expose their adornment except that which (necessarily) appears thereof and to wrap (a portion of) their headcovers over their chests and not expose their adornment...* *{Quran 24: 31}*

The Arabic word used in the Quran *khimaar* refers to a garment that covers the head specifically, and inherent in the word is its specificity for the head. Just as a helmet is specific for the head, or a sock is specific to the foot, or gloves to the hands. There is no need to add a qualification with khimaar that it must cover your head, just as if you are told to put on your socks, you do not need to be told where. Head coverings were already present in pre-Islamic Arabia and worn by men as well as women. In fact men in Arab countries still wear a head cover, with a head ring, as part of traditional attire. Hair is part of a woman's adornment and the instruction is pretty clear – keep the adornments covered, which starts with covering the head. But what Allah adds here is that this head garb must also extend over their chests, what in the Arabic is given as *juyoob*. This had to be specified as pre-Islamic head dresses did not extend over the chest, but used to fall behind a woman's back. *Juyoob* is the centre part of the chest, which also needs to be covered. At some point historically, scholars referred to this head covering (*khimaar*) that cascades over the chest as '*hijab*', and this word has been used since.

Allah adds:

> *O Prophet, tell your wives and your daughters and the women of the believers to bring down over themselves (part) of their outer garments. That is more suitable that they will be known and not be abused. {Quran 33: 59}*

This is referring to having an outer garment (*jilbab*) that will envelop their bodies, so concealing the shape of the body, and drapes right down[24]. The wisdom to the whole ensemble is then given: this serves to make it clear that they are women of modesty (i.e. that is how they will be recognised) and to avoid them being targeted by sexual harassment, as their beauty is no longer exposed.

The woman covers herself when she will be in view of men. She does not need to wear the *hijab* if she is amongst women only. Nor where the male folk present are her close relatives, defined as those whom she cannot marry (called *mahram*). These, Allah specifies as her father, brother, son, grandparents, maternal and paternal uncles, and her blood nephews (i.e. from sons of her brother or sister), as well as her father-in-law. Neither need she cover in front of little boys i.e. pre-puberty. Of course, she does not wear it in front of her husband!

The veil (*niqab*) is the covering of the face in addition to the covering of the head, so that only the eyes are left visible. It is a highly emotive topic, especially for the Western media who portray this as a symbol of oppression. That the head and body must be covered is **unanimously** agreed amongst all scholars i.e. *hijab* and *jilbab* (loose garments covering her body, concealing her shape). There is difference of scholarly opinion as to whether the face must be included in the covering (i.e. *niqab*). Some scholars hold that this is not required whilst others hold that it is. This difference of opinion has to be respected. Both sides agree that covering the face is an act of greater piety. Shaykh Akram Nadwi has pointed out that the practice of covering the face was cultural at the time of the Prophet, and in fact predated the advent of Islam. It was also something that men used to do, especially those from the upper echelons. This cultural aspect means that where the niqab fits within society accustomed to it, then it may be used; but where it is highly alien it should not be worn. So for example, it is worn by many women in Pakistan, and a woman wearing it does not look out of place. The opposite is true of, say, the USA. To don a face veil

---

[24] The Quranic ayat here uses the word *Jalaabeeb* which is plural of *Jilbab*

would attract a great deal of quizzical looks and possibly hostility.

It is important to dispel a myth prevalent in the West that women who do wear the *niqab* have been compelled to by the male folk in their family, and hence that the *niqab* is a symbol of oppression. This is completely untrue. Women who do use the face veil do so out of their *own* belief that this is Allah's command upon women, or do so for its greater virtue. It is entirely their own choice, and not a matter of coercion by their husbands or family, who more often prefer them *not* to wear it. So much for coercion by their men folk! This is a choice for the individual woman as to how she wishes to dress, and should be respected by society. Amongst Muslims, this difference of opinion should also to be respected.

'No harm in looking!' - Well, there is!

Modesty in behaviour is unfortunately frequently overlooked due to people's preoccupation with dress code. Lowering one's gaze when interacting with the opposite sex is expressly mentioned in the Quran. This applies to both men and women, and in fact the command is given to men first:

> *Say to the believing men to lower their gaze and guard their private parts; that is purer for them; surely Allah is Aware of what they do. {Quran 24: 30}*

This is not referring to everyday sight, where we are looking as we go about our way. It is that second look after seeing someone attractive, or holding extra eye contact with a colleague. Here it is about enjoying their beauty. This is not permissible and is sinful, as it violates this command. Note how Allah concludes this verse by pointing out that He is well aware of what they, namely menfolk, do, including taking that furtive second look. Therein is the test for men - curb that thirsty urge to gaze at women. If women think that men have got off lightly - they have to cover but men do not - let me point out that the desire for men to look at women is extremely strong. Even elderly men, pious men, male scholars of Islam struggle to keep this under control.

Observe also, how the command given to men and then to women is absolutely identical here, in these sequential verses (24: 30-31): 'lower the gaze' is followed immediately by 'guard the private parts'. Allah is making clear how there is a sequence that begins with the look and ends with illicit carnal relations. We already discussed the mini-encounters above. Women do not look at men with lustful gazes, as men do. So what is the relevance of telling them to lower their gaze? The danger is in prolonged eye contact, because the emotional seed gets planted when both engage in extended eye contact – it takes two to tango. This applies to both men and women. Thus, to avoid cupid's arrow from firing, practically this means breaking eye contact deliberately and frequently when speaking. Again Allah's order has wisdom and benefit in it – it is keeping people from even putting a foot onto the slippery slope that risks triggering the cascade.

Interaction between men and women is meant to be purposeful only and not casual such as between friends. When speaking, there is a very important difference between men and women, which needs to be appreciated. Women tend to be more bubbly and effusive than men. When interacting with men, their vivaciousness can be seen as quite attractive, and risks sending inadvertent signals. To this end, women need to be aware of this, and when speaking to men, should take care that their voice is neither flirtatious nor unguarded, and they should avoid excessive laughter.[25] The principle here is again, not to set foot on the slippery slope. Dressing conservatively, but then engaging in idle banter with raucous laughter is modesty defeated. The principle is not to flirt, do not tempt nor be tempted.

Free mixing therefore, where men and women interact purely for sociability, needs sensibility and guarding from both sides. Scholars hold different opinions as to the permissibility of free mixing for purely social reasons. The more stringent view is that it is not permissible, whilst the alternative view regards it as permissible provided Islamic etiquette is followed. Both sides need to be highly conscious that it is very easy to

---

[25] Quran 33:32

develop feelings for each other. They should control their gaze, body language and conversation, and break eye contact frequently. A man and woman being alone together in private is definitely discouraged, as there is a clear invitation to temptation.

Being mindful of what one looks at has another key corollary. In modern times, pornography has become far too easily accessible. Just a few clicks without having to leave your bedroom. Coupled with a mindset of 'no harm in looking' has led to a staggering proportion of the population, especially men, not just viewing it regularly but even being addicted to it. Studies have found between 50 to 99% of men watch pornography regularly[26] – so between one in two men to virtually all males watch it. The problem affects Muslim communities too[27].

Images, especially shocking or indecent ones, once seen, do not leave the mind. They act like a slow poison on the brain. The damaging effects of pornography are being increasingly documented. Rather than curbing desires, which is a pivotal principle in Islam, it will instead drive them up. Aside from addiction, many people's idea of sexual relations, especially youngsters who watch it, has been warped. The result is unhappy relationships as expectations with regards to intimacy are completely unrealistic. Islam is clear on this – there is harm in looking at indecent images, and it is forbidden.

Bottom Line:

- Control the gaze – avoid prolonged eye contact by frequently glancing away.

- Men need to avoid the 'check her out' glances.

- Dress modestly - for women this means cover the head and chest and

---

[26] https://bit.ly/2Ul9ARj
[27] https://bit.ly/2vQYJFq

don an outer garment to cloak the body shape.

• Behave modestly.

• Take great care when mixing with the opposite gender

• Viewing indecent images and videos is categorically prohibited.

Kindness

This trait is of phenomenal importance. The two attributes of Allah mentioned in the Quran well in excess of any of Allah's other attributes are *Rahmaan* and *Raheem*. In essence, they mean overwhelmingly kind and extremely compassionate – kindness and compassion well beyond human comprehension. *Rahmaan* is used 57 times, and *Raheem* 116 times. Not only is this Allah's nature, but He expects this of us too.

Kindness is wanting to see good for others and trying to facilitate this. ***Spreading goodness is the absolute tenet of behaviour of a Muslim.*** It extends to all people and creatures. The Prophet's overarching manner was one of exquisite kindness. There are countless references in the Quran to act with kindness, and countless examples from the Sunnah of the Prophet. The Prophet narrated the story of a prostitute who gave a parched dog water drawn from a well, with her shoe as a vessel and her headscarf as a string to lower it down. She was forgiven her sins and admitted to Paradise.[28] This was despite her being engaged in a highly sinful living. The single act of kindness was given weighty value by Allah.

Even in dealing with enemies or oppressors, kindness carries gravitas. Allah counsels us to repel evil with goodness i.e. kindness:

> *And they are not equal, the good deed and the bad deed. Repel (evil) by that (deed) which is better; and lo and behold! the one*

---

[28] Sahih Bukhari, Sahih Muslim

between whom you and him is enmity will become like a devoted friend. {Quran 41:34}

This was exemplified by the Prophet. There were many vitriolic enemies of Islam who committed gross atrocities and incredible evil when they were in a position of power over the Muslims. When Muslim numbers swelled and they came into the ascendancy, the Prophet could have held them to account and rightfully exacted justice and retribution. Instead he showed overwhelming benevolence and forgave them their past actions. This conquered the hearts of the disbelievers and enemies. Willingly, virtually all of them accepted Islam.

On another occasion, the Prophet visited the city of Taif to bring them the message of Islam. The people responded with malicious hostility and aggression, even encouraging their children to ridicule the Prophet. Ridicule turned to violence and they started pelting the Prophet with stones, forcing him to flee from there, bleeding and bruised. After escaping them, the angel Jibreel (Gabriel) appeared before the Prophet and offered to crush the city and its insolent inhabitants. The Prophet, however, turned this offer down. Instead he prayed for them, that good and righteous descendants would emerge in later generations. Indeed this is what transpired, but not before the same people of Taif actually came in later years to accept Islam of their own accord.

The importance of this quality cannot be overemphasised. We must strive for exemplary heights of kindness. Kindness to near relatives takes priority over others. Parents are in pole position, followed by spouse, siblings, children, extended family, then neighbours. The value of this trait and how it fits into the scheme of our obligations can be seen with another incident from the Prophet's time. Ritual prayer is tremendously important and is given huge weight by Allah. The Prophet's love for it led him to describe it as the coolness of his eyes and he used to take his time, performing it to a standard par excellence. It is after all a time to connect with your Maker. The Prophet was leading the prayer on one occasion when a baby started to cry. He transformed the measured sedate pace of the prayer into a much swifter affair to reach its rapid conclusion. Upon completion, the

Companions asked what had happened to cause this change of gears. He explained how the mother of the crying baby would have become agitated and desperate for the prayer to conclude so she could attend to her infant. Despite his love for the prayer, kindness dictated completing the prayer as soon as possible to alleviate her anguish.

Examples of kindness by the Prophet abound. The biggest enemy of Islam was a two-faced man called Abdullah ibn Ubayy. He was the leader of a group of people known as the hypocrites; these were people who claimed to be Muslims but were the furthest from Islam and spent their efforts trying to destroy Islam from the inside. Abdullah Ibn Ubayy had enjoyed great prestige prior to Islam and had been poised to be made king of Medina. The arrival of the Prophet and the conversion of the Medinites to Islam ended his aspirations. While purporting to be Muslim, he orchestrated many treacherous acts against the Prophet and Islam right up until his death. In usual circumstances one cannot tell who a hypocrite is; they may pray and fast, so outwardly they appear like any other Muslim. But in Abdullah ibn Ubayy's case his deeds were so blatant that his status as a hypocrite was absolutely confirmed, and he was known to be so amongst the people.

Abdullah's son, however, was a true Muslim. Upon Abdullah's death his son beseeched the Prophet to undertake the funeral prayer for his father and pray for his forgiveness. Now, Islamic funeral prayers are only offered for Muslims, and hypocrites are not only classed as disbelievers, but they are to receive the most severe punishment of all from Allah on the Day of Judgement. Despite this, the Prophet acceded his request. Umar bin Khattab, a very close Companion, questioned the Prophet why he would agree, given the deceased man was the greatest enemy of Islam and displayed nothing but evil. As he was known to be the greatest hypocrite, he was therefore not eligible for the funeral prayers. The Prophet remained undeterred and Umar continued to protest until finally the Prophet responded that 'if I had to pray more than seventy times so that Allah would grant him forgiveness, then I would do that.' 'Seventy times' is an Arabic expression not literally meaning seventy but much, much more; it implies a massive amount. In English an equivalent expression would be 'a million times' or 'a gazillion times'. Such is the value of kindness as was exemplified by the Prophet, that he would have exhausted himself trying to seek pardon for a man who committed gross atrocities against Allah, His Messenger and His people, and as a result, would be expected to be condemned to the lowest level of Hell.

With kindness goes generosity. The Muslim should spend generously on their family. They host their guests with great hospitality. They spend generously in charity on the less fortunate and needy. In fact, all spending in this way is referred to as 'charity' (called *sadaqa*), and Allah promises that spending in this manner will not decrease your wealth because He will actually increase it.

Bottom Line:

• Spreading goodness is the backbone of moral conduct for a Muslim.

• Develop kindness to the highest possible level.

• Be extra kind to your parents, and near relatives.

• Be generous.

Control Your Temper and the Need for Patience

Losing one's senses is the starting point to irrational decisions or unacceptable actions. This may arise from alcohol and intoxicants. Suggestive loud music can produce the same effect. It can also stem from losing one's temper. Sadly, there are many instances where a person has committed a regrettable action after becoming consumed with rage. Severing family ties, breaking off lifelong friendships, divorce, violence, and even murder.

The Prophet repeatedly warned against anger. When asked for some good advice by one Companion, he counselled him 'Do not get angry'. A bit surprised by the simplicity of the answer, the Companion repeated his question several times, looking for something more substantial. But the answer he received each time was 'Do not get angry.'[29] Of the multitude of extremely important wisdoms the Prophet could have imparted, he emphasised the need not to lose control. This is a vital trait that every Muslim must adopt.

In the Quran, Allah describes amongst the different qualities of those whom He will deem successful:

> *Those who spend (in God's Cause) when in prosperity and in adversity, who repress anger, and who pardon the people; verily, God loves the good-doers.* {Quran 3: 133-134}

> *And those who avoid the greater sins, and illegal sexual intercourse, and when they are angry, they forgive.* {Quran 42: 37}

Anger is a consequence of unrealistic expectations. We get upset with someone because we expected better from them, whether in behaviour or work. We get angry when our six-year-old scribbles on the wall. By this age, we were expecting some sense, so we lose our temper. A friend turns up late every single time when meeting up. On a particularly important occasion he is late again, despite being warned to be on time. So we lose it. Controlling anger requires lowering our expectations about people or things around us. The six-year-old is still a child, not an adult, so will do silly things. The friend has always been late and will continue to be so; no point expecting they will change (tell him to come an hour earlier than the due time). Anger is a natural emotion, but letting it out as uncontrolled rage, or acting in anger, are being cautioned against. We need to keep a lid on our anger.

The opposite of anger is patience (called *sabr* in Arabic), which is *not letting our emotions get on top of us*, regardless of the emotion or the

---

[29] Sahih Bukhari

circumstances. Someone has let us down, or a tragedy has struck, but we do not allow anger, depression or despair to overcome us. Emotions are natural but we do not let them overwhelm us. Just as Allah tells us in the Quran not to get angry, conversely He tells us to be patient and forbearing:

... and bear with patience whatever befalls you. {Quran 31: 17}

Allah loves the patient ones. {Quran 3: 146}

So be patient. For sure, the (best) outcome is for the pious ones. {Quran 11: 49)

As life will comprise hard times as well as good times, Allah and His Messenger are teaching us how to handle the dips. The Prophet passed by a woman who was grieving for her son by his graveside. He counselled her from behind to have patience and be mindful of Allah, but so overwhelmed by her grief was she, that without looking she retorted, 'Go away, you have not had such a calamity befall you.' The Prophet, who actually buried six of his seven children in his lifetime, left her be. When someone informed her that it was the Prophet himself who had been counselling her, she was horrified and hurried to his house to apologise. 'I did not recognise you,' she said to which the Prophet replied, 'For sure, patience is shown at the first stroke of the calamity'.[30] In other words, when tragedy strikes, keep the emotions under check from the outset. No matter how painful they are, do not let them get on top of you. Muslims need to have a switch between their emotions and tongue.

Bottom Line:

• Anger is a natural emotion but acting on it is unacceptable.

• We must not let our emotions control us, we need to keep on top of them.

• Patience (*sabr*) is an important virtue and a trait Allah loves.

---

[30] Sahih Muslim, Sahih Bukhari

Relationship with Parents

Parents are not VIP's, but actually DIP's (Dangerously Important People). Their rank far, far exceeds that of anyone else. Kings, queens, presidents and prime ministers do not come close. Humility towards one's parents, obedience and service towards them are *commanded*. In short, excellence in behaviour is required. Parents display a miniscule portion of Allah's kindness and compassion in how they provide bottomless love for their children, in how they protect them, feed and clothe them, educate them, nurture them until they are independent. They sacrifice themselves night and day, with their wealth, their health, their time, their energy. Just as man is generally oblivious to the multitude of blessings provided by Allah, similarly children are generally clueless about what their parents have done for them. In both cases there tends to be ungratefulness and complaints, instead of sincere heartfelt gratitude.

The mother carries the greatest respect, quite ahead of the father. Two of Allah's greatest attributes, *Rahmaan* and *Raheem*, mean extremely kind and extremely compassionate, and are derived linguistically from the root word, *Ra-Ha-Ma*, meaning to be compassionate. The mother shows enormous mercy to her children. It is no coincidence that the Arabic word for uterus, the organ that links her to her children, is *rahm*, and derives from the same root, *Ra-Ha-Ma*.

Excellence in behaviour starts with great respect and humility before them. Allah commands not to even roll one's eyes or huff at anything they may say. As one gets wiser and more mature, one's parents tend to become more rigid in their views and difficult in their ways. Getting on with them becomes trickier, as one comes to think they know better and frustration boils over when parents simply do not seem 'to get it'. But Allah notes this and orders us to remain humble before them, and to love them, honour them, and serve them. Specifically we are not to get on with our own lives, and to ignore them or their needs. The Quran captures this beautifully:

And, out of kindness, lower over them the wing of humility, and say: 'My Lord! bestow on them Your Mercy just as they cherished me in childhood'. {Quran 17: 24}

Note the amazing imagery used here. When one attains maturity, one gains wings of independence and can fly away, leaving behind the nest and one's parents. Instead, at this point, one lowers their wings, stays with them, and shows humility and love.

The verse that precedes this is:

Your Lord has decreed that you worship none but Him, and that you be kind to parents. Whether one or both of them attain old age in your life, say not to them a word of contempt, nor repel them, but address them in terms of honour. {Quran 17:23}

The command to be kind to parents in this verse is coupled with the most fundamental command of all, namely to worship Allah alone, without partners. This coupling is also seen in many other places in the Quran, impressing the eminent status of parents.

There are many narrations of the Prophet relating to parents. One particular story, however, completely captures the magnitude of reward here. The Prophet informed some of his Companions about a man from Yemen named Owais al-Qarni, who would come sometime after him to perform Hajj (major pilgrimage).[31] The Prophet exhorted them to seek this man's prayers of forgiveness to Allah, for themselves. Wow – a man so esteemed that the closest Companions of the Prophet would seek out his invocations to Allah for forgiveness for themselves.

Owais al-Qarni, on the other hand, was a very simple man with little means, who looked after his mother. He yearned desperately to meet the Prophet, learn from him, indeed serve him, and even to go to battle under him. For any able Muslim man, living at the time of the Prophet, there

---

[31] Sahih Muslim

could have been no greater dream than this – absolutely none. However, Owais' mother refused to allow him to go, and leave her. He made diligent plans to have some other family members or neighbours look after her, but she was afraid of being without him, and she remained adamant that he must not leave her side. Owais respected her and obliged, dutifully looking after her. He did not get to make the trip to meet the Prophet.

The Prophet passed away and in time, Owais' mother passed away too. Owais finally made his trip to Mecca for Hajj. It was now the period of Umar bin Khattab, the second ruler (caliph) to succeed the Prophet. Umar and other Companions would search for Owais al-Qarni during Hajj every year. The tribe of Qaran on this occasion directed them to an unassuming man without any special standing in the tribe. Upon finding him, they relayed the glad tidings the Prophet had revealed about him, and as per the Prophet's instructions, they requested Owais to make prayers (*dua*) to Allah to grant them Allah's forgiveness and mercy.

The Companions of the Prophet, especially the closest ones, such as Umar and Ali, were of the highest standing and rank. Yet a devoted son's *sincere service* to his mother, allowed him to reach their rank. Such is the reward of honouring, obeying and serving one's parents. Allah decreed obligations on man as means of bestowing heavy rewards (see later, *Why do we Pray*). The obligation of serving one's parents is a command but carries the greatest rewards from the domain of moral conduct.

There is another important side point to note about this story of Owais al-Qarni. From society's perspective, he was a very ordinary man. He was not outstanding in any obvious manner, for instance in terms of education, job, status in community, or lineage. His lofty status with Allah, however, shows that any person can reach this astonishing relationship with Allah. Such people are called *awliyaa*; this status can be achieved by ordinary people in addition to the prophets. It is a matte r of sincere intention, sincere gratitude and devoting one's life in the best manner to please Allah. What deeds can seem trivial to others or even to oneself, can carry profound weight with Allah.

There is also a profound message in his story warning us against arrogance and prejudice. How so? The people of his tribe had no idea about him and did not hold him in any special regard. In fact, he was a man who had had leprosy, which would, if anything, have stigmatised him in his community (though from which Allah had cured him, leaving a small white patch on his skin). Yet here was a *walee* (singular of *awliyaa*) living amongst them. Many a person probably thought they were better than Owais. Similarly, we have no idea who is a *walee* of Allah amongst us. Who has that sincerity of worship and true love for Allah in their heart, or is undertaking some deed that Allah gives magnanimous gravitas to? They may have that special relationship with Allah, but walk about amongst us like very ordinary folk. They might not know themselves. That person could be a cleaner, a porter, a taxi driver, or just a mum, or a son or a daughter. We have no idea but we might easily feel we are better than them because of our job, education, home, etc. Arrogance lurking in our hearts – beware.

Whilst children should strive for obedience, how should parents behave with their children? Parents are in a clear position of authority. The concept of rights and obligations is very important, and is discussed emphatically in the next sections. The Prophetic way is not to demand one's rights, but to uphold kindness and compassion with all. Obligations are used to make sure one is fulfilling one's own duties. Parents need to be mindful that expecting such high levels of obedience can easily turn their children into quasi-slaves. Children are a trust from Allah. A parent's role is to educate them, instil faith and values in them, and train them to be upstanding in their behaviour and of service to humanity. Whatever commands they issue to them must have these goals at their core. For example, assigning them chores in the house teaches service and humility. However, ordering them around night and day, and keeping them at your beck and call is unwarranted. Overburdening them is a form of oppression. Not only will the parents be held to account by Allah for this injustice, but they risk rebellion from the children and their going astray, which is the worst possible outcome.

On the other hand, there can be issues spoiling children. Certainly, love and kindness are central to upbringing children. The Prophet was deeply loving of his children and grandchildren and used to play with them, as well as teach them good manners. However, where love becomes excessive, parents can give in to all the demands of their child, providing all their wants along with excessive comfort, instilling selfishness, self-centredness and lack of regard for others. Failing to teach good behaviour, and the importance of striving in effort and hard work to achieve goals is a failure of the parents. Spoilt selfish individuals will not be of service to anybody.

Bottom Line:

• Excellence in behaviour towards parents is obligated.

• The magnitude of serving one's parents cannot be quantified.

• There is no greater reward than in the honour and service of one's parents.

• One should rush to do things for them, that please them, *before* they themselves even ask.

• People can attain a special relationship with Allah (and become a *walee*) through sincere intention, worship and undertaking deeds that may seem trivial but carry great weight.

• Beware of arrogance and looking down on others – you have no idea who is a *walee* walking amongst you.

• Parents: children are a trust from Allah – train them to be God-conscious upstanding human beings. They are not slaves, do not overburden them. Equally, do not spoil them.

Women in Islam

Men and women have been created from the same spirit, and are equal in the eyes of Allah. It is a misconception that Huwa (Eve) was created from the rib of Adam. Both were created from the one spirit, and not one from the other. A man does not have any superiority in rank over a woman simply by the nature of his being a man, and vice versa. Both have the same opportunities to achieve Allah's good pleasure, and attain the highest levels of Paradise:

> *Whoever does works of righteousness, **man or woman**, and has Faith, verily, to him will We give a new Life (i.e. Paradise), a life that is good and pure and We will bestow on them their reward according to the best of their actions. {Quran 16: 97}*

> *Surely, Muslim men and Muslim women, believing men and believing women, devout men and devout women, truthful men and truthful women, patient men and patient women, humble men and humble women, and the men who give sadaqa (charity) and the women who give sadaqa, and the men who fast and the women who fast, and the men who guard their private parts (against fornication) and the women who guard (theirs), and the men who remember Allah much and the women who remember (Him) - for them, Allah has prepared forgiveness and a great reward. {Quran 33: 35}*

Women have the right to education, owning wealth and property, and are fully entitled to inherit. They can work outside the home, and can own and run businesses. They have the right to turn down any marriage proposals they dislike. These rights were given to women more than 1400 years ago with the advent of Islam. Whilst spiritually they are equal, men and women are different to each other physically, mentally, and emotionally. As such, they have been assigned different roles and responsibilities by Allah. Men must shoulder the responsibility of earning a living and providing for the family. In contrast, no woman is obliged to earn a living, either for herself or the family. Her financial upkeep is not her responsibility at all, but lies with her father, subsequently her husband and later her son. In their absence, her brother, or grandfather, and failing them, other male members of her extended family, with final responsibility lying with the State.

This does *not* mean that she is not allowed to work. Rather, she does not need to 'work for a living' but working is, instead, a *choice* for her. This is an honour that Allah gives women. If she wishes to work and support herself this is entirely her decision.

Women have been recognised as being equal spiritually to men, with rights to match, only relatively recently in other faiths and societies. Islam granted this almost one and a half millennia ago. Unfortunately, in the modern age, Islamic countries are dominated by rather patriarchal societies and governments, and women are often considered inferior and denied their due rights. This is not a proper application of Islam. More representative is the key role women scholars have played throughout Islamic history; they learnt and then taught the sacred disciplines, including hadith transmission. One example is Nafisa bint al-Hassan (762-824 CE), the great granddaughter of the Prophet, who learnt from the great scholar Imam Malik ibn Anas, and then went on to teach two of the greatest scholars of Islam, Imam al-Shafi'i and Ahmad ibn Hanbal, who founded the respective schools of *fiqh* (legal rulings) bearing their names. Another is Umm al-Darda al-Soghra who taught the great scholar Hasan al-Basri, as well as the caliph (ruler) of the time, Abdul Malik bin Marwan. The scholar Shaykh Akram Nadwi discovered more than 8000 female scholars of hadith throughout history, which he compiled into a magnum opus of 53 volumes.[32]

---

[32] Shaykh Akram Nadwi: Al-Muhaddithat: The Women Scholars in Islam

Husband and Wife Relationship

It is critical to appreciate first and foremost that the marital relationship is built upon love, mercy and respect for one another. *Not rights and obligations*. Love is wanting to see the other person happy for no personal gain. Allah describes the husband and wife as being 'garments' for one another.[33] This powerful imagery captures the essence of this relationship. The closest substance to our bodies is our clothes. Clothes hide our shame, beautify us, and protect us from the outside. Nobody will be closer to a person physically, mentally, or emotionally than their spouse. Allah says:

> *And one of His signs is that He has created for you, spouses from amongst yourselves so that you might take comfort in them and He has placed between you, love and mercy. In this there is surely evidence (of the truth) for the people who reflect carefully. {Quran 30: 21}*

In other words, the marital relationship is one in which both the husband and wife find companionship, love and mercy, and derive comfort from each other. The embodiment of Islam was the Prophet. He treated his wives with great respect and was extremely loving and caring towards them. He used to joke and play with them, as well as help in the household chores. He used to consult them on important matters, and take into consideration their viewpoints. This is what an Islamic marriage is. Note how household chores were a responsibility for both the husband and wife, not the wife alone. When the Prophet married his daughter, Fatima, to Ali, his cousin and close Companion, he divided the household chores between them.

The Prophet strongly recommended men and women to get married. Marriage is a great blessing from Allah, which should be availed. This is also the only permitted relationship in which one's physical (intimate) desires are met. It is the nucleus for a family and raising children. Marriage

---

[33] Quran 2: 187

is not portrayed as a bed of roses; it will have ups and downs. After marriage, spouses discover not only that their partner can press their buttons, but in fact that they have buttons they did not even know about!

For this reason, the Prophet explained that marriage is half of faith, i.e. *when disagreements inevitably arise*, one has to show the best of moral character to their spouse. Handling this conflict is immensely important. Displaying exemplary kindness at a time one may not be feeling very charitable is the test. An invaluable approach at times when one's spouse has hit the ceiling is consciously not to get angry. Anger met with anger is a recipe for disaster and escalation. One person needs to step out of the arena, mentally, to break the conflict. Keeping quiet, active listening and being an absorbent sponge is called for. Taking on some of their chores, helping with some troublesome task, a little humour or even just making them a cup of tea will go a long way to cooling the situation and open the door to resolution. Once the emotional flare-up has subsided, acknowledgement and kindness will allow the situation to heal.

Whilst the spirit of the marriage is the key, there are rights and obligations in the marriage. As already mentioned above, rights and obligations are *NOT* the way to run a marriage. So what is the point to those rights and obligations? They have two uses. Firstly, each spouse needs to look at their *own* obligations to the other, and ensure they are fulfilling them. This way the obligations are used as a yardstick for oneself to check they are not falling short on their responsibilities to their spouse. They should not dwell on their rights, and neither be ever watchful as to if their spouse is living up to their 'requirements'. So to be clear, the husband's perspective on his rights and obligations should be to ensure he fulfils *his* obligations to his wife, not demand his rights from her. The same goes for the wife. In other words, rights and obligations should be used to make sure one is holding up their end. The second use of rights and obligations is if the marriage hits trouble and the couple need to have mediation. The mediator will then have a set of rules to navigate the roles and responsibilities of the husband and wife.

Having made that clear, the husband is obligated to provide his wife accommodation, independent from his family, so she has her own space. He must provide for her, which includes food, living expenses and a similar quality of life she was used to prior to getting married. In addition he must provide additional money for her to use as she wishes. She is not obliged to cook or clean for him. In fact all of these responsibilities are inherent in a few famous verses from the Quran relating to husband and wife:

> *Men are caretakers of women with what Allah has bestowed on some of them over others, and with what they spend out of their wealth. {Quran 4: 34}*

> *... and for men there is a degree over them (women)... {Quran 2: 228}*

Wait just a minute – aren't these verses bandied about to suggest that that Islam holds men as superior to women? It turns out these verses are heavily and erroneously misquoted. The Arabic word *qawwaamoon*, used in the first verse to describe men, comes from the root verb *Qaa-Ma*, literally meaning 'to stand'. But here the usage implies to stand over, as in to supervise and look after; men serve as the caretakers for women. A caretaker does not own his charge, but he is responsible for making sure that it is maintained and well looked after. Men are completely responsible for the upkeep of the females in their care, a husband to his wife, a father to his daughters (and a son to his mother and a brother to his sisters, if he is their only close male relation). Allah makes this clear by stating that 'they spend out of their wealth'. In the second verse, the 'degree' for men over women actually means men have a greater degree of *service* to women. The verse does not imply that men have a degree of superiority over women.

Spousal relationships and intimacy can only exist between husband and wife. As discussed above (see *Modesty*), carnal relations outside of marriage are a major sin in Islam. Intimate relations between a husband

and wife are rewarded – yes, you read that right, *rewarded.*[34] This is a revelation for most Muslims as the abhorrence of fornication is so well ingrained in Muslims that the act within marriage becomes equated to one of necessity, not one of reward. It is not held as sinful or repulsive as in some other faiths. The reward is there because both the man and woman are fulfilling their desires in accordance to the command of Allah.

The wife's obligations are to protect her husband's home, his reputation and her chastity. She is also meant to answer his call for intimate relations, *where reasonable.*[35] This might sound strange especially to those used to western values. So, why is this so? This has to be understood very carefully. Again, men and women are programmed differently and function differently. Generally, intimate relations are a big aspect of life for men. Much less so for women, who multitask and juggle numerous roles and chores throughout the day to do with their children, home, husband, work, etc. As a result they could easily go for long stretches without physical intimacy.[36] Marriage is the only permissible outlet for intimate relations. A healthy intimate relationship is an important part of a successful marriage. This obligation is meant to be a *reminder* to the women to keep up on this part of the marriage, as they serve as the gatekeepers for this. Otherwise the marriage will face difficulties as resentment and dissent builds up and the husband may seek other outlets to fulfil his unrequited desires. Adultery is the worst-case scenario. The woman must keep aware of her husband's needs and should use this as a yardstick to prevent her imposing hardship on her husband.

The benefit of this approach in marriage has been noted by non-Muslims as well; for instance, Laura Doyle in her book, *The Surrendered Wife*, which coaches women on achieving a successful marriage, has a chapter specifically encouraging the wife to pay due attention to this and making

---

[34] Sahih Muslim
[35] Sahih Bukhari
[36] https://wb.md/2ydyV7p

herself available[37].

The husband meanwhile needs to be reasonable in his requests. Where his wife is tired or unwell, she would not be obligated and neither should he expect or seek it. If he finds the wife always seems to be too tired, he needs to reflect on why. Is she overburdened in the house, with chores and the children? He might need to pitch in more to give her some relief. The wife on the other hand should also evaluate where her energies are going and how to prioritise her husband. If she has chosen to work outside the home, and her job is demanding, constantly draining her energy so that she is always too tired for her husband, she needs to redress this. The husband should not be second to her job, and constantly neglected. This would be unfair on her husband, and a form of cruelty.

In the home, as in any company or team, there has to be a leader or a boss. This role has been delegated to the husband and *is restricted to family matters*. When there is a decision to be made, there should be discussion and consultation between husband and wife. Any final decision is then made by the man. It is important to stress this relates to family matters only. He does not have the right to order the wife in other areas that are personal to her. It is her right what she chooses to wear, even whether she wears the *hijab* (headscarf) or not, whom she has as friends, how she wishes to spend her personal time and money, when and where she prays. She is fully entitled to go to the mosque if she so wishes. Note also, the husband as the leader of the home, is a default position that Allah sets out. Allah does not set this as an obligation. If the dynamics of the husband and wife are such that they both agree that the wife is the one to have the final say, there is nothing wrong with this.

It must be stressed again that married life and family life is not meant to be run according to rights and responsibilities. Just as in every other aspect of life, the spirit of Islam is essential in the relationship. Kindness, love

---

[37] Laura Doyle. Chapter 20 in, *The Surrendered Wife* (Reading, Pocket Books 2006), 206-221

and the highest conduct overarch the relationship. Let's take another example of obligations being misunderstood. Generally, the husband must provide for the family, whilst any income the wife makes is entirely hers. But consider if the husband earns a modest living and is struggling to provide for the household, the children's schools and a standard of living for the wife and family, having to take on two jobs, or even loans. The wife on the other hand is wealthy due to her business or portfolio of properties. If she takes the view that the husband should struggle on with the upkeep of the family, as this is his obligation and she is not required to contribute, not only has she missed the spirit of kindness and mercy but she is actually harming the husband, by not relieving him of his stress, when it is in her power to do so. As well as missing the *spirit* of Islam she is guilty of an injustice on her husband.

Whilst marriage is highly recommended and a great blessing, marriage is not an obligation. For some people marriage fails to materialise for whatever reason. That is a tough test, especially if one has tried long and hard to find a soulmate. But marriage is not the be-all and end-all of life.

One continues in life striving to fulfil one's obligations to Allah and fellow man in other ways.

Parenting in Islam

Parenting and raising children is a matter of utmost importance in Islam. Children have to be raised with great diligence, and not just educated, but their character needs to be moulded to produce God-conscious human beings with the highest levels of moral behaviour. The degree of importance can be understood from reflecting upon the meaning of what seems to be an unconnected verse in the Quran:

> *...whoever kills a soul... it is as if he had slain all of mankind. And whoever saves one – it is as if he had saved all of mankind. {Quran 5: 32}:*

Why is killing one person like killing all of mankind? Each person is capable of having a family, and his children will go on to have families, with their children subsequently having their own progeny, and so the cycle continues. Over generations and generations, this one person will have given rise to countless other humans, like a nation all of itself (see Figure 1). If that person has been killed before he had his children, then it is as if a whole nation will never come forth now, and has been wiped out.

By analogy, a child brought up without due care and attention, who is left to go astray and becomes a disbeliever, is likely to have children who will be disbelievers, and the end result of the ongoing cycles is that he has spawned a nation of disbelievers. Conversely, each righteous child will hopefully produce a nation of righteous believers, just like saving one life is equivalent to saving all of mankind. Parenting is all about propagating nations of believers.

The mother plays the bigger role in the upbringing of the children, and has been given more suitable traits, namely a very loving, self-sacrificing and caring nature. A woman has the capacity, even when she is exhausted or sick (even seriously sick), to soldier on and take care of all her children, cook, feed, clean and comfort them. Anecdotally, men, on the other hand, are often crippled from the 'man flu' and need to be taken care of, regardless of what else is happening around them. This is not to say that men are not loving and caring, or have no role in parenting (fathers have a key role in parenting too), but women have these traits instinctively built into their motherhood par excellence.

Islam frees the mother from the financial responsibility and burden to provide for the family precisely to allow her to focus on this task. Modern culture, especially feminism, in the pursuit of apparent equality, expects the woman to have a flourishing career and an independent income of her own - any person's worth in society is based on power, position and prosperity. These all stem from a career. Motherhood is increasingly being delayed as career is prioritised; at worst, it is viewed as an inconvenience and a digression from her career. Childminders and childcare facilities are used to solve this 'problem'. The upbringing of the children is thus outsourced. This is not the view in Islam. A mother carries great status and great responsibility in Islam – she is to produce the next generation. This is not to be belittled. Instead she is given the honour and respect to go with this, along with the necessary worldly means.

It is worth reflecting on the physiology of human male and female reproduction. Men can reproduce throughout their lives. Even a 90-year-old man can father children. Women on the other hand have a body clock, and typically around the age of 50 years their menstrual cycle stops, and along with it the ability to have children. Why is this so? Note that, generally, this is not the case in the animal world, where, barring a few exceptions, animals as a rule retain the ability to reproduce as they age right up until their death.

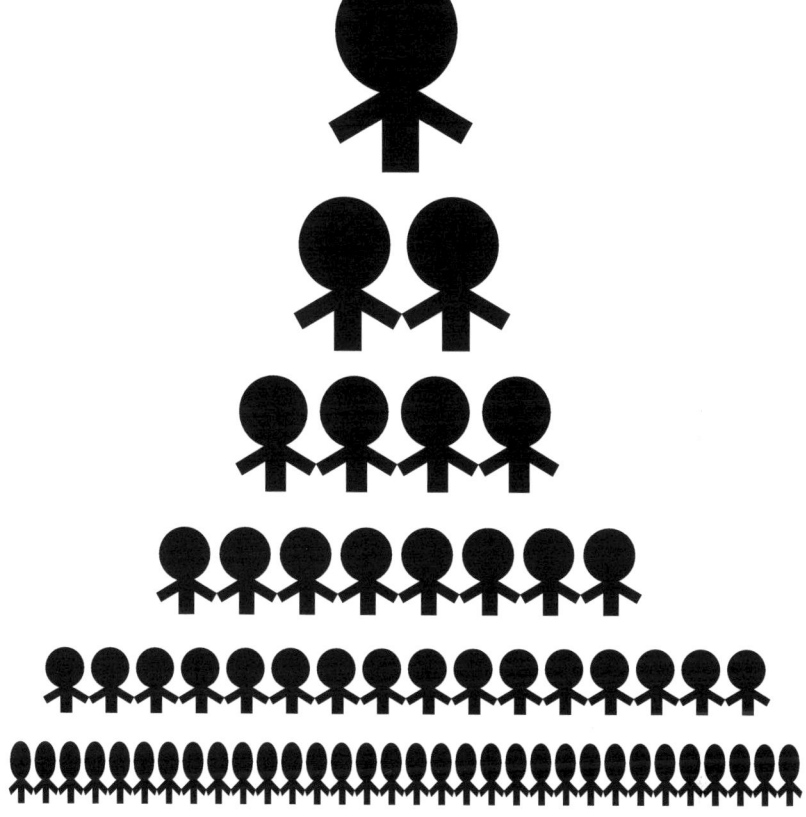

Figure 1a: A pyramid of people over time

In this figure each person gives rise to two children, starting with the person at the very top (the spouses are not shown, just the progeny that arises from each person). The fifth subsequent generation therefore comprises 32 progeny. Thus, one person gives rise to a whole nation with time.

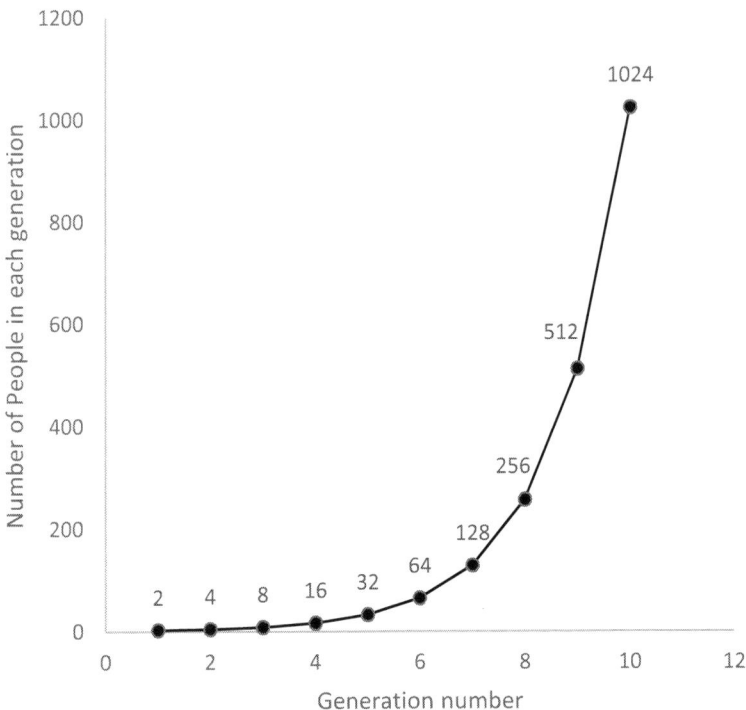

Figure 1b: The maths of two children per person - graph of y = 2^x

For the mathematically inclined, the graph for each person having two children is exponential, being y=2^x. The generation numbers have been plotted against the number of people each generation contains. Generation number zero is the original person. Notice how at 7 generations, there are now more than 100 offspring and at 10 generations there are 1024. These are the numbers if each person has *only two* children each. If each person has, say, 4 children, then the graph (y=4^x) is even more dramatic, by the fifth generation the children number 1024 and by the 10th generation, more than a million!

Allah has placed signs in His Creation to point to Him and for us to reflect. The father is important in raising children, but the mother clearly plays the bigger role. One key reason for the female body clock is to ensure that women will have enough years ahead of them to raise the youngsters and inculcate the right values and faith. A woman having a baby at 50 years old, living until 80 years, still has 30 years to raise the child. In this there is a sign. The body clock is there to emphasise the role mothers play in rearing. This is a job of serious focus and commitment. This sign fits exactly with what Islam tells us. The priority role of women is to raise God-conscious children, and they are freed from worldly worries and distractions for this specific role. It also brings home another point. No woman knows when her cycle will cease. It can stop well before the assumed 50 years. With the modern push for women to have careers, they are at risk of delaying children to the point they miss the boat. This has been noted and reported as one of the serious issues facing modern women.[38]

So parenting is a big deal in Islam. It is about producing nations of believers and the mother is built for this role and freed from worldly responsibilities to concentrate on this. But what is in it for the mother, and the father in fact? As we shall cover later, each person receives reward for each good deed, or sin for bad ones. But they also receive the rewards and sins that other people do where they have taught the knowledge or are responsible for those deeds, good or bad respectively. For instance, you teach someone how to fish and you receive the same reward whenever that person catches fish with which he feeds himself, his family, or sells to earn his living. If you are a hardened gangster and you teach a new member how to kill, you will receive the same sin every time he uses these new skills to attack people.

A friend asks to borrow your van so he can transport some charity goods to the local charity shop. You will receive the same reward of his good actions. If he needs it to pick a consignment of liquor to distribute to the

---

[38] https://bit.ly/2WIJo4V

local off-licences, and you know that, you will earn yourself sin.

Now, any good that a child does because their mother taught them so, will result in the mother receiving the same reward as the child receives. And this reward continues to accrue even after she dies. Wow! That's a lot of reward flooding her account now, if she is picking up the same good deeds that all her children are doing during their lifetime. The children get their rewards and the mother the same, that is the Generosity of Allah.

But hold your horses, there is more! Whatever good deeds her children's children do (i.e. her grandchildren), also comes back to her. In fact every generation that follows now, the reward of their good deeds is duplicated for the previous parents, which means this mother receives all of the good deeds in equal measure. If you look at Figure 1a again, now view the pyramid of people from the bottom up. The reward of *every* good deed of *every* person in *every* generation is passed upward to *every* parent. You can see the person at the top of the pyramid, the mother, is receiving exponential level of rewards, everything from the generations that have descended from her. Think about this – if she taught her children to pray, every prayer they do, she gets equal reward. She taught them how to do the ablution, every time they make ablution, she receives equal reward. She taught them to give charity; she receives equal measure every time they do so. She taught them to read; everything they read and put to use in their whole life, she will receive equal rewards. There is no limit here. *Her account has exploded from good deeds*. This is the astonishing, mind-blowing prize for parenting.

The converse is also valid. If she has taught wrong things to her children or neglected her parenting, whatever sin results from the children doing bad deeds also passes in equal measure to her. For example, if she feels alcohol is not a problem and allows her children to drink, she acquires the sin (in equal measure) of them drinking alcohol and any ill consequences that ensue. Note the mother is responsible for her intention and the effort she puts into raising her children. Not guaranteeing they turn out well – Islam is effort-centric not result-centric. Occasionally children turn out bad or disbelievers despite all the hard work of the parents – this is a test from Allah. Prophet Nuh (Noah) had a disobedient and disbelieving son, who drowned in the flood. If it can happen to prophets, it can happen to anyone.

Whilst the focus so far has been on the mother, the father receives exactly the same. Whatever good he teaches his children, he will benefit the same with the good deeds of the children. And any evil he teaches, he will reap the same sin as they do. But the father has to shoulder the responsibility of earning the livelihood along with his fatherhood, so his level of teaching the children directly will naturally amount to less than the mother. However, he will accrue the rewards of his wife as the mother in equal measure if his intention is to earn a living and so support her in the parenting. So the father is not left behind.

Bottom Line:

• Marriage in Islam is built upon love, kindness, and the highest moral character.

• Marriage is a great mercy and also a test – like all gifts.

• The husband shoulders the responsibility for providing for his family.

• The wife has been freed from worldly responsibilities to allow her to focus on the critical task of motherhood.

• The mother makes her best effort to produce her nation of believers.

• The prize of diligent and righteous motherhood is receiving *equal reward* of *every* single good deed from *every* child of *every* generation that follows her.

• The father supports the mother in her role by providing for the family and through his fatherhood.

• In matters of the family, the husband and wife discuss matters but the husband has the deciding say.

• The act of intimacy between husband and wife is rewarded.

Love in Islam

Modern culture has us believe that love is the ultimate entity in this world. People are ready to sacrifice anything to find 'true love'. After falling in love, you get married (or not, as marriage is increasingly portrayed as unnecessary in the modern age) and spend your lives happily ever after. The problem is that people can then fall out of love too. When life becomes mundane, and the honeymoon period is over, there can be a need to find excitement again; how? By falling in love all over again, but with someone else. The risk is cheating, adultery, divorce, or all three.

In Islam, love comes *after* marriage. There is no dating in the Western sense. When one feels the need to get married, they start the search for a spouse. The Prophet advised to choose a spouse based on their piety, beauty, wealth and lineage. Marriage is a complete package, and so all factors are considered to ensure a sound match, but the Prophet counselled that piety should be given the most weight.[39] The boy is allowed to meet the girl in an appropriate manner, namely with one of the girl's guardians present. He finds out from people who know her what she is like. The girl and her family do likewise. If things are looking promising, there is an engagement period to get to know the prospective spouse They both assess compatibility to each other during the engagement period. These meetings are done with the sole genuine intention of seeking a spouse and getting married. They are both still technically strangers to one another, so meetings must continue to have a guardian of the girl present. If all seems favourable, either side can propose and if accepted, the marriage ensues.

Love is a product of the subsequent companionship. It is fortified by the passage of time along with intimacy. It continues to mature with the arrival of children. This is true love. It gets stronger with time, not weaker. This was beautifully exemplified by Nadiya Hussain, the 2015 winner of television's *The Great British Bake Off*. A Muslim and mother of three,

---

[39] Sahih Bukhari, Sahih Muslim

she had an arranged marriage at the age of 19 years. She described in a recent interview how there was no love in her marriage in the beginning. This is natural in an arranged marriage; after all, the couple do not really know each other. She explained, 'I didn't know my husband, and then we had two children, and then I fell in love with him.' She and her husband symbolically renewed their marriage vows in December 2018 to reflect their love for each other.[40]

Note this does not mean Islam equates to arranged marriages. An arranged marriage is a cultural practice and an acceptable model of marriage if it suits both parties, including their families. Increasingly common in the modern era is to have an introduction made by a mutual party or an agency to allow the boy and girl and their families to get to know each other and assess suitability for marriage.

However, if a boy and girl are already acquainted with each other and like each other, they can seek marriage. They might know each through schooling, professional work, community work, they may be neighbours, or extended family. Khadija, a noble and wealthy businesswoman in Mecca, hired Muhammad, who was not a Prophet at the time, to manage her trade. Working with him, she was highly impressed with his honesty, integrity and character. After undertaking due diligence, she went on to send him a marriage proposal. He accepted and she became the first wife of the Prophet.

Bottom Line:

• In Islam, love comes after marriage, not before it.

• Love between spouses is a great blessing and a sign of a Creator.

• In seeking a spouse, the complete package should be assessed as a suitable match, but piety should be given the most weight.

---

[40] https://bit.ly/3buWgzA

Homosexuality and Islam

Homosexuality, namely people of the same gender engaging in sexual *acts*, has been categorically prohibited in Islam. There has never been any debate on this matter amongst scholars throughout the centuries. However, recently there has been a move from certain orientalists, Scott Kugle in particular, to re-evaluate and reform Islam. Kugle, who is gay himself,[41] espouses that re-examining the Quranic texts that prohibit homosexuality actually reveals that it is compatible with Islam. This viewpoint has been adopted by 'progressive Muslims', who are more inclined to follow western values as they view them as intellectually superior.

So have centuries of scholars been wrong? Are these Quranic verses open to re-interpretation? Let's recap a few basic points from *Lenses of Islam*. The Quran provides guidance and principles *for all mankind until the end of time*. It is not a thesis nor a lexicon of law that it goes into great specifics and details. Therefore only matters of serious importance and key principles get mentioned in the Quran. But where Allah wants to particularly emphasise an issue, it gets repeated, sometimes many times. There is nothing superfluous in the Quran; every single verse, word and letter is there with intention and specific purpose.

With regards to homosexuality, this issue is mentioned in the Quran no less than eight times, referencing the time of Prophet Lut (Lot) and his people of the town of Sodom. These people are referred to as evil in their behaviour, and homosexuality was rife. After numerous warnings, they were finally punished and destroyed, whilst the Prophet Lut and his family, bar his wife, were saved. Here is one example, summarising the story:

> And (mention) Lot, when he said to his people, 'Do you commit indecency with eyes wide open? **Do you have carnal relations with men rather than women?** Nay! you are a people behaving

---

[41] https://bit.ly/2ydjaNJ

foolishly.' The reply of his people was but to say, 'Expel Lot's family out from your town! Truly they are people who keep themselves pure.' So We saved him and his family, save his wife; who was destined to be of those who remained behind. And We brought down upon them a rain (of stones); horrible was the rain for those who had been warned! {Quran 27: 54-58}

Of the eight occasions this story is recounted, their homosexual behaviour is highlighted seven times: five times being explicitly stated immediately in the narrative, and on two occasions being clearly implied. So, of all the evil they were engaged in, and for which they were destroyed, Allah picks out homosexuality specifically and consistently. Any sensible reader cannot conclude anything other than the fact Allah is declaring homosexuality a clear sin. Bearing in mind that repetition in the Quran serves for powerful emphasis, this point is made categorically and without any possibility of alternative viewpoints.

To make this clear, let's take a simple example. You are looking into secondary schools for your child. You ask ten neighbours and friends about your local high school, to which you receive the reply from eight of them, 'Oh, that school is really bad; they have a problem with bullying'. Now, it could be the school also has problems with poor academic results, truancy, lack of facilities, poor hygiene, bad food, bad teachers, lack of values, very poor attitude from the children, and a host of other reasons. They might even have a serious drugs problem. Indeed, there may be several problems which overlap. But the thing that everyone is highlighting, as the worst issue by far, is the bullying. The message is: Do not send your child there because of the bullying problem. Similarly there can be no doubt that Allah is pinpointing homosexuality as a grave sin, enough that He destroyed a nation **specifically** for it.

For an in-depth analysis the reader is directed to Mobeen Vaid's scholarly essay, which comprehensively reviews this issue and refutes Scott Kugle's flawed analysis.[42] We will review later the importance of knowledge and authentic teachers, as well as common mistakes Muslims make.

It is important to note that the above summary relates to *sexual acts* between people of the same gender. *Same gender attraction or desires* is a different matter. Desire has been made one of the clear tests of this world by Allah. As discussed above, Islam could be summarised as submitting to the Will of Allah by curbing our desires to within the boundaries Allah has set. Desire could be for money, power, fame, food, possessions, sex, etc. In matters of attraction, for the vast majority of people this is between a man and woman (i.e. heterosexual desire).

Desire is a natural inclination and not in one's control just like one's feelings; there is no sin in having feelings, though *one must take great care to manage these* (see *Closing the Door,* and *No Harm in Looking*). It is acting upon the emotion where one is held to account. If a boy and girl have attraction for one another, they are not sinful unless this translates into physical acts such as fornication, or them indulging in interactions which would heighten the desires (for instance, going on a date).

For a minority of the population they experience desires for the same gender. Whilst this is unimaginable or even repugnant to many Muslims as well as non-Muslims, this forms a test for these individuals. In similar manner, same gender attraction will become sinful only when acted upon or allowed to develop. The test is harder unfortunately, for whilst a man and woman may be able to marry and thereby an intimate relationship becomes *halal* (permissible) for them, this is not an option for those with same gender desires.

Muslims challenged and struggling with this tendency need to remain steadfast and work on it. Absolutely paramount is not attempting to validate this behaviour through 're-interpretation' of the Quranic texts. Changing what is clearly prohibited to permissible is a serious

---

[42] https://bit.ly/2WHzUqC

transgression that risks rendering the individual a non-believer, because one is overruling God's command. Managing these feelings, and seeking judicious and sympathetic help if necessary, will form part of the solution. Slip ups can happen and seeking forgiveness for them and repentance (*tawbah*) are the great tools from Allah to rectify oneself and then strive on. These desires, or even acts, need to be kept veiled and private. There is no publicising or rejoicing in them, contrary to Western opinion where 'coming out' is seen by many as a joyful rite of passage to much fanfare. The issue should only be discussed where help is being sought to manage it. Muslims, especially Muslim leaders (imams), need to be aware that these people need support and compassion. They are battling their desires whilst trying to obey and please Allah. Brother Yousef's article brings home the reality of their struggle.[43] Afflicted with same gender attraction whilst recognising that acting upon these is against Allah's Commands, he relates his personal struggles and runs a support network for similar people.

So how are Muslims to deal with gay people in their communities or workplaces, especially those living in the West where these alternative lifestyles are open? Indeed, sometimes it is pushed with more than a degree of militancy. Muslims need to bear in mind that judgement lies with Allah alone. Their job is to behave with kindness with all around them. Maintain excellent conduct. If gay individuals choose to be vocal and ascertain their views, Muslims should politely tell them they do not agree with their lifestyle, though Muslims respect all and everyone's right to lead their lives however they choose. What people do in their own privacy is their business. However, Muslims must not support activities and agendas that promote this lifestyle.

---

[43] https://bit.ly/2UEa5F5

Bottom Line:

• Same gender sexual acts are strictly forbidden, just like fornication or adultery.

• Same gender desire can arise in a minority of individuals who can be pious Muslims – this is a test for them, and they need compassion and support to help them manage this.

When It Does Not Work Out: Divorce

Divorce can arise sadly even between a good and pious couple. The couple may have a lot of difficulty seeing eye to eye, personalities might clash, and the marriage may become unviable. Bitter arguments and resentment become entrenched, and a cycle of resentment sets in. The outcome may be divorce. Islam recognises this, and gives clear guidance. Allah orders the man to be kind and deal with his wife gently and equitably. No matter how bitter the resentments, he must remain fearful of God, and therefore mindful of committing cruelty and injustice on his wife. He must maintain kindness at times when blood may be boiling on both sides. Exactly the same applies to the wife.

Divorce can be undertaken by the husband or the wife. When the husband issues a divorce, this is called *talaaq*. The couple separates. The wife is to wait for the completion of three menstrual cycles (this duration is called *iddah*) before she can marry anyone else (a non-menstruating woman will wait for three months). One reason for this is to ensure that if she is pregnant, the paternity of the child is clear. It also serves as a time period to review how they feel being separated, and to allow emotions to settle. By the end of this time, they either reconcile and get back together again, or formalise the separation into a divorce. If they wish to get back together after the *iddah* period is over, then a new marriage has to take place with a new contract and formal ceremony.

There is a limit to this process. Two divorces can be issued by the husband along these lines. If he does so for a third time, the divorce is permanent.

It will now be prohibited for the couple to get back together. After a third divorce, the only way the couple can remarry in the future is after the woman has been in a marriage to another man, with whom she had consummated the marriage.[44] This has to be a genuine marriage, not a sham marriage to facilitate return to her ex-husband, and the consummation is partly to ensure this. A sham marriage arranged with another man to get around the permanent divorce after three pronouncements receives a severe curse by Allah upon those party to the trickery.[45]

What is the wisdom here? Firstly, it is important to appreciate the historical context. Before Islam, men could issue a divorce then take their wife back, without any limit. Cruel men would do this repeatedly as a means of tormenting their wife. Islam curtailed this to two occasions, giving leeway for reconciliation and the couple getting back together with genuine intentions. Preserving the family unit is paramount. After a third divorce, however, it is clear either that the couple have a serious relationship problem, or that the husband is oppressive. It is likely that they are harming each other and their children by continuing in this toxic partnership. Islam now forces them to move on from each other.

There is a misconception amongst some Muslims that divorce should therefore be issued by giving three utterances of divorce to render it permanent immediately i.e. the man says, 'I divorce you. I divorce you. I divorce you.' This is not the case. To shoot off three pronouncements of divorce belies ignorance and stupidity. Uttering one statement of divorce will lead to a full divorce unless there is a reconciliation in the *iddah* window. There is no need to fire off divorce number 2 and number 3.

If three pronouncements have been done in one breath, and the couple come to regret it, wishing to get back together again, they have landed themselves in a real quagmire. Does this amount to one overall

---

[44] Quran 2: 230
[45] Sunan Abu Dawood, Sunan Ibn Majah

pronouncement or three? In the first scenario, the door is open for reconciliation, but in the second the divorce is sealed with no possibility of reuniting, unless the woman ends up getting divorced following a subsequent marriage to a different man. They will need to consult an imam or scholar to untangle their hideous mess. The consequence of this ignorance and foolhardy practice has opened up desperate divorced women to abuse and exploitation from charlatans offering sham marriage to 'allow' them to return to their ex-husbands.[46] This is expressly prohibited as mentioned above, and one ignorant practice is being compounded by another.

A wife also has the option for divorce, which is called a *khula*. Here, she files the divorce in court, and presents her case, analogous to English divorce law. Again, there is a misconception that a woman is at the mercy of her husband, and in a difficult marriage she is helpless to end the marriage unless he initiates the divorce. If the woman finds the husband unbearable or the marriage intolerable, she can file for divorce herself. Again, she fulfils a waiting period (*iddah*) before being able to marry another man.

Bottom Line:

• If husband and wife have irreconcilable issues, both have the option to effect divorce.

• They can reunite after a divorce on two occasions, but after a third divorce their divorce is permanent.

• A man's three divorce pronouncement in one go is supreme ignorance and should not be done.

---

[46] https://bbc.in/2Ul7Oj7

Forced Marriages and Honour Killings

Both of these two issues receive a great deal of coverage in the media. It has already been mentioned that a woman can turn down any marriage proposal she does not like. This is her right, and it cannot be overruled by her father or her family.[47] It follows quite clearly therefore that forced marriages are absolutely not permitted in Islam. There was a case at the time of the Prophet of a young lady who was forcibly married to a man by her father and she came and sought the Prophet's judgement. The Prophet was unequivocal: the marriage was invalid.[48]

Honour killings are where women have been killed by their family or community because they have done something that has been deemed shameful. Often the 'shame' is the girl likes a particular boy, is involved in a relationship, or has refused to accept the family's decision to marry a particular man (forced marriage). These killings are simply murder. There is no mitigation of this crime because the family felt their 'honour' had been disgraced. This is not Islam. The perpetrators are answerable for their heinous crimes in this world to the justice system, as well as to Allah in the Next.

Daughters Are a Blessing

The issue of honour killings and forced marriages stem from unfortunate cultural (not Islamic) perspectives that see girls as inferior to men, and a burden on the family. The Prophet strongly dispelled these notions. On raising daughters, he said:

> *Whoever supports two girls till they attain maturity, he and I will come on the Day of Resurrection like this and the Prophet joined*

---

[47] Sahih Bukhari, Sahih Muslim
[48] Sunan Ibn Majah

his fingers to illustrate closeness in the Afterlife. {Sahih Muslim}.

Indeed, the Prophet himself had four daughters (Zainab, Umm Khulthum, Fatima and Ruqayya) and was survived by only one of them (Fatima). He had three sons who died in their childhood. This dispels another misconception in some Muslim or Eastern cultures, which is the desperate need to have boys. Continuation of the family name, which requires having sons, is viewed as a matter of necessity. Actually, it is not the family name that is important, but producing God-fearing upstanding Muslims. The rewards of producing pious children (and all the subsequent generations) will pass to the parents in equal measure as the children (see *Make Use of Five before Five* later). This has nothing to do with family name.

Maintain Family Ties

Families are the cornerstone of successful communities and society. Well-functioning families are there for each other, and help out with each other's problems. The word in Arabic for blood ties, *rahm*, is taken from the same root as the names of Allah that mean extreme mercy and compassion (*Rahmaan* and *Raheem*). Blood relations are a mercy from Allah. How can we know that? An orphan on the street or in an orphanage, yearns for a family. People he can call his own, who would be there for him, regardless of what they can provide materially or not. An orphan would give anything to belong to a family, even if that family was destitute themselves. Islam is about spreading as much goodness as possible amongst people, and so building as many healthy relationships as possible. The familial relations are therefore God-given bonuses in this regard.

Furthermore, in the very early days of Islam, a man named Amr ibn Abasah came to find the Prophet and learn about his message. He asked the Prophet 'what have you been sent with?' namely, what is your mission? The Prophet's opening line was 'to join the ties of kinship' followed by 'to break the idols and proclaim the oneness of Allah, so nothing is to be worshipped alongside Him'. Acknowledging that God is One and to be worshipped alone is the most important tenet of Islam. But the Prophet did not give this as the very first point. On many occasions he would change the order of an answer or teaching to give due emphasis to a particular value. Here the purpose of mentioning the maintaining of familial relations, before the worship of One God is to give this aspect of moral conduct due weight.

Every bounty serves not only as a gift, but also as a test. Families can also be a source of tremendous testing. Offended pride and jealousy unfortunately play a major role in throwing familial relationships into terrible strain. Awkward in-laws, family feuds, insinuations or perceived insinuations. A cousin did not invite you to a function at their house, stinging your 'honour'. A brother-in-law receives a massive pay out after his start-up company is bought out by a giant corporation, turning him into a multimillionaire overnight. He will go onto a life of luxury whilst you slave away for your daily living – 'Why him? Why not me? I deserved it more.' Resentment sets in, bitter arguments ensue, and estrangement follows. The family ties are broken. I am fairly confident that there has never been any family in the history of life where difficulties and issues have not been present. Handling awkward family members can be extremely challenging, a source of terrible stress and misery for so many people.

So with families, whatever issues come up (and there will be issues), the ties of kinship are to be maintained. There are numerous teachings from the Prophet warning of the gravity of cutting ties. We must keep in touch, ask after each other, be there for each other, help as best as we can. Difficult though that may be, the bigger picture is to be kept in focus. Recall again that knowing how to be of help to others necessitates having a rapport in order to know the situation and needs of others.

Importantly, we might think that maintaining ties means that we have not closed the door on the others. We are happy if they want to call us, but we do not initiate any connection ourselves. This is not enough. *It means reaching out to them, even if they are refusing to keep ties with you.* The Prophet explained:

The one who maintains a relationship with his relatives only because they maintain a relationship with him is not truly upholding the ties of kinship. The one who truly upholds those ties is the one who does so even if they break off the relationship.
{Sahih Bukhari}

Allah sternly warns, in the Quran, of His Curse and the punishment of the Hellfire for those who break off ties:

And those who break the Covenant of Allah, after its ratification, and sever that which Allah has commanded to be joined (i.e. the bonds of kinship), and work mischief in the land, on them is the curse; And for them is the unhappy home (i.e. Hell).
{Quran 13: 25}

As with any rule of Allah, it serves as a test but also carries wisdom and reward. It is not difficult to see the wisdom here. Harmony in the community is a pillar in Islam, and thus ensuring harmony in the family and extended family units, which are the building blocks of the community, is essential. As for the reward, the Prophet said:

Whoever would like his provision to be increased and his life to be extended, should uphold the ties of kinship.
{Sahih Bukhari and Sahih Muslim}

So keeping contact with family members and being cordial and hospitable even though they may be insulting and abusive, is met with an increase in one's wealth and one's lifespan. Who does not want to live longer and be richer? The concept of obligation versus our own will is present here as well. Modern societies, particularly in the West, often break ties with annoying family members but cement friendships into quasi-familial relationships. For example, a man severs ties with his blood brother over some petty dispute, vowing never to speak to him again. At the same time, he feels his best friend is always there for him, and his 'true' brother. This is replacing the Will of the Creator with one's own will and choice. Whilst having strong friendships is certainly to be encouraged, severing family ties is a serious transgression.

Bottom Line:

• Breaking off family ties is a serious transgression.

• Maintaining family ties means reaching out to family members even if they wish to break off.

• Families are a blessing as well as a test.

• Strong families make for stronger communities.

Look After and Be Good to Your Neighbour

A neighbour is defined as one who lives within 40 houses of you, on each side. It is quite clear then that actually a large number of people who live around are actually your neighbours, not just the few who live immediately next door. Neighbours have been given many rights in Islam. Allah commands goodness to neighbours whether near or far.[49] In fact, the rights of the neighbours are such that Aisha, one of the wives of the Prophet, stated that she was suspicious at some point that a decree would come that would entitle neighbours to a share in inheritance as well.[50]

The Prophet narrated the example of two women. One undertook the bare minimum in terms of obligatory worships of prayer, fasting, charity, but was excellent in her conduct to her neighbours. She was rewarded with Paradise. On the other hand, a woman who undertook tremendous extra acts of worship, i.e. extra prayers on top of the obligatory, extra voluntary fasts on top of the obligatory, extra charity in addition to the required, was in the Hellfire, due to her abominable treatment of her neighbours. This epitomizes the importance of one's neighbours, as well as the value of kindness as a trait.

The Prophet taught that a man is not a believer if he fills his stomach whilst

---

[49] Quran 4:36
[50] Sahih Bukhari, Sahih Muslim

his neighbour goes hungry.[51] One has to have sincere concern for their neighbour. The theme of harmony in the community can be seen here as well, and will be discussed further later. Note again that in order to actually aid someone, one has to know that the other is in need of help. People have their dignity and will often be shy to ask for help. It is therefore a prerequisite that one should build rapports with all those around themselves to know their situation and circumstances and therefore be aware if they are in need of assistance.

Looking After Orphans

Orphans are the neediest group in society. Young and vulnerable, they may have no parents at all, or a widowed mother looking after them. Their responsibility will fall first to the extended family and, failing that, to society itself. There are extensive references in the Quran and numerous teachings of the Prophet on the importance of looking after and raising orphans in society. There are mighty rewards promised to the one who raises an orphan. The Prophet said that such a person will be as close to him in Paradise, as the index finger is to the middle finger.[52] Ponder this for a second. Living next door to the Prophet firstly implies you made it to Paradise. Secondly, you have been granted the highest level of Paradise. Finally, there can be no greater reward than being a neighbour of the Prophet.

As an act, this is one we should seek out actively. Even if one does not physically take on the guardianship of an orphan, this has become readily accessible, at least financially, with the development of orphan sponsorship agencies and charities, globally.

The worth of a society is based on how it treats its neediest members. Here, rather than being left behind, the most desperate group is being nurtured

---

[51] Al-Adab al-Mufrad by Sahih Bukhari
[52] Sahih Muslim, Sunan at-Tirmidhi

to give them the opportunity to be positive contributing citizens. Thus, society tends to them and they can in turn serve society. So the cycle of positivity rolls on.

Make Use of Five Before Five

The Prophet advised that there were five blessings to capitalise on, before they disappeared:[53]

1. Make use of your youth before you become old

2. Make use of your health before you become sick

3. Make use of your wealth before you become poor

4. Make use of free time before you become busy

5. Make use of your life before you are overtaken by death

The essence of advice here was to rush to do good deeds. It is easier to study, whether Islam, worldly knowledge or a vocation, and to undertake beneficial works, when one is young, healthy, and single. There is ample free time, physical ability, and energy, and expenses are limited to oneself. These blessings or opportunities may go with time, at which point one will deeply regret not having made the effort earlier. A spouse, and later children, will heavily preoccupy one's time. The finances will also be impacted; now expenses proliferate. This need to be focused is summed up finally by the last point. Life itself is a blessing - hurry to do good works, for once death arrives, the opportunity for performing any more deeds comes to an end.

Note how time is a blessing and not to be wasted. When at a loose end between appointments or errands, people often talk of having to 'kill time'. This is a failure to appreciate the true blessing and value of every minute

---

[53] Mustadrak of Al-Hakim; Musnad of Imam Ahmad

one has been given on the earth. A free moment can be spent remembering and praising Allah (see later *Constant Remembrance of Allah with Dhikr*). Reciting short simple phrases glorifying Allah draws tremendous rewards. The Prophet described such phrases as 'being light on the tongue, but heavy on the scales.'[54] On the Day of Judgement, every person will desperately wish for their scale to be overflowing with good deeds. In this way, the Muslim does not waste any minute of the day. Once a person dies, their ability to perform any good deed or act of worship comes to an end. So, every second is meaningful.

This attitude of being in constant state of remembrance of Allah also increases God-consciousness (called *taqwa* in Arabic), something Muslims strive for. Why? Because the more God-conscious one is, the more they will appreciate His favours, thank Him, and seek to obey Him, and therefore try to perfect their character. Indeed, actual ritual acts of worship, such as fasting, serve to increase this God-consciousness. *Taqwa* is discussed further later on.

This idea of rushing to do good deeds is also mentioned by Allah in the Quran, where He describes the ones achieving greatest success as being those who 'raced' to goodness – *sabiqoon* in Arabic.[55] Allah tells of mankind being assembled into three groups on the Day of Judgement. The People of the Right, who are the good. The People of the Left, who are the wrongdoers. The People standing Right in Front, the *sabiqoon*, who are the esteemed champions. They were the ones who stayed focused on the race and grabbed every possible opportunity they could to do good.

---

[54] Sahih Bukhari, Sahih Muslim
[55] Quran 35: 32 and 56: 10

Everything is a Loan from Allah

We do not own anything in this world. Not our homes, nor our jobs, nor our spouses, nor our children. We do not even own our bodies. Everything has been entrusted to us by Allah and, like any trusts, we must preserve and safeguard them. With regards to our children this means raising them as Muslims, instilling the right values and faith. This is a responsibility of the utmost importance in Islam. In the last section we saw the Prophet counsel sound advice, but in fact he also warned:

> *A servant of Allah will remain standing on the Day of Judgment till he is questioned about his age and how he spent it; and about his knowledge and how he utilized it; about his wealth from where he acquired it and in what (activities) he spent it; and about his body as to how he used it. {Sunan at-Tirmidhi}*

With regards to our bodies, we must look after our health. Eating appropriately, getting good exercise and leading healthy lifestyles are an obligation. Just as, if a friend loans us his car, we use it but also look after it. It would be appalling and unacceptable to utilise the car and then return it with scratches on the paintwork, dents on the bodywork, and a filthy mess inside.

Obesity is not part of Islam. Obesity is a reflection of poor diet, both in quality and quantity, as well as inadequate exercise. It is truly rare to be overweight due to a genuine medical diagnosis. Those who are overweight need to take responsibility for this and strive to correct their lifestyles. Obesity will lead to ill health (diabetes, heart disease, respiratory conditions, arthritis, etc) and worst of all, a vicious cycle can develop. Once one chronic disease takes hold, like arthritis, the ability to exercise disappears and the obesity gets worse. Ultimately one will have to give account for one's abuse of their body on the Day of Judgement. The Prophet cautioned:

> *There are two blessing which many people lose: health and free time for doing good. {Sahih Bukhari}*

In other words, people tend to take their health and free time for granted and miss the opportunity to do good with them. When the health is replaced by chronic illness, disability, or old age, there will be regret over how the past was wasted. The value of capitalising on free time was discussed in the previous section.

Similarly, wealth is loan from Allah. The money does not truly belong to us, we are guardians entrusted to look after it, and utilise it in a righteous manner. Hence there is obligatory charity (called *zakat*) that must be paid every year. Additionally, there is very strong encouragement to give additional voluntary charity monies. In matters of inheritance, Allah has decreed how the majority portion (two thirds to be exact) is to be distributed prescriptively amongst family members. Only one third of one's wealth is open for distribution as to their own wishes.

Materialism is the antithesis of Islam. Wealth and worldly possessions are not the focus of life. The heart must remain detached from these. Our worldly assets need to be utilised in the best manner for humanity. Owning beautiful things is not prohibited. Allah loves beauty. Spending on our families is also part of our responsibilities to mankind. But there needs to be a limit on spending. Extravagance and opulence are out. Balance is the key, and Allah describes His dutiful slaves as:

> *And those who, when they spend, are neither extravagant nor miserly, but practise a middle way between those (extremes) {Quran 25:67}*

Eliminating desires to *own* wealth and property is called *zuhd*, and is a station Muslims aspire to. Note the importance of intention here (covered in more detail later): there is a distinction between the desire to have wealth so that one may spend it on charitable causes (in other words, using wealth as a tool for good), which is a healthy outlook and one that is rewarded, compared to the desire for wealth for the sake of possession (materialism), a highly blameworthy trait. A Muslim is not owned by wealth or the world, but uses it as a tool for good.

A beautiful modern-day example is of Sonny Bill Williams, the New Zealand All Blacks rugby player who was part of the Rugby Union World Cup winning team in 2015. Whilst doing a lap of honour following the prize ceremony, a 14-year-old lad was forcefully knocked over by a security guard as he ran on to the pitch to celebrate. Concerned about the feelings of the boy, Sonny Bill Williams rescued him and handed over his medal to the 'little fella', as a souvenir.[56] Anyone else who had just received a World Cup Championship medal would have held it dear to their heart, the most prized item for them in the whole world at that moment in time. Their life's dreams and aspirations finally realised in the pinnacle moment of their life. But this was not so for Sonny Bill Williams, who showed tremendous concern for the feelings of others (kindness) along with *zuhd* (not being owned by your possessions). At the time I read this story I did not know anything about him, but I strongly suspected he was Muslim, as he had personified *zuhd*. I came to learn later that indeed he was, having converted to Islam in 2009. The moving video of him putting his medal over the little guy's neck set the internet alight.[57]

Bottom Line:

• Everything we have in this world is a loan from Allah, including our body and our children.

• We will be accountable for obesity and unhealthy lifestyles.

• Materialism is completely against Islam.

• Our hearts need to be detached from the desire to own things (*zuhd*).

• The world, including wealth, serves as a tool for us to use for good.

---

[56] https://bit.ly/3aiMikK
[57] https://bit.ly/2WNbXy0

Make the World a Better Place and Leave the World a Better Place

A Muslim's conduct is aimed at making the world a better place. A Muslim must spread goodness everywhere. Allah also rewards passing on knowledge that is beneficial. In fact, when that knowledge is utilised, the reward not only goes to the person actually performing the good deed, but is also duplicated for the person who taught it initially. If many people are taught, and they in turn use it and teach many others, quite clearly the reward actually increases exponentially for the original teacher. This reward will continue to accrue for the person, *even after they have died.* This is very important because, as mentioned previously, a person's ability to perform good deeds themselves comes to an end with death.

Two other things can benefit someone after their death. One is having raised and left behind pious children. The children can supplicate to Allah for their parents, to bestow forgiveness and mercy on them and elevate their position in the Afterlife. Furthermore, their good deeds will also be credited to their parents in equal measure. Imagine the exponential chain here yet again. The good deeds of the children in turn will benefit their parents, so their grandparents, so their great grandparents. And so on. This is also applicable to any teachers of the children. They benefit from whatever they taught the children, but can also benefit if the children make supplications for them.

The third thing is ongoing charities. A person sets up or contributes to a charity in their lifetime, then as long as that charity remains functional and delivering benefit to people, the reward will continue to accrue for that person even after their death. This could be building water wells for deprived rural communities. As long as that well provides water, the reward amasses for the one who built it or sponsored it. Constructing a mosque is another example: here the reward of *every* act of worship of every worshipper performed in that mosque is also credited to those who built it, physically or financially. Setting up a school for underprivileged children. A shelter for homeless people or battered women. A rehabilitation facility for drug addicts. There are countless possibilities.

<u>Bottom Line:</u>

• Leave the world a better place by:

  – Imparting beneficial knowledge

  – Raising pious children

  – Setting up charities and beneficial works that will be ongoing.

• These three things will continue to accrue good deeds for a person even after death.

Always Think Positively of Your Fellow Man

Assumptions are the road to animosity. Negative assumptions that is. Unfortunately this is our automatic response.

In any given situation, the Prophet taught us to make excuses for our fellow man, and to think positively of them, always. This is the opposite to backbiting, which implants negative impressions of others in our hearts. Here, taking a positive view of others, and giving them the benefit of doubt where they may have said or done something dubious, helps to foster cordial relationships and so keep families and communities strong.

You might have someone at work whom you thoroughly despise. You cannot see eye to eye on any matter. They are a thorn in your side. You lock horns over each and every matter. Just thinking about them makes your blood boil. Then you discover, one day, that outside of work, they maintain an inner-city shelter for drug addicts. They bought the property themselves, and run it completely at their own expense. A place where the addicts can simply have a safe room to crash out. Your colleague is not even looking for reform here, but the shelter serves to provide thoroughly humanitarian help to desperate people – pure altruism. This cannot fail to change your view of them. Now when an issue comes up, you know that the person is sincere, though they may have a different perspective. This makes for a much more civil and respectful relationship. And your softening in the interactions is very likely to be reciprocated. Here, consciously keeping a good view of them from the beginning despite despising their behaviour, would allow building a good relationship rather than a strained one.

All people have faults. Allah has created man as the pinnacle of His Creation, and every person is capable of tremendous good. The person committing the worst sins can suddenly turn over a new leaf, and bring extraordinary benefit to mankind. There are numerous such stories throughout history, including from the time of the Prophet. In the modern day, there are similar examples of those who were vociferously active against Islam propagating anti-Islamic rhetoric. At the time of writing, Joram van Klaveren, formerly a far-right MP of the Dutch Freedom Party, was busy researching Islam and halfway through writing a book with the specific intention of maligning it. As he came to realise the truth of the message, he became convinced and has converted. The Freedom Party campaigns on a specific vitriolic anti-Islamic ticket. He follows Arnoud van Doorn, a former official of the same party, who had been distributing a film slandering Islam. He converted in 2011, and then undertook Hajj a year later. His son went on to convert as well in 2014. Arthur Wagner, a politician in Brandenburg who used to be a member of a German anti-Islamic, far-right party similarly converted, with his story reported at the beginning of 2018. Who would have thought that anti-Islamic politicians campaigning on anti-Islamic platforms would have become Muslim themselves?

We are taught, therefore, not to hate the person, but hate the action (as discussed in *Humility*). If we dislike someone, we should keep in mind that there is very likely a good side to them that we simply have not seen yet.

Bottom Line:

• If someone is doing bad or committing sins, hate the action, not the person.

- Always give people the benefit of doubt, make excuses for them.

- Keep a positive impression of everyone.

Equality amongst Mankind

Racism has plagued every nation throughout history. Only relatively recently have developed countries acknowledged racism as being morally wrong, and legislated against it. There have been dramatic changes, for example, in the UK and the USA in just the last few decades. The Race Relations Act in 1965 was the first time public discrimination was officially outlawed in the UK; almost simultaneously the USA introduced the similar Civil Rights Act of 1964. Islam, however, brought the value that every person is equal, in both dignity and rights, regardless of race or nationality, *1400 years ago*. In the famous sermon the Prophet gave at Hajj (major pilgrimage), just a little while before he died, he said:

> *O people, your Lord is One and your father Adam is one. There is no favour of an Arab over a foreigner, nor a foreigner over an Arab, and neither white skin over black skin, nor black skin over white skin, except by righteousness. {Musnad Ahmad}*

The Prophet's poignant instructions in his last major speech are explicit in barring discrimination. Allah Himself states in the Quran:

> *O mankind, indeed We have created you from male and female and made you into peoples and tribes that you may know one another. Indeed, the most noble of you in the sight of Allah is the most righteous of you. Indeed, Allah is All Knowing and Fully Aware. {Quran 49: 13}*

The verse was revealed following the Prophet's conquest of Mecca. At the time of prayer, he asked Bilal, an esteemed Companion who was of Ethiopian descent and a former slave, to give the public call to prayer (called *adhan*). Some of the pagan Quraish Arabs made disparaging and racist remarks about Bilal, unable to bear a position of honour being given to a man who was not only non-Arab but also black and previously a slave. Allah revealed this verse in response, to make clear that all of mankind is descended from a single Father and Mother (Adam and Eve) and their offspring have gone on to become different races and nations. So not only is all of humanity related to one another, but the purpose of being of different skin colours, languages and customs is to allow one to show tolerance and patience. Allah then explicitly states that it is righteousness i.e. piety and moral character that ranks with Him, not a person's race or lineage. He further follows this up by warning that He knows everything and is aware of everything, namely what people harbour in their hearts, not only the good but the bad too. Islam made clear everyone is equal, and discrimination has no place in society.

This is seen in practice, in Islam, for example, in the conduct of the congregational ritual prayer. People stand in rows behind the leader of the prayer (called imam). There are no special or reserved places. People of all backgrounds and classes stand shoulder-to-shoulder with one another. The president of the nation can be sandwiched between a janitor and a porter. A white man will stand shoulders with a black man, next to an Asian man, next to a Chinese. This is the universal dignity Islam gives to all people. Observing this when he undertook his own Hajj opened Malcom X's eyes to the real Islam. It was a pivotal moment that changed his belief, and led him to realise that the white man was not the devil as he had been taught by the organisation known as the Nation of Islam, but that all humans are truly equal. On his return to the US, he broke from the Nation of Islam and began to speak against all forms of racism and the need for racial integration.

Excellence in Your Work

A job or profession is an honour from the Almighty to earn an honest living. One has to be grateful for this blessing. Allah dignifies all honest work, as the Prophet told us that there is no better meal we can eat than the one we have earned with our own hands.[58] The Prophet goes on to give the great example of Prophet Dawood (David). Prophet Dawood was a kingly prophet who had empires, vast armies and wealth. Yet, despite his kingdom, he used to work daily with his hands to earn his meals, rather than relying on his wealth. In the Quran, Allah uses this example of Prophet Dawood to illustrate that it is Allah's Favour that He bestows a job on a person, giving them the means to earn their living.[59] Otherwise, they would be dependent on others, taking loans or begging, and to accompany this would be the loss of their dignity. Note that the job must be one that is permissible i.e. not engaged in prohibited acts e.g. making alcohol, gambling, etc.

In the story of Prophet Dawood there is another important lesson. Allah tells in the Quran how He bestowed the gift of iron on Prophet Dawood, and the ability to mould it and fashion it.[60] Allah ordered him to make chainmail armour, and told him to be sure to perfect each of the links. This example is given to show that one must strive for excellence in their jobs. We must do our best in our work, regardless of what that job is, whether it be as a scientist, doctor, or taxi driver, porter, or cleaner.

There is wisdom here. Everyone striving for the highest level in their work will lead to progression of knowledge, development, innovation, and enterprise. This is how society will progress. The scientist will make new discoveries, the inventor will make new technologies, the entrepreneur will develop businesses and bring the innovations to the people. But everyone has their part to play, even those in less glamourous jobs. Take the janitor. An obvious example is hospitals: doctors and surgeons treat patients, but the cleaners ensure the hospital is clean and thereby reduce infection rates. But imagine a simple office not having a cleaner, or having one that does a very poor job. With no one to maintain the toilet facilities, dust and sweep the floors and clear the garbage bins, it would become an

---

[58] Sahih Bukhari
[59] Quran 34: 10; https://bit.ly/2JgUMNp
[60] Quran 34: 11

unpleasant place to work. Going to the toilet, a matter of human necessity, would become a disgusting and unpleasant experience. People would not be able to focus in such an environment, or would simply choose not to work there. The fact that one does not have to worry about cleaning the toilet or clearing the rubbish allows each one to concentrate on what one really needs to put their efforts into.

No one is an island, and nobody works in true isolation. Every person is weaved into the intricate fabric of society, and relies on countless people to exist. The key players in any enterprise have a whole host of people supporting them, including right down to their human needs. When visiting NASA in 1962, John F Kennedy asked a janitor what he did there, to which the janitor famously replied 'I am helping put a man on the moon.'[61] The janitor understood he was part of the team that was striving for greatness, literally striving for the moon, and he needed to do his part.

At the time of the Prophet, a woman called Umm Mihjaan used to clean his mosque. One night she died. The Companions, not wishing to bother him over the death of a cleaner, buried her promptly themselves and prayed the accompanying funeral prayer. The next morning the Prophet was most upset to learn of her passing and that no one had thought it important to inform him at the time. He then asked to see her grave, and prayed the funeral prayer himself personally over her grave.[62] This shows the importance of everyone's contribution to the community and the dignity the Prophet gave to each individual. We need to do the same – appreciate and dignify everyone's roles.

Ultimately the combined effort for excellence will lead to service of humanity and progression of mankind. Now here is a very important point to grasp: If one's *intention* is to excel at their job so as to serve humanity and thereby please Allah, then *one's work becomes a form of worship.* I took a taxi on one occasion in Chicago. Whilst making conversation with

---

[61] https://bit.ly/2UxP521
[62] Sahih Bukhari; Sahih Muslim

the young African American taxi driver I asked him if he did this full time. No, he replied, he was mainly a film producer. He drove a taxi to make ends meet whilst looking for his big break, but then he added that he was looking to provide his passenger with an experience, not just transporting them from A to B. Close your eyes, he said, and you will not be able to feel the car move, no sense of acceleration or braking, as he would make the journey so smooth. I tried that, and to my astonishment he was absolutely right. He had transformed a rush hour journey normally full of stops and starts and numerous jolts into an impressively smooth performance. It was an experience indeed. Similarly, a taxi driver can take pride in his car, keep it clean, provide a smooth and pleasant journey to his customer, knowing that he is facilitating his transport needs, contributing to his customer's mood, and so providing positive assistance to the customer's work or social relations.

At the time of writing, the coronavirus pandemic is sweeping across the world. There is great fear and anxiety about its rapid spread and virulence. Panic-buying in shops is resulting in superstores with empty shelves. Yet its effect on society is highlighting just how everyone is part of the fabric of society and the role they play. The shopkeeper, anywhere from the local corner shop to the superstore, is now vital to providing goods to the population. The shelf-stacker, the checkout agent, the truck driver and the humble home delivery driver are vital links in the chain that allow society to procure their bare necessities of groceries and goods. The petrol stations with their attendants are essential to allowing the trucks to function. The IT professionals are essential to making sure the whole IT network that runs the processes function without hitch. The internet providers and the support staff are critical to support the necessary information and communication flows. Schools have shut down, and education is moving to an online mode. Everyone is a cog in the machinery of modern society. The modern lifestyle, with all its conveniences, is only possible because of each person's contribution. One needs to keep this intention in mind: that they are playing a role in the service of the community, not just making a living, and their work transforms into worship. The pandemic has also issued a poignant reminder to society against arrogance: those whose jobs have been deemed 'unskilled' and contemptible are now suddenly found to be vital for society to exist.

There is a serious misconception amongst many Muslims that when they need to become more religious, the only way is praying more, growing a long beard or donning a *hijab*, frequenting the mosque more, or going for Hajj – reducing Islam to rituals and symbolism. Service to humanity and striving for its progression are deemed to be 'worldly' and therefore a distraction. This is a terrible trap. There is no doubt about the value of the ritualistic worshipful aspects of Islam or, for example, seeking to emulate the Prophet in appearance. But this is the classic lack of understanding about the profound weightiness of moral conduct and the need to help humanity, and how it relates to worship without being ritualistic. Allah provides everyone with talent and opportunity. We need to put these to best use. They are not to be wasted. We will be accountable for how these were utilised.

Bottom Line:

• An honest job is an honour bestowed by Allah.

• Allah tells us to strive for excellence in whatever we do, including our profession.

• Everyone is provided with customised ability and opportunity, and everyone must give account for how these were utilised.

Abstain from Alcohol, Intoxicants and Gambling

Intoxicants, including alcohol, result in a loss of senses. Uninhibited behaviour follows, which can culminate in unacceptable decisions and actions. People can undertake actions while intoxicated that would horrify them when sober. The mildest outcome might be personal embarrassment, whilst the most serious could be a criminal offence such as rape, or violence. The law of many countries mitigates a crime that resulted due to intoxication. This is not the case with Allah. Allah holds a person fully accountable and culpable. It was their decision to drink. One drink led to another, until they became drunk. Any consequences that arose remain fully their responsibility. Intoxicants of any sort are therefore expressly prohibited.

Four Quranic verses were revealed in relation to alcohol and intoxicants, separated by many years. The first was:

> *And from the fruits of the palm trees and grapevines you take intoxicant and good provision. Indeed in that is a sign for a people who reason. {Quran 16: 67}*

This verse comes amongst verses in which Allah talks of the different types of beverages that derive from nature: rainwater from the sky, milk from the udders of cattle, alcohol from dates and grapes, and honey from bees. Allah is giving these as signs for man to reflect.

The next verse to be revealed came after Umar bin Khattab and Mu'adh bin Jabal asked the Prophet for a ruling on alcohol, concerned about how it led to drunkenness, debauchery and depravity.

> *They ask you about alcoholic drink and gambling. Say: 'In them is a great sin, and (some) benefit for men but the harm is greater than the benefit'. {Quran 2: 219}*

Allah is now introducing the concept that both intoxicants and gambling are vices and sinful. What is the '*benefit*' referred to here? People feel good after taking intoxicants, plus for the farmer, producing wine from grapes brings a much greater revenue than just from the fruit – what Allah referred to as 'good provision' in the first verse. Gambling might lead to money and riches if the gambler wins his big one. However, the impact on the individual and society at large will be damaging in the end. So the harm is far greater.

Alcohol had not yet been completely prohibited. The next verse to be revealed brought the first restriction:

Believers, do not pray when you are drunk, but, instead, wait until
you can understand what you say. {Quran 4: 43}

As ritual prayer (*salat*) is five times a day, that leaves very little room for
one to drink to intoxication and then sober up in time for salat. This was
ordering Muslims to limit their drinking without giving an outright ban.
However, this verse was abrogated (i.e. replaced) with a subsequent and
final verse on alcohol, where its prohibition was made clear and definitive:

O Believers, intoxicants (i.e. alcohol and other agents), gambling,
the stone altars and (divining) arrows are all abominable acts
associated with satanic activities. ***Do not even come near*** *them so*
that you may have everlasting happiness. {Quran 5: 90}

Satan only wants to cause between you animosity and hatred
through intoxicants and gambling and to avert you from the
remembrance of Allah and from prayer. So will you not stop?
{Quran 5: 91}

The rationale for this method was gradualism (as discussed at the outset –
see *Islam as a Journey: Slow and Steady Wins the Race*). Alcohol was a
big part of life amongst Arabs just like all nations, and indeed continues to
be for most nations today. Gradualism, known in Arabic as *tadaruj,*
allowed people to slowly digest the idea of alcohol as a vice and not
impose a prohibition that would overwhelm them. The concept is
introduced, then a limited prohibition made, and ultimately a complete ban
over the course of many years.

It is important to note the linguistics of the final command. Allah does not
say 'Do not drink alcohol'. He says '*fajtanibuh'* from the verb *ijtanaba,*
meaning to keep away. The meaning of 'Don't come near' is exactly the
same way as Allah prohibited fornication (see *Modesty*), and is a far
stronger command than simply 'Do not drink'. English translations often
render this verb as 'avoid' which some readers interpret as a mild
precaution and not a prohibition. This demonstrates the problem of
translations, and how they may be misinterpreted. Not only is the
prohibition unequivocal and stern, but Allah explains why in the

immediate verse that follows (5:91) – communities are ripped apart through its consequences. The word used for intoxicants is *khamr*, literally meaning wine. However this is used as a surrogate for all intoxicants. The Prophet explained:

> *Every intoxicant is khamr, and every khamr is forbidden.*
> *{Sahih Muslim}*

> *(The Messenger of Allah) cursed ten people in connection with wine: the wine-presser, the one who has it pressed, the one who drinks it, the one who conveys it, the one to whom it is conveyed, the one who serves it, the one who sells it, the one who benefits from the price paid for it, the one who buys it, and the one for whom it is bought. {Sunan at-Tirmidhi and Sunan Ibn Majah}*

The Sunnah (teachings of the Prophet) is therefore also clear on this. Anyone connected in any way to intoxicants is cursed, so serious is this matter.

The concept of abrogation is seen here. Later verses may replace earlier ones, or earlier rulings. Casual reading of the Quran may lead one to conclude that alcohol is permitted in Islam because of earlier verses that do not give outright prohibitions. The importance of thorough knowledge of the Islamic sources is seen in deriving permissibility and rulings in matters. It can also be seen how verses can be taken out of context to 'prove' a pre-conceived notion.

The wisdom behind the prohibition of intoxicants is readily evident. If one examines the detriment that alcohol and drugs cause in modern society, it is clear they are a major root cause of crime, ill health, and social chaos. The National Institute of Clinical Excellence, a key NHS advisory body, notes 'alcohol is one of the biggest avoidable risks for disease and death. Between 2010 and 2011, alcohol misuse led to 1.2 million hospital admissions and 15,000 deaths. Alcohol misuse also carries an economic burden costing the NHS around £3.5 billion per year, with annual cost to society in England of around £21 billion.'[63] The Chief Medical Officer's latest guidelines on alcohol records 'The risk of developing a range of illnesses (including, for example, cancers of the mouth, throat and breast) increases with any amount you drink on a regular basis.'[64] A Global Burden of Disease Study, a comprehensive health study of 195 countries and almost 30 million people over more than 15 years concluded 'alcohol use is a leading risk factor for global disease burden and causes substantial health loss.'[65] It concluded that 'results show that the safest level of drinking is **none**'.

Alcohol is a particular challenge for young Muslims growing up in Western societies. Good times and good fun are closely linked with alcohol. This may allure the teenager and young adult. Or they may feel the pressure to conform, and not be seen as the odd one out. They should be ever mindful of the possible disaster scenarios that can follow a night of drinking and 'a bit of fun'. Imagine a guy waking up the next morning and finding, whilst smashed out of his senses, that he had engaged in some sexual behaviour, not something he would have done usually, or had been sexually abused. Even worse, imagine if this was with, or at the hands of, another guy. Worst of all, this got filmed on someone's mobile and was now posted up on social media. Imagine the embarrassment, guilt and stress to follow.

Note how gambling is also prohibited alongside intoxicants in these same verses, and with the same principle of gradualism. Gambling is seen as a vice by many, even from a secular viewpoint. Islam is a religion of effort. The making of money from pure chance goes against the principle of Islam. However, the bigger issue is the social detriment. Seduced by big jackpots that will transform their lives, gamblers who are most often from the lower socioeconomic classes are willing to bet valuable money that would otherwise be spent for the good of the family. Heavy financial

---

[63] https://bit.ly/33MO62W
[64] https://bit.ly/3dzjkiL
[65] https://bit.ly/2UDtYwa

losses can occur. Families and lives are ruined. The resentment of losing leads to bitterness, quarrels and possibly violence. Families and communities suffer. Islam's position is clear: gambling is a no-no.

Strict Prohibition on Usury (*Riba*)

Dealing in usury (financial interest) is expressly prohibited. Loans in Islam are a matter of charity, done to help someone out. The money loaned is returned after the agreed period, *exactly* to the same amount. Giving or receiving more than this is usury (called *riba* in Islam), and is severely outlawed. The reason is that charging interest opens the door to oppression. Compound interest can spiral out of control, and quickly the debt becomes insurmountable. Unscrupulous lenders can impose overbearing and unachievable terms for desperate borrowers. The debtor is at the mercy of the lender when he duly fails to return the money. Historically this has led to enslavement, with the borrower and/or his family becoming slaves or bonded labourers to the lender. Islam condemns oppression and closes any possible pathways to it. The gravity of usury is seen from the Quranic verses prohibiting it:

> *Those who consume interest cannot stand (on the Day of Resurrection) except as one stands who is being beaten by Satan into insanity. That is because they say, 'Trade is (just) like interest.' But Allah has permitted trade and has forbidden interest....*

> *...But whoever returns (to dealing in usury) - those are the companions of the Fire; they will abide therein....*

> *...O you who have believed, fear Allah and give up what remains (due to you) of interest, if you should be believers. And if you do not, then be informed of a war (against you) from Allah and His Messenger.*

> *But if you repent, you may have your principal – (thus) you do no wrong, nor are you wronged.' {Quran 2:275-279}*

The language is blunt and stern. Allah makes clear that there is no problem with trade and business, but usury is a major transgression. His Curse is upon those engaged in usury and they are destined for the Hellfire. This is the case whether one is the lender charging interest, or one is the borrower, paying the interest, again indicating the severity. In fact in one hadith of the Prophet, he adds that even the transcriber and the witnesses of the transaction, are also guilty parties.[66]

Sharia Law

The principles of Islam and its framework of legal rulings are known as the sharia. It encompasses every aspect of human life and covers issues of belief and worship, through to personal matters, through to community affairs. The sharia has been derived from divine sources (the Quran and the Sunnah) combined with human endeavour (examining early Muslim societies' practice, and logical reasoning).

The sharia's governing principles are: right to life and wellbeing, right to property, right to dignity, right to religion, right to family.

Sharia law is frequently given bad press by Islamophobic agencies, which report on its 'barbaric' or 'medieval' practices. The majority of sharia law is related to worship – how to pray, when to pray, the necessary ablution for prayer, rules of fasting, giving charity, etc; followed by rules of societal affairs – marriage, divorce, family life, businesses, transactions, inheritance, etc. There is only a very small section on criminal matters. Of this, there is an even smaller section on very specific crimes, known as the *hudood*.

Crimes and *Hudood* Laws

Any crime committed is dealt with by a court and a judge, who, if the

---

[66] Sahih Muslim

defendant is found guilty, issues an appropriate punishment. The punishment is at the discretion of the judge. This process is familiar to all. There are, however, a handful of specific crimes in Islam, known as the *hudood*, where the punishment is not the judge's discretion, but is divinely decreed. Examples include cutting of the hand for certain types of theft, and stoning to death for adulterers. These are what get widely publicised in the media. These negative and emotive reports do not make any attempt to understand them, as they seek to spread misinformation and malign Islam. We shall examine the *hudood* carefully to be clear about them.

The *hudood* laws serve as deterrents *for fully established Muslim communities*. The punishments are deliberately very harsh, but the burden of proof has been set very high to ensure they are actually not administered. For the crime to be classified as of the *hudood* category, there are general conditions that need to be fulfilled, as well as conditions specific for that crime. It is important to understand the applicability of the *hudood*, and their purpose.

The *hudood* and their punishments are: fornication (100 lashes); adultery (stoning to death); falsely accusing someone of fornication (80 lashes); certain types of theft (cutting off the hand); armed robbery (crucifixion and /or cutting off the hands and feet from opposite sides); and consuming alcohol or intoxicants (40 or 80 lashes).

The applicability

General conditions:

Society has to be Muslim and well established. That means that the people are educated, knowledgeable about their religion, and have jobs and incomes to sustain their families. Society is not facing any turmoil, such as war or famine. Law and governance are well established. Unlawful behaviour is therefore not arising from desperation or necessity.

The individual committing the crime has to be a Muslim adult of sound mind, fully aware of what he or she is doing and what the consequences are, if caught. If he / she claims ignorance of the penalty of the crime, then the *hudood* sentence cannot be imposed.

Additional key principles in determining a case as *hudood* or not are:

1. *In any shadow of a doubt*, the *hudood* punishments must not be applied. The Prophet said 'ward off *hudood* through ambiguity.'[67]

2. Islam is the way of mercy. Where *hudood* cases are presented, doubts must be sought *ardently* <u>by the judge</u> in the case to *avoid* the penalty. It is not the job of the defendant or his advocate to try to produce the doubts. Even the defendant denying the crime is counted as sufficient doubt to deem the case not *hudood*.

3. Do not seek out crimes or sins committed in private. What people do in their own privacy is their own business, for which they remain accountable to God. It is not society's business to interfere or administer punishment, unless there is public disturbance, or the individual seeks to publicise their crimes and promote anarchy in the community.

Just from these few principles, without even getting into the specific criteria necessary to establish each of the *hudood* crimes, it is clear that *hudood* punishments are not meant to be applied.

Specific conditions:

For establishing each *hudood*, there are extensive specific criteria. For theft, for example, criteria include that it must be a physical theft i.e. not an accounting swindle, embezzlement or a cybercrime. The stolen item must have been secured in a safe place by the owner, so it was not left lying around, open to see. The item should have a certain minimum value, so stealing a loaf of bread is not a *hudood* theft. It must have been clearly

---

[67] Sunan Ibn Majah

witnessed by two people.

The issue of witnesses is actually very important in setting an unachievable threshold. For fornication / adultery, there is a requirement of four witnesses. Furthermore, it is not sufficient they found the defendants together naked. Each witness needs to have clearly seen actual penetration. It is quite clear that this criteria will be next to impossible to fulfil.

In fact, by now, it is unmistakeable to the reader, that the conditions to establish a crime as a *hudood* are unattainable, and its principles work to the same effect. The idea is not to absolve the criminal who has perpetrated the crime. If the evidence convicts him, he must be punished. But it is to demote the seriousness of the crime from category of *hudood*, where a harsh penalty *must* be imposed by divine decree, to one where the crime is non-*hudood*, and so allowing the judge to impose a penalty at their discretion, and thereby avoid one so harsh.

The purpose

The punishments are deliberately harsh to ensure they serve as firm deterrents in society. This can be seen in a simple modern day example. Parking your car on a yellow line is liable for a penalty ticket with a fine. People often take the chance, hoping they will get away with it, especially if they just need to pop into a shop. However, imagine if the penalty was changed to the car being seized and then crushed. The outcome – not a single person would park on a yellow line, ever.

The question then arises why have such harsh penalties been ordained, yet they are not really to be applied? Dr Jonathan Brown, the American scholar of Islamic Studies, beautifully explains the underlying wisdom:

> *Perhaps these stringent laws, which God's mercy has made almost impossible to apply, exist primarily to remind people of the*

enormity of the sins that they usually get away with.[68]

In other words, people will commit such offences and they will be safe from the divinely-ordained worldly punishment, but they need to be conscious of just how severe Allah deems the sin. They should be gravely concerned with what awaits them in the Hereafter.

So what happened at the time of the Prophet? How did he apply these rulings? The *hudood* of adultery for example, was **never** applied because the perpetrators were caught. There were, however, a few cases, where the transgressors came forward themselves and confessed out of their own guilt. The Prophet actively sought to turn them away, or find excuses that would absolve them. He went to great lengths to avoid application of the *hudood*, but the piety of these people drove them to pursue the punishment themselves, until it was carried out. The magnitude of the sin weighed on them so heavily that they wished to have the punishment exacted in this world, not in the Next.

Bottom line:

• Sharia law is the framework of Islamic principles and rulings relating to human activity.

• A tiny minority of these rulings deal with specific crimes known as *hudood.*

• The *hudood* crimes have divinely decreed harsh penalties but, out of Allah's Mercy, their application is *deliberately* engineered so they are *not* to be administered.

• The *hudood* penalties serve as a profound deterrent for society, as well as to impress on people the severity of their sins.

---

[68] https://bit.ly/39oezF8

Closing the Door

It will be readily apparent by now to the reader that Allah has ordered us to be upstanding in our moral character. We are to follow His rules which serve as guidance for us, not only as a means of obeying Him but also for our own benefit. Temptation is present in this world as a test for us. Temptation could be for illicit relations, wealth, drugs or alcohol. A valuable principle is to avoid being in the situation that would expose us to that temptation in the first place. It is easier to deal with temptation if we are not exposed to it, rather than pulling ourselves away, once in the thick of it. If we want to eat healthier, it is far easier not to buy the biscuits, cakes, deserts and sweet stuff, and so not have them in the house at all, rather than trying to resist having just the one then two, then three. Before you know it, the entire packet is finished - we have all been there!

In this way, we are closing the door to temptation. Allah has given this principle Himself in fact. With regards to fornication He says:

> *Do not even come near to fornication. It is indecent and an evil act. {Quran 17: 32}*

Whilst for alcohol the final verse revealed to prohibit it completely was:

> *O Believers, intoxicants, gambling, the stone altars and divining are all abominable acts associated with satanic activities. Do not even come near them so that you may have everlasting happiness. {Quran 5: 90}*

Both of these prohibitions are not given as 'Do not do', but are given in an even more stern fashion – '*Do not even approach*' these vices, which is precisely what *closing the door* is. In other words, do not even allow yourself to be exposed to the situation where temptation may arise.

This translates into not going to the club ('clubbing'), disco or party where there will be uninhibited free mixing along with alcohol, suggestive loud music, and possibly drugs. Similarly, a guy buddying up with a girl to work together on homework or class assignments, risks being alone together in certain situations, with possibility of leading onto fornication – so avoid this. The guy partners up with a male buddy, and the girl with a girl friend. If their pairing is unavoidable, then all meetings are kept in public and strictly none are undertaken where they would be secluded.

This is a crucial strategy and it is important to realise there is a mental element here as well. Sins do not tend to just happen out of the blue. Usually there has been a lead up to it, such as constant external peer pressure to go clubbing, or to have one (alcoholic) drink just one time. However, mentally, one can also dwell on sinful scenarios or feelings. For example, the guy who starts getting affectionate feelings for a girl in his class. If he dwells on these, they will expand and permeate until he is totally overwhelmed and all he can think about is 'the most beautiful girl in the world'. This buds into action eventually when he asks her to join him for a coffee or pizza. He is on the slippery slope now, as discussed in *Modesty* and *No harm in looking*. The door needs to be closed on these mental thoughts and whispers too.

Bottom Line:

• In order to avoid temptation, do not allow yourself to be exposed to it in the first place – close the door on the situation.

• Also close the door on thoughts and whispers that will lead to enticement.

Ease in the Religion

Allah has prescribed a way of life, and has given rules. For the majority of time, for the majority of people, these will be the boundaries to stay within. However, there could be times where these limits may impose excessive hardship on people. Allah is extremely merciful and compassionate, He is *Rahmaan* and *Raheem* (see '*Kindness*') and He makes abundantly clear that He does not wish hardship in the religion:

And Allah wants to lighten for you (your difficulties); for mankind was created weak. {Quran 4:28}

Ablution, which is ritual cleansing, requires water to wash the face and limbs. It is a prerequisite for the ritual prayer. So what if water is not available, for example whilst travelling? Allah permits dry ablution where sand or dust is wiped lightly over the face and limbs:

> *... **Allah does not want to place you in difficulty**, but He wants to purify you and to perfect His grace upon you so that you may give thanks. {Quran 5: 6}*

Allah is making easy the ritual cleansing. If water were absolutely required no matter what, then a traveller on a long journey through the desert, for instance, may have to compromise on his drinking water to perform ablution, putting themselves at risk. Allah removes this dilemma.

In the month of Ramadan, when all adults are obligated to fast, Allah gives exemption to several groups: the sick, the traveller, and by extension others for whom fasting would be onerous, such as pregnant women. He says:

> *...So whoever sights the month (i.e. the new moon of the month of Ramadan), let him fast it; and whoever is ill or on a journey - then an equal number of other days (i.e. of what they could not fast). **God wants ease for you, and does not want hardship for you**; and that you fulfil the number, and glorify God that He has guided you, and perhaps you will be thankful. {Quran 2:185}*

The principle is not to follow our desires and lusts, and to stay within Allah's prescribed limits. But where there will be undue hardship, He relaxes the boundaries. The Prophet also expounded on this numerous times. When he sent his Companions away to teach people Islam, he told them:

> *Cheer the people, and inspire them not with aversion, and* **make** **(the religion) easy for them**, *and do not make it difficult for them. {Sahih Bukhari and Sahih Muslim}*

> *Facilitate things to people (concerning religious matters), and do not make it hard for them and give them good tidings and do not make them run away (from Islam). {Sahih Bukhari}*

Combining ritual prayers in times of necessity or undue hardship, such as travelling, is also permitted and was practised by the Prophet. Travelling here refers to undertaking a significant journey, for instance going abroad, not our regular commute on the Underground or the city's metro system. Juristic scholars have given it a more precise definition. Combining of prayers was not done, however, as a matter of convenience e.g. whilst shopping. Similarly, consumption of pork is strictly prohibited for a Muslim. However, in cases of famine and starvation, pork becomes permissible.

Aisha, one of the wives of the Prophet, said: 'If there were two alternatives, the Holy Prophet used to adopt the easiest, provided there was no sin in it.'[69] This is very important to appreciate. Some Muslim groups have developed rigid and uncompromising practices that impose tremendous burden on their followers. This goes against Allah's wishes for us. And the Prophet warned:

> *Islam is very easy and whoever overburdens himself in his religion will not be able to continue in that way. So do not be extreme, but try to be near to perfection and receive the good tidings that you will be rewarded. {Sahih Bukhari}*

In other words, following rigid religious practices will lead to a breakdown of that person because it will be unsustainable on a personal level, or it will strain and break relationships around them. This was also illustrated

---

[69] Sahih Bukhari, Sahih Muslim

by another episode in which three men visited the wives of the Prophet to inquire about his worship and so gain inspiration.[70] Feeling desperately inadequate with their own level of worship in comparison, each of them took a vow to boost it. The first man vowed never to sleep, but to pray all night long instead; the second declared he would fast every day; the third stated he would never marry and therefore never engage in intimate relations. The Prophet upon learning of this counselled them not to be excessive, but to follow his way, a way of balance. He prayed at night, but also slept for part of it. He would fast some days but also eat on others. He did not forsake marital relations. The message is to remain balanced and not to overburden oneself, this is what Islam prescribes.

Unfortunately, some Muslim groups go even a step further and have converted many permissible (*halal*) actions into prohibited (*haram*). They view this as a matter of being thoroughly scrupulous and super cautious. This is actually a very serious matter for it is not just going against Allah's decree of ease in the religion, but is actually altering His Laws.

Bottom Line:

• Allah has prescribed ease in His religion, out of His immense Mercy.

• The Islamic way is one of balance and the middle way.

• The Prophet advised always taking the easier option of what were permissible.

---

[70] Sahih Bukhari

Encouraging Good and Forbidding Evil

Allah says in the Quran:

> *You (i.e. Muslims) are the best of peoples ever raised up for mankind; you enjoin Al-Ma'roof (i.e. that which is good) and forbid Al-Munkar (i.e. that which is bad), and you believe in Allah. {Quran 3:110}*

This is often coupled with the saying of the Prophet:

> *Whoever among you sees an evil action, let him change it with his hand (by taking action); and if he cannot, then with his tongue (by speaking out); and if he cannot, then with his heart (by feeling that it is wrong) – and that is the weakest of faith. {Sahih Muslim}*

The principles espoused here are that Islam is based on justice, integrity and equity. Corruption is not permitted and is not to be accepted. These principles apply to *all Muslims*, not just to the rulers or those in authority. Muslims are not to turn a blind eye. They are all to be active in upholding a just society. Indeed this quality, Allah is pointing out, marks Muslims out from the rest of mankind.

Unfortunately this verse and hadith are misconstrued by certain over-enthusiastic Muslims, who take this as a licence to stand up and browbeat those found to be committing a sin. For example, slamming a fellow Muslim for drinking alcohol or mixing freely with the opposite gender. In fact, speaking up when it may even be harmful to themselves, is seen as a sign of courage and a badge of piety. The one 'standing up' feels proud and righteous, and similar minded observers congratulate them on taking the stand.

Allah's Guidance through the Quran and the teachings of the Prophet form a framework for perfection in character and conduct. The Prophet himself had the best character, which was to be emulated by all mankind. In the overarching framework of Islam, softness and kindness are key in interacting with others. The Prophet was always gentle and compassionate when dealing with anyone, including his enemies. There was never any harshness or confrontation. The show of power and the need for force was only seen on the battlefield, the battles themselves being eventualities for self-preservation where negotiation and diplomacy had failed. The Prophet sought to convey the message of Islam and what was right and wrong, *in the best manner, using a judicious and soft approach*, to be as effective as possible. Blunt self-righteous and confrontational dialogue was never his way. This should not be the way of any Muslim. Allah says:

> *Invite (mankind) to the way of your Lord **with wisdom and beautiful preaching**; and reason with them in ways that are best and most gracious: for your Lord knows best, who have strayed from His Path, and who receive guidance. {Quran 16:125}*

Inviting someone is always done pleasantly. We invite acquaintances to dinner in a warm manner. Never is an invitation done with belligerence, debate and self-righteousness. When a Muslim encounters wrongdoing, it is important to judge what intervention can be made and its likely effect. If the overall result will be to worsen things, either for the person in the wrong or society at large, then that intervention is not the right approach, and an alternative should be sought.

Consider these two examples. An elderly lady is being mugged. It is imperative to intervene if one has the physical capability. If physically infirm, then raise an alarm and get help. One should not turn a blind eye.

On the other hand, consider a Muslim drinking alcohol. If it seems they are teetering with this weakness, or are trying it out, then a gentle reminder may work well. But if addressing this may have the converse effect of turning them further away from Islam ('these Muslims only spend their time telling us everything is wrong!' or 'here comes the *haram* police again') then it may be better to leave this for now. Everyone is on a journey and they may not be ready to make that change for now. On a subsequent occasion, encourage them to learn more about Islam generally, and perhaps join you for an Islamic talk. Good counsel from sound and righteous teachers may inspire them and soften their heart to the path favoured by Allah. As they come to gain more knowledge and associate with good company, the increase in God-consciousness and love for God will lay the foundations for wanting to avoid sins. Giving up alcohol will then naturally fall into that journey.

Bottom Line:

• *All Muslims* are responsible for upholding a just, fair and moral society.

• Corruption is not to be tolerated.

• Intervention against wrongdoing should be judicious and well-measured, so as to be effective.

• Brow beating and confrontation is not the Prophetic way, but softness and kindness is.

• Interventions may need a long term approach.

PART III
PRINCIPLES OF BELIEF
AND WORSHIP

How do We Know God Exists?

1. Something cannot come from nothing

If we wake up one morning and find a hammer on our bedside table, we would wonder who put it there. We would engage our mind to recall who had been in the room the day before, or could someone have been in the room during the night? Did we use it and forget to put it back? If we cannot think of an answer and we live with family we would finally conclude a family member is guilty. And we would then go off to scold whoever had been irresponsible in not putting it back. If we live alone, we would get somewhat alarmed at the prospect that an intruder had gained access to our bedroom. What we would not accept is that it simply appeared out of nowhere. In fact we would not entertain this idea at all.

Yet with regards to nature, the perpetual cycle of life make some people oblivious to the question where did all this life come from in the beginning. Some might say 'well the hammer obviously had to be placed by someone, but nature and the universe is different.' For instance, a flower originated from a seed which originated itself from a parent flower, which itself came from a seed and so the cycle goes on and on. The natural processes they argue, explain the existence of our universe. But if we keep going backwards, at some point this cycle had to have a beginning to it. There must have been the very first seed, or the very first flower that initiated this cycle of life. Where did it come from? Just as we would not accept that a hammer popped out of nowhere, similarly we cannot accept that nature or the universe popped out of nowhere. Someone *must* have put it there to start with, no?

A desert Bedouin remarked that 'the camel's droppings testify to the existence of the camel, and the footprints testify to existence of the walker. A sky that holds the stars, a land that has fairways, and a sea that has waves. Does not all of this testify to the existence of the Kind, the Knowing (i.e. God)?' So the trees, the mountains and the sky indicate the existence of a Supreme Being who is responsible for them. Something cannot come out of nothing. Everything in this universe has a causal agent, namely something that is responsible for it. All that is in this universe had to have been put here by someone.

This was obvious before the advent of science. Some might now put forward the argument that 'Ah with science now, we can explain the first seed / flower. There was the Big Bang and then evolution!' Invoking the murky black box of the Big Bang / evolution narrative does not actually answer the question. It merely shifts the question along, and/or is a pretence at giving an answer. It still leaves massive questions unanswered. The Big Bang advocates that the universe originated from a single particle that contained all the mass and energy of the universe, which then rapidly expanded giving rise to matter, then stars, galaxies and planets. But who caused the Big Bang in the first place, where did this particle of singularity, as it is known, come from? How did life subsequently originate from inanimate inorganic chemicals? In actuality, scientific advancements *confirm* the existence of God – they certainly do not lead one away from the idea of a Creator. In fact not only the existence of God, but they lead to an increasing wonderment at His ability. The atheistic narrative prevalent today is a misportrayal of science.

2. The incredible order in the universe – order does not come from chaos

The universe is directed towards chaos and disorder. This is apparent from our own daily observations. Our bedroom will tend to get messier, the kitchen counter gets cluttered, the garden will become an unkempt jungle with time. Only someone's intervention will restore order: someone needs to tidy the bedroom, someone needs to wash the dishes, and someone needs to mow the lawn and weed the garden. This is also recognised in the laws of the universe. All reactions take place due to an increase in entropy, which is a thermodynamic measure of disorder of any system. If a chemical reaction will result in increased disorder of energy distribution, the reaction is viable. So chemical reactions and the universe are geared towards disorganisation and chaos.

However, the universe is ***exceptionally*** ordered at every level from astronomical, right down to the atomic level. Galaxies, stars, our own Sun and planets trace defined orbits. Humans and animals are made up of organs which perform specialised functions, such as the heart pumping blood all around the body, the lungs harvesting oxygen from the air, the gut processing food to extract its nutrients. Every organ has an intricate architecture built up of highly specialised cells. Each cell is a little factory made up of subcellular structures called organelles which comprise: the nucleus, the information centre of the cell; mitochondria, the power-house energy production centres; ribosomes, the protein-producing machinery; cytosol, the chemical reaction cauldron of the cell. Each of these organelles have incredible structures themselves and deal with giant molecules (called macromolecules) such as proteins, DNA, RNA. These molecules themselves are astonishingly complex. Molecules are made of atoms, which themselves have exquisite order of the nucleus and electrons. The degree of complexity present in life and the universe is mind-blowingly staggering. In fact, there is no word or even phrase in the English language that captures the utterly incredible and profound complexity. To even appreciate this complexity to a minor degree requires some contemplation, and in fact science helps enormously.

How did this order arise? And who maintains this order, after all once things have been organised initially, everything should continue to move to disorder and chaos? Someone has to not only produce this order but also maintain this order – surely, evidence of a Supreme Being.

Those who do not believe in God may counter and say 'Ah well wait a minute, the universe had unique intense and extreme conditions in the beginning, and there has been an incredibly long time, billions of years, to allow the development of the universe and life.' Let's consider this: Suppose Neil Armstrong, the first man on the moon, had just planted his feet on the moon, 'one small step for man, one giant leap for mankind… oh wait, whats that…?' he says as his eye caught something in the moondust: a piece of pottery. This is perhaps the simplest object that can be made – some clay that has been moulded and shaped, baked and then decorated. This could surely have come out of the extreme random processes of the Big Bang, no? The intense heat and pressures, particles smashing together, new nuclei, new atoms, new molecules being forged. Why not during the birth of the moon, some clay matter formed, got shaped by the pressures, and baked by the heat. Coloured fluids also formed during this intense period, and randomly smeared on the clay, like paint, but they happened to create a pretty pattern. So the incredible processes of the early universe and the profound passage of time are all there.

Honest reflection here is required - would any rational person ever accept that this was a residue from the random processes of the Big Bang and subsequent celestial bodies' formation? If such an instance had occurred it would have been taken as evidence that an intelligent life form already existed and was responsible for it. In fact such a discovery would have turned the media and earthly civilization into a frenzy as this would be taken as incontrovertible evidence of extra-terrestrial life i.e. aliens; in other words *someone* was responsible for putting it there. Why? Because the degree of order seen, even in something as simple as a piece of pottery, can only be explained by the action of someone. If anyone suggested this was Big Bang residue, they would have been branded fools.

Another example to consider was the discovery of large intricately designed geometric circular patterns on the sandy seabed floor off the coast of Japan's Amami Ōshima Island in 1995. The patterns span approximately 2 metres across and comprise a central circular area which itself contains a maze-like design, enclosed by a series of outer rampart-like rings which themselves are etched with radially arranged ditches, with the crests decorated with shells and coral. The symmetry and geometrical design of these ornate patterns are breathtakingly beautiful, even a human artist would be proud. People were bamboozled as to their origin. Could the intricate order have come from random processes such as oceans currents acting on unusual seabed geography? Clearly not. Somebody or something purposeful was responsible. In fact so strong was this sentiment that even aliens were proposed as one explanation. Eventually a scientific team unearthed the mystery - the tiny male of the white-spotted Japanese pufferfish.[71] This little guy, no more than 10 centimetres in length, excavates furiously using its fins over a two week period to produce its astonishing aesthetic artwork, all to court the female. Once attracted, the female would come and lay her eggs in the centre.[72] The point to observe here is that incredible order, *even if simply a pattern in the sand*, requires an explanation involving a purposeful agent; random purposeless processes do not do.

The argument has been made that order can be the outcome of a reaction rather than disorder when energy is applied to a system. In the case of our earth, the energy of the Sun is proposed as being the primary external source of energy. This argument is unsatisfactory. Energy only increases order in a system *where it is directed*. Undirected energy input will continue to increase disorder in the system.

Take the messy bedroom. Inputting energy alone such as a tornado will do nothing to tidy the room. The directed energy of the mother who comes in and cleans up will bring order. Similarly the directed energy of a gardener will restore an unkempt garden to a landscape one. The undirected energy from exploding a massive bomb in the garden will only worsen the state. If we take our example from above of the seabed geometric circles, we would not accept this could have arisen from the high energy of a grenade exploding on the sandy seabed floor, or even a cyclone roughing up the seabed. The directed energy of the male Japanese pufferfish is required. The Sun can provide necessary energy but it cannot produce order per se; a separate directing agent is needed.

Order does not arise from random chaos – it requires an organiser. In fact not only is someone responsible for the order in the first place, He must also be responsible for *maintaining* it, as the constant natural direction is to disorder.

---

[71] https://go.nature.com/2wFnZiq
[72] https://bit.ly/2xrfl7i

All the exquisite order in the universe requires a Creator, an Organiser and a Maintainer.

3. The balance in the universe

In the atom, the negatively-charged electrons are held with just the right electromagnetic force from the positively-charged nucleus to keep it in orbit around the nucleus rather than whizzing off. With the development of quantum mechanics, referring to the electron being 'in orbit' is disliked as the electron can be in different levels around the nucleus, rather than in a set orbital plane. However the point remains that the electron has energy and it is moving at great speed. Why does it not actually fly off? It is held 'captive' by the electromagnetic force from the nucleus, but this force is just right. Too much and the electron would crash into the nucleus and bind there permanently just like opposite poles of a magnet click together. Too little and the electron would break free of the atom altogether. Where did the electron acquire this energy? And how does the nucleus apply just the right electromagnetic force?

The earth and the planets of our solar system orbit the Sun. In the same manner as the electron in the atom, the earth is moving at great speed. Yet the gravity of the Sun acting on the earth, which is just the right the distance from the Sun, holds it in orbit. Again, how is it that the gravity is perfectly balanced against the motion of the earth? Too much gravity or if the earth was moving with less speed, the earth will be drawn into the Sun where it will be destroyed. Too little gravity or if the earth was moving faster, the earth would break free of its orbit and drift into outer space. How did the earth acquire just the right speed, and enter into orbit at just the right distance, and the Sun exert just the right gravitational pull?

The natural laws of the universe are the rules according to which the universe runs. These have been elucidated by scientific study and continue to be so. In the development of the universe after the Big Bang and formation of the earth with its ability to hold life it has become clear that these parameters are actually extremely precise. So precise in fact, that had the parameters been even slightly different, off by the most minuscule amount, there would have been no universe, no earth, and no life.

The earth is at the perfect distance from the Sun to allow temperatures that allow water to exist as a liquid, and allow life to flourish. The earth rotates so that temperatures can vary through the day and night. Otherwise the side facing the Sun would be baking hot and the non-facing side would be freezing cold, permanently – life could only flourish at the fringes where these two extremes meet to allow mellow temperatures. The moon is the perfect size, shape and distance from the earth to stabilise the tilt of the earth's axis, and to influence the ocean tides to the right level allowing circulation of the Sun's thermal energy through the ocean water, and mixing of land and ocean sediments. Jupiter our giant planet neighbour serves as a protector for the earth, drawing asteroids towards itself that could otherwise result in catastrophic impact with the earth, terminating all life. The earth's core contains molten iron which circulates resulting in plate tectonics as well as a magnetic field for the earth. The magnetic field serves as an important shield for the earth, warding off damaging radiation from the Sun in the form of solar flares, or from supernovae (exploding stars).

There are four fundamental forces that operate in the universe: gravity, electromagnetic force, strong nuclear force (what binds nuclear particles together), and weak nuclear force. At the time of the Big Bang the forces driving the singularity particle apart had to be appropriately weighted against those pulling it back together again. Too much driving force and basic atoms of the universe and stars would not have formed, culminating in a universe of vacuous space and little matter, therefore no stars and planets. Too strong the attractive forces and the universe would have collapsed back on itself, resulting in no universe at all. It transpires that the ratios of these four forces are *exceptionally* precise.

For instance, if the ratio of strong nuclear force to electromagnetic force was off by even 1 in 10^{17} no stars would have formed. The other parameters are similarly pinpoint.[73]

The balance is so overwhelmingly precise that it simply cannot have arisen from random and purposeless processes. The natural laws of the universe have been very finely-tuned to give rise to a universe and life. Fred Hoyle was the late astrophysicist who coined the phrase 'Big Bang'. A lifelong atheist, he ultimately came to a conclusion at odds with his disbelief in God, that the extreme degree of balance in the universe could only be explained by a superintellect.[74] 'My atheism is greatly shaken' he conceded when reflecting on the calculations demonstrating the extreme improbability of the laws to produce this universe and life.

4. The innate need to worship the Creator

This is built into every single human, a feeling that there is a Higher Being that deserves to be worshipped. All civilizations throughout history have worshipped a God or even gods of some description. Where did this feeling come from? Only recently has been the advent of atheism, erroneously spurred by the scientific theories of Big Bang and evolution. Even many atheists, however, feel there is a cosmic force or energy at work in the universe, so have actually arrived at a proxy-God. So where did this innate drive to worship a Higher Power come from?

The origin of this drive has been explained in the Quran. Before Adam was sent down to the earth, all souls that were to ever live were brought forward from his loins. They stood before Allah who addressed them, asking 'Am I not your Lord?' All the souls answered 'Yes we do testify.'[75] Allah took a covenant from every single soul and explained that this was done to stop

---

[73] https://on.wsj.com/3dx561M
[74] The Universe: Past and Present Reflections, *Engineering and Science*, November 1981
[75] Quran 7: 172

man from claiming ignorance when he returns to Him on the Day of Judgement. This encounter that the soul of every single person has experienced, although not in our memories, has burnt the feeling deep into every human that there must be a God. This is called the *fitrah* in Islam, the inherent need to worship the Creator.

This *fitrah* exists in every person. Atheism is a learnt belief. Those who come to declare there is no God have buried their *fitrah* and taken on an unnatural state.

5. Moral code and altruism

Moral code is the in-built awareness of what is right and wrong. Every person from every civilization has a sense of what is right. Altruism is helping others without any material gain to oneself. An act done for 'a greater good', in other words an act based on the moral code. This desire to help others is also innate and firmly built into all mankind. So much so, that it extends to helping strangers, and sometimes putting one's own life at risk. Numerous people have lost their lives in the endeavour of saving others. Many a person has donated one of their kidneys to a family member or even to a non-family member, all for the sake of doing good for others. Why is this?

This has been a very prickly thorn in the side of the evolutionary scientist. Natural selection is the key principle in evolutionary theory, which purports that animals evolve over time, based on the survival of the fittest members i.e. the most well adapted animals will outcompete the rest of the herd, and their offspring will survive. Survival of the fittest implies that each organism looks out for itself without regard for others around it. Evolutionary theory cannot account for behaviour that puts one's life at risk. Recently hypotheses have been postulated about how this behaviour actually benefits the whole group/community even though harmful to the individual. These hypotheses, however, are based on established communities, for instance bees and the structure within a bee hive with a queen bee and worker bees. This social ordering is not to be confused with moral code. The animal is acting within a social structure here, not according to a moral conscience of what is right and wrong. Even with regards to the social organisation, there is no explanation whatsoever for how this arose *originally*, especially at genetic level. How did the first gene evolve to produce this astonishing social order in ants or bees?

Moral code is specific to man. Recall earlier the story of creation, when Allah tells the angels He is about to make a new species, they respectfully ask Him why. Allah creates Adam and then demonstrates to the angels the strength of man's moral code by showing them, not only man's ability to learn but crucially, the character of the pious humans to come.[76] Man has been given the ability to do an extraordinary amount of good. The moral code is what sets man apart from the rest of God's creation.

There is no evolutionary benefit to be found for the moral code, there are no scientific explanations for it. Yet even those who deny God still tend to live their lives according to the moral code. Whilst denying accountability and an afterlife, when asked 'what is the purpose of life', an atheist or agnostic will answer that 'it is to do good'. So where did this moral code come from?

The follow up question of what is the point of doing good if it does not count for anything (i.e. there is no accountability after death) meets with an uncomfortable blank. If man is just a result of random processes and particle interactions, who turns to dust and particles after death, then there seems to be no purpose to doing good in one's life. Yet the moral code is an overwhelmingly powerful aspect of humanity. People are ready to sacrifice their own life for achieving a greater good, or what is right. This extends even to a sworn enemy, who you think on most days you would be happy to see dead. But if they were truly in mortal danger requiring you to risk your life to save them, it is very likely you would do so.

---

[76] Shaykh Akram Nadwi's explanation of Quran 2: 30-32: 'What did Allah teach Adam? The great misunderstanding' (Cambridge Islamic College) https://bit.ly/3bs95dX

Some atheists may argue that doing good simply makes one feel fulfilled and good about themselves. In other words, there is no truly altruistic deed. These deeds are done for one's own satisfaction. This is an inadequate explanation. The hero who dies saving a little girl from being run over, knowing full well it will cost him his life, was not looking for fulfilment but sacrificed himself for 'good'. The courageous hero who charges a deranged gunmen hellbent on killing as many office workers as possible, knowing it will result in his own death but will allow his colleagues to escape is not seeking fulfilment. There is no feeling good about an act if one is dead.

And herein is the mind-blowing power of the moral code. Not only does it drive man to do good, but it *leads* man to realise that the good *must* have a purpose to it. This drive to do good is too powerful, to the cost of one's own life, to be dismissed as being about fulfilment. A life of good acts followed by death, crumbling bones, turning to senseless dust makes no sense at all. It must be that the good deeds have a higher purpose and so will count, and therefore there *has* to be God who will take account. The moral code therefore actually has two parts:

1. Do good

2. Believe in God, accountability, and an afterlife (the purpose of doing good).

Many people especially atheists either fail to derive, or choose to deny, the necessary consequence following on from the first part.

Here is the next mind-blowing part. Allah talks in the Quran specifically of what He requires man to do:[77]

1. Believe in God, accountability and an afterlife

2. Do good.

---

[77] Quran 2: 227; 5: 9; 5: 93; 19: 96; 41: 8

The instructions of the moral code and the instructions of Quran are eerily identical! Is this a coincidence? In fact Allah emphasises this by repeating it more than fifty times, along with similar statements, adding each time that those who do this will be the successful ones, the ones who attain Paradise.[78] The moral code is burnt into every person's being and the Quran emphatically embeds the same. How can this be? Is this mere coincidence?

Some might say 'well the moral code was already there, someone has simply taken this observation and written it into their book'. But as we shall see later the Quran is certainly not the product of a human mind. Is not the Writer of the Book (Quran) the same as the One who wrote into people?

6. Consciousness, language and intellect

Every living organism is made up of cells. In complex organisms such as animals the cells are organised into specialist units called organs to perform set functions. The heart has muscle cells arranged to pump blood. The intestine has epithelial cells to digest and absorb nutrients from food. The brain has nerve cells (called neurons) to control the body, collate sensory perception, and respond with movement or action. Humans have the same general anatomical arrangement as higher animals, including the brain.

Yet humans have cognitive functions that set them worlds apart. They have consciousness, the awareness of themselves and the world around them. Man is unique in that he can think about his own thinking.

Man has intellect, and can reason. Whilst communication exists amongst animals, it is rudimentary, compared to man whose development of language allows him to express his thoughts, wishes, emotions, intentions to others as well as forms the basis for his own reasoning. How does a

---

[78] For example – Quran 2:25; 29:7; 47:2; 31: 8;

collection of brain neurons result in all this high level cerebral activity?

How does it give rise to consciousness? Why is it not seen in animals who have a similar brain structure? For example, primates such as chimpanzees have the same brain structure as humans, as well as some basic language ability. But as author John Hands notes: 'The claim that a single chimpanzee using a stone to crack open a nut is the same kind of thing as a large international team of scientists cooperating to invent and construct the Large Hadron Collider in order to discover how fundamental particles interact is, I suggest, somewhat less than valid.'[79]

Evolution theory pertaining to this would suggest a continuum, such as we see with organs like the eye. Various levels and degrees of functionality and capability are found across species. However, man's intellect and language ability are massively superior to that of all other species in a way that evolution theory cannot explain.

In short, man's consciousness, language and intellect are scientifically unexplainable. It follows that the One who created man, endowed man with these abilities.

7. Living organisms contain complex information

Every living organism contains DNA (deoxyribonucleic acid) which is the genetic information that runs the cell, just like a blueprint for a machine. The DNA resides in the nucleus of the cell[80] and is in the form of a code which is translated by cellular protein machinery into proteins, which are the actual functioning complex molecular units of the cell.

We need to stop here for a second and consider what is information. Defining what is information is actually surprisingly difficult, though we

---

[79] Cosmosapiens: Human Evolution from the Origin of the Universe (Duckworth Overlook, 2015).
[80] In eukaryotic cells (i.e. those with a nucleus) such as in animals. In prokaryotes such as bacteria, the DNA lies in the cell as a ring.

all instinctively know what it is. In essence, it is thoughts, ideas or data, and it has to exist in the form of some language. Its transmission also requires language to do so. For example, books contain information and this information is in the form of letters from the alphabet arranged as words, words appropriately ordered to make sensible sentences, sentences sequenced to produce themes as paragraphs, paragraphs correctly organised to generate a logical flow of ideas.

Here is the thing. Information can only come from a conscious mind that supplies the information. This is always the case. *Information can never result from randomness*. This is a profound but critical concept. Monkeys on typewriters, or computers running random letter generators will never produce *information*. At best, the odd word will come up, but coherent comprehensive sentences will never arise that transmit information. And there is no chance for even a single paragraph, let alone a meaningful page.

DNA is real information just like computer code or a book. Computer code is a good comparison. Computer programs (apps) are written in a language by a computer programmer. The computer code they use is uninterpretable to lay people but the programmer understands the coding. What they write in the code dictates the computer's actions, such as displaying certain graphics or text, or making calculations, or moving figures, etc. Similarly DNA has a language, where its alphabet comprises the four building blocks of DNA called nucleotide bases, let's call them A T C and G for simplicity. A triplet code exists, so that each triplet of letters codes for one of the twenty amino acids. Amino acids are the building blocks for proteins. For example, CAG codes for the amino acid Glutamine. ATG codes for Methionine. The sequence of DNA nucleotide bases, therefore, codes for a sequence of amino acids which constitute a protein. Every protein in a cell has been manufactured by using the production information coded in the DNA. Every cell on this planet contains DNA, or arose from DNA. DNA is like the coding manual for all the cell's proteins. For further reading, Dr Stephen Meyer covers the concept of information and just how mind-blowing DNA is, providing a compelling argument for the existence of a Creator, in his book, *Signature in the Cell*.

DNA cannot have arisen from random processes. DNA cannot have evolved. Information ***always*** needs a programmer or an author. DNA therefore also needs a 'programmer'. The inescapable question arises who put this information in the form of DNA in every living cell of every living organism?

8. Islam

Islam itself is an evidence for the existence of God. The revelation of the Quran and the guidance Islam encompasses can only derive from a Creator. I will cover this in more detail later (*Is Islam the Right Religion*).

Bottom Line:

We know God exists because:

1. Something cannot come from nothing – everything has to have a cause including the universe and life.

2. The incredible order throughout the universe cannot come from randomness.

3. The balance in the universe is far too exquisite – some Great Artist must be responsible.

4. Every person has a profound in-built desire to worship the Creator – the *fitrah*.

5. The in-built desire to do good (altruism based on the moral code) must imply accountability to come, and therefore One who will take account.

The Quran's emphatic instructions exactly mirror the moral code embedded in man's fabric.

6. Intellect, language and consciousness of man must have been endowed upon man.

7. DNA is real information. Information can only arise from a conscious mind.

8. Islam itself is evidence of a God.

Who is God?

God is One, One alone, and He is unique. He has no comparison and is nothing like anything in His Creation. He is All-Knowing, All-Seeing and All-Hearing. That means He knows every detail of the universe, including what is in our hearts; He sees absolutely everything; from the farthest reaches of the universe, to the smallest detail of the atom. He hears absolutely everything. He is the Provider for all of His Creation. He is Generous and Kind beyond bounds. He never tires or sleeps. He is in complete control of everything, from the most infinitesimally small to the infinitesimally big. He is the Ever-Living, and has no beginning and no end. He has no parent, no child, no family. God is Allah.

God has ninety-nine names each of which describes one of His attributes. These are a great way to come to know Him. We know this from Allah Himself who says in the Quran:

> *Call upon Allah or The Most Kind. Whichever name you call – to Him belong the best names. {Quran 17: 110}.*

This is further expounded by the Prophet when he said 'Allah has ninety-nine names...'[81] It is believed that the most supreme of these names is Allah, which encompasses all the traits of the other names. There are sometimes more than one name to reflect a particular quality; the different names reflect subtleties in the attribute. Here are a few examples of His attributes with the name(s) that goes with it:

- Extreme kindness: *Ar Rahmaan*, and *Ar Raheem*
- Generous – *Al Kareem*
- Provider – *Ar Razzaaq*

---

[81] Sahih Bukhari, Sahih Muslim

- Forgiver – *Al Ghaffaar*, *Al Ghafoor*, *Al 'Afuww* (the last one actually means the Pardoner and Eraser of sins)

- All-Seeing – *Al Baseer*

- All-Hearing – *As Samee*

- All-Knowing – *Al Aleem*

- The One who responds to the person calling Him – *Al Mujeeb*

- The One who is exceedingly loving – *Al Wadood*

- The One that fulfils exclusively all needs – *As Samad*

Allah's attributes are who Allah is. Note that this has *always* been the case. Allah's qualities did not arise as a result of what He created. For example, He is the Forgiver. He has always had this attribute, and He created humankind to exhibit this aspect. Importantly, He did not develop a forgiving nature because He created man. He has qualities of being generous (*Al Kareem*), wanting to bestow (*Al Wahhaab*), and being a giver (*Ar Razzaaq*). Again this is who Allah is and has always been so. He created man to utilise and demonstrate these qualities. He did not become generous because of man.

Time is a creation of Allah, just like all the laws of the universe. Allah is therefore free from the paradigm of time. There is no past, present or future for Allah. The question of what existed before Allah is an invalid question as time does not exist for Allah. He created time as one of the laws of this universe.

Allah is free from any need, carrying the name *Al Ghani*. All the worship that all of mankind does for Him neither benefits Him nor increases any aspect of His Kingdom. **ALL** worship is actually done simply because Allah deserves it, His majesty is such. In contrast, we are the needy. Our worship benefits ourselves, as it is the means to gain Allah's pleasure. Although Allah has no need of us, He gives complete appreciation to whatever effort we make, no matter how big or how little, one of His names being *Ash-Shakoor*, the One who appreciates fully:

And whoever does good voluntarily, for sure Allah is the All-Appreciative, the All-Knower. {Quran 2: 158}

People naturally wonder what Allah actually looks like. Scholars have debated this issue, as Allah has mentioned features about Himself, such as that He has Hands, a Face or that He speaks. He is able to see everything and hear everything. Importantly, however, He also says:

*(He is) Creator of the heavens and the earth. He has made for you from yourselves, mates, and among the cattle, mates; He multiplies you thereby. **There is nothing like Him**, and He is the All Hearing, the All Seeing.. {Quran 42: 11}*

Allah is giving the clear message that He resembles nothing whatsoever in all of creation. The mainstream scholarly debate settled on the conclusion that Allah does have the features He describes, but they are not what we are familiar with and we can never come to realise them by using our imagination; so there is no point trying. The scholar Imam at-Tahawi (d. 933 CE) summarised the basic tenets of belief (creed) for a Muslim in his short work, Aqeedah Tahawiyyah.[82] This is a must read for all Muslims, but best studied with a teacher. In it these concepts are crystallised as:

Imagination cannot conceive Him, and intellect cannot grasp Him {#8}

He is different from any created being {#9}

In other words, we accept what Allah says about Himself, whilst we simultaneously acknowledge that picturing Him is beyond our abilities – so we should not lose our minds in abject speculation.

The successful ones, in the Hereafter, do receive the ultimate gift in Paradise – they get to finally see Allah Himself:

---

[82] https://bit.ly/2V0kvPx

Some faces will be radiant on that Day. Looking at their Lord. {Quran 75: 22-23}

Similarly when the Prophet was asked will we really get to see our Lord on the Day of Resurrection, he replied, 'you will see Him the same as you see the full moon or the sun on a clear day'.[83]

Some people put forward the view that there are many roads that lead to Rome, and it does not matter at the end of the day what faith one follows, just as long as you believe in a Creator. There are two problems with this belief. The first is that Allah wants man to know Him for who He is, as He is. This means recognising Him and giving Him the reverence and worship He deserves to the best of our ability. To direct one's worship somewhere else actually is an insult to the true Creator. For example, some may appreciate how fortunate they are and the incredible blessings bestowed upon them, but then, noticing how the Sun is the source of all energy on our planet, direct their worship to the Sun. Worse is to direct it to manmade objects such as statues, or animals such as cows or snakes. Clearly this is not the same as actually thanking the true God and Creator, who has created everything in the universe including the Sun. Instead of worshipping the Creator worshipping something in His creation is a manifest insult to Him.

The second issue with this belief is that worship of Allah also entails obeying His commands and instructions to us (see later, *What Does It Mean to 'Worship' God*). Obedience necessitates knowing what He has commanded through the guidance He provided man. Again when He has given specific guidance with specific orders, it is an affront to Him to declare that all faiths are quite similar and any of them will do as they all preach 'goodness'.

---

[83] Sahih Bukhari, Sahih Muslim

Allah says:

> *...This day I have perfected for you your religion and completed My favour upon you and have approved for you Islam as your religion... {Quran 5: 3}*

This was the final verse revealed of the Quran, and Allah makes clear that Islam is the way He has ordained on mankind. Through His Revelations of the Quran and the Sunnah, Allah explains who He is and what He expects of us, not only in terms of worshipping Him but also our conduct in this world.

Why Have We Been Created?

In the previous section we note that Allah has attributes that define Him and pre-exist all of what He created. Each person has certain qualities which they will display because that is the nature of who they are. For example, an artist will paint. 'A painter' who has never painted anything cannot be titled 'a painter'. A mechanic will fix things, an inventor will invent things. A person cannot identify themselves as an inventor if they have never invented a thing. In similar fashion, Allah is The Creator (*Al-Khaaliq*), so He creates. He is the true Creator, meaning One who produces something from truly nothing. That is His nature. He is also *Al-Bari*, the one who takes matter and makes things from it, like a carpenter takes timber and constructs a beautiful, ornate table. He is also *Al-Musawwir*, the One who fashions, shapes and proportions things.

We are here because of who Allah is – Allah is the Creator and we are a product of His Creativity. Allah exhibits all of His qualities with His creation. For instance, He is Loving, Extremely Kind, Forgiving, and Generous. All of creation especially man is the recipient of these traits.

Having created us, Allah gives the purpose of our existence explicitly – to worship Him. He says:

And I did not create jinn and man except to worship Me.
{Quran 51: 56}

Allah is quite clear. But angels also worship Allah, and they do so without tiring or committing sin. So what is the need for man? And how come man is actually of a higher level even than the angels? We need to reflect on this a bit deeper.

The first key difference is that man has been given free-will. Man can make his own choices and decisions, and act upon them. Angels were created pure by Allah, and follow His command without any choice and therefore without deviation. So man is free to choose what he wants.

Secondly Allah has endowed man with faculties and intellect to comprehend the world around him. This is unique to man. Angels do not have this. Man can appreciate, at least to some degree, the incredible complexity and astounding beauty of the universe. The mind-boggling diversity of life forms, the natural laws, the size of the universe, the amazing patterns seen in nature and mathematics such as the golden ratio, the Fibonacci sequence. The way life develops from embryo to foetus to baby, then how the baby grows and is proportioned in just the right way. This will lead him to marvel at the One who created it all, how sublime and magnificent must He be. Observing the world and pondering is extremely important. This is one of the special features Allah gives man, and man must try to appreciate the Almighty as much as possible. Combining this with reflection will lead one to come to know who God is and how blessed one is. One comes therefore to love God, and to worship Him willingly.

But what is more, is that man's relationship with the Creator is subject to a variety of testing scenarios, as man undergoes trials and tribulations. In these times, he continues to affirm his recognition of God, and maintain gratefulness and obedience to God, even though his circumstances may be difficult. Man's rank and status, therefore, stem from his coming to know God, and his *WILLING and LOVING* worship of God, *even in times of hardship.*

Man's free-will has a corollary too; he can choose to be deviant, and not worship God. This world therefore serves as a testing ground, where man proves himself one way or the other i.e. does he acknowledge his Master and gain His Master's good pleasure? Or does he deny his Master and instead earn His displeasure?

Bottom Line:

• We have been created because Allah is The Creator, so He creates.

• Allah gives our purpose explicitly – to worship Him.

• Man has free-will, and the ability to observe and reflect. This should lead to willing and loving worship of Allah.

Who Created the Creator?

Because we observe cycles of creation in this world, people confuse themselves by asking, 'If there is a Creator, well, who created the Creator?' The question has a phonetic ring to it, and atheists delight in using this to try and unhinge believers. This question is akin to walking into a fancy bakery and seeing hundreds of delicious pastries and cakes displayed on the counters. You might then ask, 'who baked all of these?' to which you may be told 'Nadiya' baked them. A follow up question of 'Who baked Nadiya then?' is clearly absurd. Baking is an ability of Nadiya. She bakes. It is not valid to then assume that she is also the object of that ability.

'Creating' is an attribute and ability that belongs to Allah alone. Creating means to produce something from truly nothing. No person is capable of truly creating. Everything in this world is derived or made from something, which ultimately leads back to the Creator. We are born to our parents, who were born to their parents, and them to their parents, and so on (cycles of creation). Ultimately, we arrive at the first humans, Adam and Eve, who were created by Allah. Manmade objects also are not created, they have been assembled from materials provided by the Creator using knowledge endowed by the Creator. A car has been made by using metal or plastic, derived from the earth, suitably moulded and assembled. No car, or any object for that matter, has been truly created by man, where he made it from absolutely nothing.

One needs to be clear that questions can be valid or invalid. For example, 'Where do you live?' is valid, but 'Why is the moon made of cream cheese?' or 'When did you start smoking?' or 'How long have you been beating your wife?' (when you neither smoke nor beat your wife) are invalid questions. The question of 'Who created the Creator?' is the same as 'Who baked our baker', or 'Who wrote the writer?' or 'Who built the builder?'. An invalid and absurd question.

Is Islam the Right Religion?

This is a key question. Whilst non-Muslims may ask this, of course, Muslims themselves will also wonder this from time to time. There is nothing wrong with this, as that is human nature. The Muslim simply reminds themselves, why. Note Allah has given us both a heart and a mind. When one is seeking guidance and answers to life's questions and examining different faiths, the faith should satisfy both the heart and mind. It is inadequate and unsatisfying, for example, to accept a faith that simply preaches love, but does not make sense intellectually (therefore all heart, no mind).

There are extensive reasons as to how we know Islam is the right way. I will give a selection:

1. The guidance for how people should live, is perfect and comprehensive

The guidance provided to mankind through revelation (Quran and Sunnah) is comprehensive, perfect and uncorrupted: stressing highest moral character, excellent dealings with parents, spouse, family, neighbours and community; social justice; looking after orphans, the poor and needy of society. It gives a complete way of life to produce upstanding individuals, strong nuclear families with strong cohesive communities, built on justice and equality. Social harmony is a central theme in Islam. The guidance is fully comprehensive, spanning every aspect of life. The reader should, by now, be gaining a sense of the guidance, having covered Parts I and II.

2. The concept of God is perfect

God is One. God is All-knowing, All-Powerful, yet Compassionate and Kind beyond comprehension. He is incredibly Loving and Merciful but also Just. He will take account of every soul, and their every deed no matter how big or how small. Allah's qualities and who is Allah, are given beautifully in His 99 Names. Some of His qualities are determinable from observing His creation, and some are not possible to know other than what He has informed us through His Revelation. As we journey through this book, some the amazing qualities of Allah should become apparent. What Allah explains about Himself makes perfect sense to us and appeals to our souls and intellect.

Note God can only be one. There cannot be more than one God. If there is more than one, what happens if there is a disagreement, who has the final say? The more powerful one? but then that implies the other gods are not all-powerful, and therefore, not gods – a paradox.

3. There is an evidence base for all the teachings in Islam

This is extremely compelling. Man's own values and ideas transform with time as evidenced by the history of societal norms. Man is prone to errors and these changes may be flawed and detrimental. For instance, the concept of marriage in modern society has been discarded and the right to live with whom one wishes and engage in whatever type of relationship is not just deemed acceptable but has actually become the norm. All the teachings in Islam can be determined from the Quran and the Sunnah (teachings of the Prophet). The reader will note that the concepts presented in this book are all referenced to Revelation (Quran and Sunnah).

4. The linguistic miracle of Quran

The Quran can only be the Word of God. **This is utterly, earth-shatteringly, mind-blowing.** This will be discussed in detail later.

5. The literary challenge issued by the Quran

As a literary work, the Quran is sublime and truly extraordinary. The Arabs were literary geniuses in poetry at the time of the Prophet. They were stunned and astounded by the Quran. The Quran laid out a challenge to the Arabs to produce even a short literary piece to match the Quran's linguistic allure. This challenge is, in fact, for all time.

> *Produce then a chapter like it (i.e. of the Quran) and call upon whoever you can besides Allah, if you are truthful. {Quran 10:38}*

The Arabs of the time failed, despite the shortest chapter of the Quran being a mere three verses in length (*Surah al-Kawthar*, Chapter 108)! Yet the Arabs were so bamboozled and mesmerised by the Quran that sworn enemies of Islam used to secretly hide outside the home of the Prophet, in the darkness of the night, to enjoy the Prophet's recitation of the Quran, such is the beauty of the Quran. They failed in this challenge to produce a short piece of the Quran's standard, as has everyone else who has embarked on it since.

6. Scientific revelations contained in the Quran

Scientific facts that have only been discovered relatively recently and are taken for granted now, were described in the Quran 1400 years ago. These include: how man and all life are made up primarily of water;[84] the Big Bang and the origin of the universe;[85] the water cycle.[86]

Human embryology is described in simply remarkable and astonishing

---

[84] Quran 21: 30
[85] Quran 21: 30
[86] Quran 23: 18-19; Quran 30: 48

detail, at a time when microscopes did not exist.[87]

7. The concept of complete justice and equity in Islam

Nobody will get away with any injustice committed against someone else. Those who oppress others are not granted forgiveness by Allah; they will have to pay back their victims on the Day of Judgement in full.

Difficulties encountered in this life, are recompensed either in this world, or in the Next. The supplications of the oppressed person or the poor person are accepted quicker by Allah than those who are enjoying comfort.

Racism has been deemed unacceptable in the West with laws legislating against it only in the last 50 or so years. Before this the mistreatment of Blacks and ethnic minorities has been blatant and abhorrent. Yet Islam abolished this categorically more than 1400 years ago. Women have been granted equality and rights in the West, again, only in the same time span as racism. Islam afforded them equality, status and honour as well as rights almost one and a half millennia ago (though some Islamic societies have used misinterpretations to justify a patriarchal society).

8. Historic revelations prophesised in the Quran

The two superpowers at the time of the Prophet were the Romans and the Persians. After more than a decade of war, the Persian emperor Kosros II was finally victorious over the Romans with their leader Heraclitus forced to take refuge in Constantinople. This was a crushing defeat for the Romans. Just as this news came through, the Quran then predicted the Romans would re-emerge and be triumphant in a few years.[88] Given the manner in which the Romans had been thoroughly quashed, this was unimaginable yet the prophecy came to pass.

---

[87] Quran 23: 12–14
[88] Quran 30: 2-4

9. Islam is applicable to all mankind

Islam is fully inclusive. The guidance in Islam is applicable to all races worldwide for all times.

10. The preservation of the Quran

The Quran is preserved in *exactly* the same form it was revealed. Revealed in Arabic, not a single change of letter, not even a vowel 1400 years on. It has been committed to memory in its entirety by countless Muslims in every generation since the Prophet. Of all world religions, this is unique to Islam. Those who have memorized it fully are called *huffaz* (singular – *hafiz*). As an example, Pakistan alone produced 63,000 *huffaz* in the *single year* of 2014.[89] The preservation in the original language is an important feature. No translation can ever do justice to the subtleties of any language. Furthermore, Arabic as a language has remarkable features which contribute to the linguistic miracle of the Quran.

11. The life and character of the Prophet

The life of the Prophet himself was a miracle. His character, his behaviour not just with friends but also his enemies, his teachings, his wisdom and his accomplishments, leave no room for doubt. Aisha, one of the wives of the Prophet, when asked to describe the character of the Prophet, said 'undoubtedly the character of the Prophet of Allah was the Quran.'[90] His kindness and gentleness were beyond extraordinary. Many an enemy was won over by extreme compassion at times when the Prophet could rightfully have exacted justice and retribution. The Prophet beautifully described his desperate concern for *ALL* his fellow humans, as being like the man next to a large bonfire on a dark night who is desperately trying to stop all moths and grasshoppers from swarming over, and being consumed in the bonfire.[91] The exquisite imagery conveys the vast numbers of creatures (implying mankind), the bedazzling attraction of the

---

[89] https://bit.ly/33SK2yq
[90] Sahih Muslim
[91] Sahih Muslim, Sahih Bukhari

fire (implying the sinful path and culminating in the Hellfire), and the despairing task of the sole person (the Prophet) trying to salvage them.

It is not possible to do justice to the sublime character of the Prophet in this book. The reader is directed to books that have been dedicated solely to describing his beautiful character and nature; see *Further reading*.

Are Other Religions Also Acceptable?

We discussed earlier how Allah states that Islam is the chosen way for mankind (see *Who is God*). Questions have been raised that the Quran talks of plurality, in other words that other religions that preach one God i.e. Christianity and Judaism, are also acceptable. In particular the verse suggesting that Jews and Christians can attain Paradise is:

> *Indeed, those who believed, and those who were Jews or Christians or Sabeans – of whom the ones who believed in Allah and the Last Day and did righteousness - will have their reward with their Lord, and no fear will there be concerning them, nor will they grieve. {Quran 2: 62}*

It is important to note that these verses refer to those who *preceded* Prophet Muhammad and his message of Islam. They are making clear the fate of sincere believers *prior* to the advent of Islam – they are judged fairly and will attain Paradise for their belief and deeds. However, these verses do not hold for those who lived at the time of Prophet Muhammad and witnessed his message, and those who have followed ever since.

The prophets of Allah start with Adam, the first human, and the line continued throughout human history including Ibrahim (Abraham), Musa (Moses), and Isa (Jesus). The messages they have conveyed have all been consistent in making clear there is only one God, with no partners, and rules and boundaries were provided as part of guidance. The divine message culminates in the Prophet Muhammad and the religion of Islam, the last Prophet with the final rules, commands, and guidance. Those who preceded Islam would have had to follow the way of the truth, and the rules laid out by the prophets of their generations. The messages of the prior messengers have been corrupted and eroded over time. Allah makes this clear and references the Jews and Christians specifically, extensively and in detail, as having altered the sacred scriptures of the Taurat (Torah) and the Bible.[92] In these same verses He explicitly tells the Christians and the Jews to accept the message that Muhammad is delivering to them which is the truth and uncorrupted. Recall from earlier the final verse revealed of the Quran:

> ... *This day I have perfected for you your religion and completed My favour upon you and have approved for you Islam as your religion... {Quran 5: 3}*

Allah makes clear that Islam is the decreed religion and the only way; these other faiths will no longer be accepted:

> *Indeed, those who disbelieve in the message after it has come to them...*

> *And indeed, it is a mighty Book for sure. {Quran 41: 41}*

Note how the first part of the verse is left incomplete, implying big trouble, just as a parent at the end of their tether might warn their disobedient seven year old child 'if you do not get your shoes on right now, then…(!!&!#!)'. The next verse to follow this continues with Allah also giving the guarantee that the Quan and Islam will be protected and preserved for all time, and this guarantee is reiterated elsewhere:

> *Falsehood cannot approach it (re: Quran) from before it or from behind it; (it is) a Revelation from (the Lord who is) Wise and deserving of All Praise. {Quran 41: 42}*

> *Indeed, it is We who sent down the Quran and We will assuredly*

---

[92] Quran 2: 75; 4: 46, 5: 13, 5: 41

guard it (from corruption). {Quran 15: 9}

Allah will not allow the corruption of the Quran and Islam. This makes perfect sense and is clearly of extreme importance as Allah has made clear that there will be no further messengers or revelation to follow Prophet Muhammad.[93] Islam is the final way for all of time. Its preservation is clearly paramount and logical.

Bottom Line:

• Islam is the only accepted religion since the time of Prophet Muhammad until time's end.

• Those people who preceded Prophet Muhammad are judged according to their obedience to the prophets and guidance of their times, and can attain Paradise.

Is the Quran a Miracle?

Hold on tight for the symmetrical structural mind-blowing miracle of the Quran.

The Quran is a miracle for many reasons. One of the lesser known miracles is the amazing structure of the holy book. It mirrors the universe. The earth rotates on its axis, the moon revolves around the earth, while the earth orbits the Sun. The Sun with its Solar System rotates within the Milky Way. Just as you find spirals within spirals in the universe, similarly symmetrical spirals within spirals are found in the Quran. This unique structure would be impossible for any man to have created, as we shall see.

Let's start by thinking about how any book is normally composed, in fact let's look at the universal sequence in producing an *exceptional* book. This

---

[93] Quran 33: 40

always starts with a great author, a literate person with tremendous literary skills. After careful planning, the book writing is commenced, starting at its beginning and working through to its end. Even if different chapters are written out of sequence as the ideas are evolving, each chapter (or section) will be written from its start to finish. There is then a process of repeated review, editing and refining, of which there are countless cycles, first by the author, then by friends or colleagues and finally numerous cycles with the publisher. Changes of words, shuffling sentences and paragraphs around. Rewriting substantial chunks. Perhaps a change in the storyline even. The end result following much blood, sweat and tears is the completed book, hopefully a masterpiece.

The composition of the Quran was nothing like this process. How so?

1. The Prophet had no formal education and so could neither read nor write. This was the norm of the time, 1400 years ago, when very few Arabs could actually read or write.

2. The Quran was revealed bit by bit to the Prophet over 23 years. The entire Quran which comprises 6,236 verses (*ayats*) was *not* revealed as a complete book in one go.

3. Revelation was *not* in the Prophet's control. Verses often came in response to questions people had posed to the Prophet, or situations that arose at the time. The Prophet had no control over these, and therefore could not have composed verses in anticipation. In Quranic studies, the reason for revelation of any particular verse is termed *asbaab al-nuzool*. We will review such an example at the end of this chapter.

4. The order in which the verses were revealed <u>over time</u> is *NOT* the same as their actual arrangement in the complete Quran. In other words, the order of verses that we actually see in the Quran when we pick up a copy is not the order that they were revealed chronologically. So how did the verses get compiled then? Whenever the Prophet received revelation of any verse, the Prophet was also endowed with the knowledge of its appropriate placement. The Prophet would explain to his Companions

where the newly revealed verses were to be placed in the sequence of what had already been revealed - sort of like, where to file them.[94]

This idea is very important to comprehend. Put differently, the Quran was not revealed starting with its beginning at Chapter 1 and finishing with its end, Chapter 114. Instead it was built like a massive jigsaw, where the pieces (each verse) seem to have been fitted together in a completely random manner. The very first revealed verses are actually of Chapter 96 (*Surah al-Iqra*).

5. The revealed verses were *never* altered. Not a single word, not even a single vowel has been changed.

6. The Quran was *never* edited. The way the verses were revealed and placed is exactly how they remained in the Quran, and how we see them today. There has been no shuffling, cropping, rewriting, re-ordering, re-phrasing of any sort.

We can conclude therefore that to our human eyes the 'emergence' of verses (i.e. the revelation of the Quran) seemed completely random and haphazard over a period of almost two and a half decades. This is rather like compiling a novel which is written over 20 plus years, but the sentences are randomly populated into the book, each sentence being

---

[94] Let's explain with a simple example. Imagine you are reviewing a 100 page manuscript and it falls on the floor scattering all the sheets everywhere. You start the process of reassembling it, picking up a leaf at a time. Each leaf you gather you slot into the appropriate place amongst the sheets already in your hand. The first two sheets you pick up are pages 48 and 61. The next one you pick up is page 59, naturally you place it between 48 and 61. When you pick up page 55, you put it between 48 and 59 now. And then page 35 goes before page 48, so right at the front for now. Page 77 goes after page 61. You continue to do this until all the sheets have been recollated. This is how the verses of the Quran were collated. So whilst the verses from the Quran did not come numbered, the Prophet had the knowledge of where to place them amongst what verses had already been revealed. The Prophet also explained how verses were partitioned to form chapters (*surahs*).

generated when someone has asked you a certain question. You produce a reply, and you then place that reply into what seems a random point in a blank book. For example, one day someone asks you about the weather and you reply 'there is a fierce gale blowing today'. Then you instruct that this sentence will go in Chapter 15, and will be line 103. At this point there may be no line 102 or 104; in fact there may not be any lines in Chapter 15 yet!

Spectacular Symmetry

Despite this apparent 'randomness', to have produced a coherent book at all is nothing short of a miracle in itself. But that is no way even *near* the whole story. The Quran's use of words, imagery, linguistic style, and structure of the Quran are spectacular and mind boggling. The Quran is clearly not from this world. The simplest aspect for a lay reader to appreciate is the structure. When sequences of verses are examined to produce *themes*, the Quran produces breath-taking symmetry. This symmetry is seen within whole Chapters, as well as within the parts of Chapters, and even within single verses, giving rise to thematic ring structures.

Let's look at examples of each, using Chapter 2 (*Surah al-Baqara* – 'The Cow'). This chapter is the longest in the Quran at 286 verses long. If the whole *surah* is broken down, the following themes are seen:

1. Faith and Disbelief (verses 1 to 39)

2. Laws given to Moses and the Israelites (verses 40 to 112)

3. Abraham was tested (verses 113 to 141)

4. Change in the direction of Prayer from Jerusalem to Mecca (verses 142 to 152)

5. Muslims will be tested (verses 153 to 177)

6. Laws given to Muslims (verses 178 – 242)

7. Faith and Disbelief (verses 243 – 286)

At first glance there seems nothing special about these themes, but there is symmetry in these themes which can best be appreciated in Figure 2. In fact, a ring structure of symmetry is found, called concentrism. What is more, *ring structures are seen within ring structures*. Take the first theme, Faith and Disbelief (verses 1 to 39) which can be broken down to the following subthemes:

1. Description of who are the believers

2. Description of who are the disbelievers

3. Description of who are the hypocrites

4. The punishment for the hypocrites

5. The punishment for the disbelievers

6. The rewards for the believers

When the themes of this section are organised, remarkable symmetry that forms a ring structure is again found – see Figure 3.

Ring structure symmetry is also seen *within a single verse* itself. Here is a single verse from Chapter 2, which is famously known as the verse of the Throne (*Ayat ul Kursi*, 2:255), which is quite long and can be broken into 9 parts:

1. Allah - there is no deity except Him, the Ever-Living, the Sustainer of (all) existence

2. Neither drowsiness overtakes Him nor sleep

3. To Him belongs whatever is in the heavens and whatever is on the earth

4. Who is it that can intercede with Him except by His permission?

5. He knows what is (presently) before them and what will be after them

6. And they encompass not a thing of His knowledge except for what He wills

7. His Kursi (Throne) extends over the heavens and the earth

8. And their preservation tires Him not

9. And He is the Most High, the Most Great.

On casual reading there does not seem to be any particular connection between any of these parts. Allah is introducing who He is and some of His qualities. But again, if we examine the themes presented, a remarkable symmetry emerges as seen in Figure 4. Note the ring structure yet again. Astonishingly, the very middle, line 5, itself splits into two and demonstrates symmetry *within* the line – Allah's talks of His knowledge of man, with the first half of the sentence referring to what precedes man (namely his past) and the second half, what is ahead of him (namely his future). This is all seen within one single (long) verse.

The reader is directed to Raymond Farrin's book *Structure and Qur'anic Interpretation*, and Nouman Ali Khan and Sharif Randhawa's *Divine Speech* for more detailed coverage (see *Further Reading*).

In fact the Quran is teeming with ring structures. There are spirals within spirals within spirals, etc. How can these remarkable symmetries have been produced in abundance by a man who could not read nor write, had no formal education, who purely recited the revelations orally in response to situations and questions that arose over 23 years, yet he 'produced' a perfect version straight away, with a mind-boggling array of symmetrical patterns and without any editing or re-ordering? Recall, that chapters were not revealed or produced in their entirety in one go. Verses that make up the chapters have been revealed *years apart*. The magnitude of intellect required to produce this is simply not human. It is inconceivable that this Book is from human effort. Remember again that this feature of the Quran is symmetrical spirals within spirals, and reflects the universe where there are spirals within spirals.

Figure 2
Example of ring structure seen in the themes of a *whole* Chapter (Chapter 2: *Surah al-Baqarah*), and note how **the right side is a mirror image of the left.**

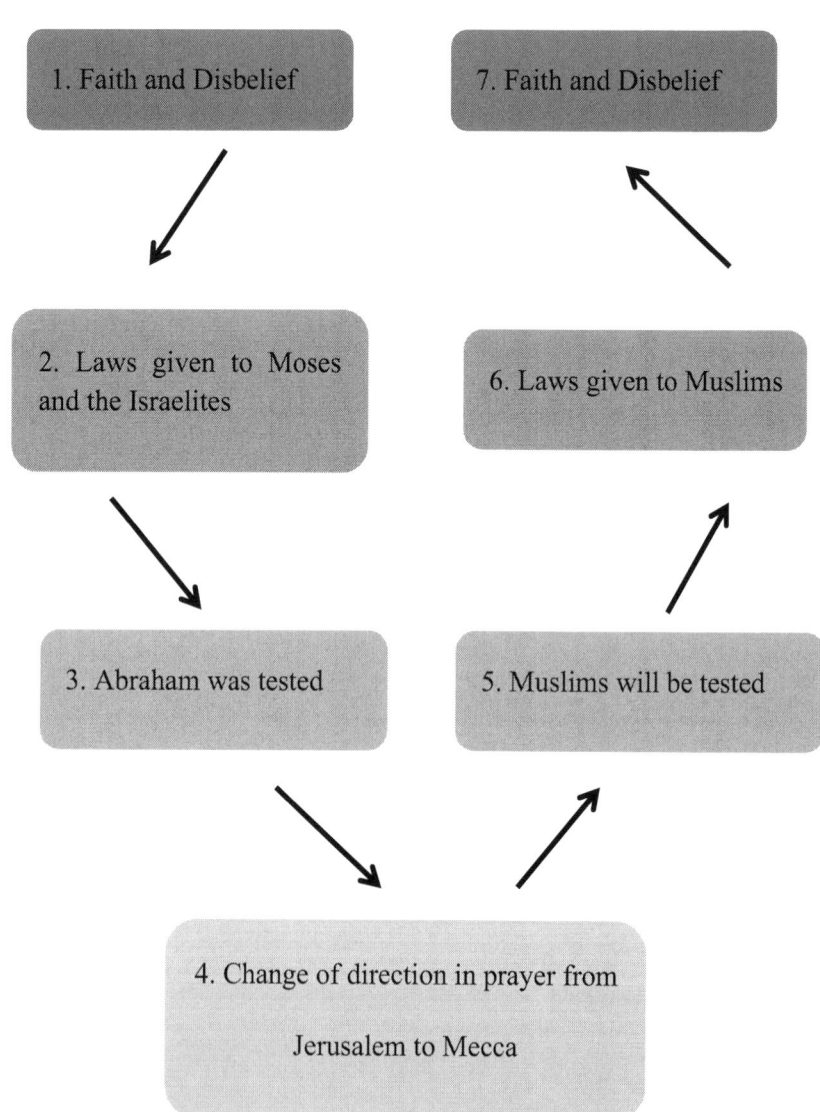

Figure 3
Example of ring structure seen within *part* of a Chapter
- Beginning portion of Chapter 2 (*Surah al-Baqara*)
- note how **the right side is mirror image of the left**.

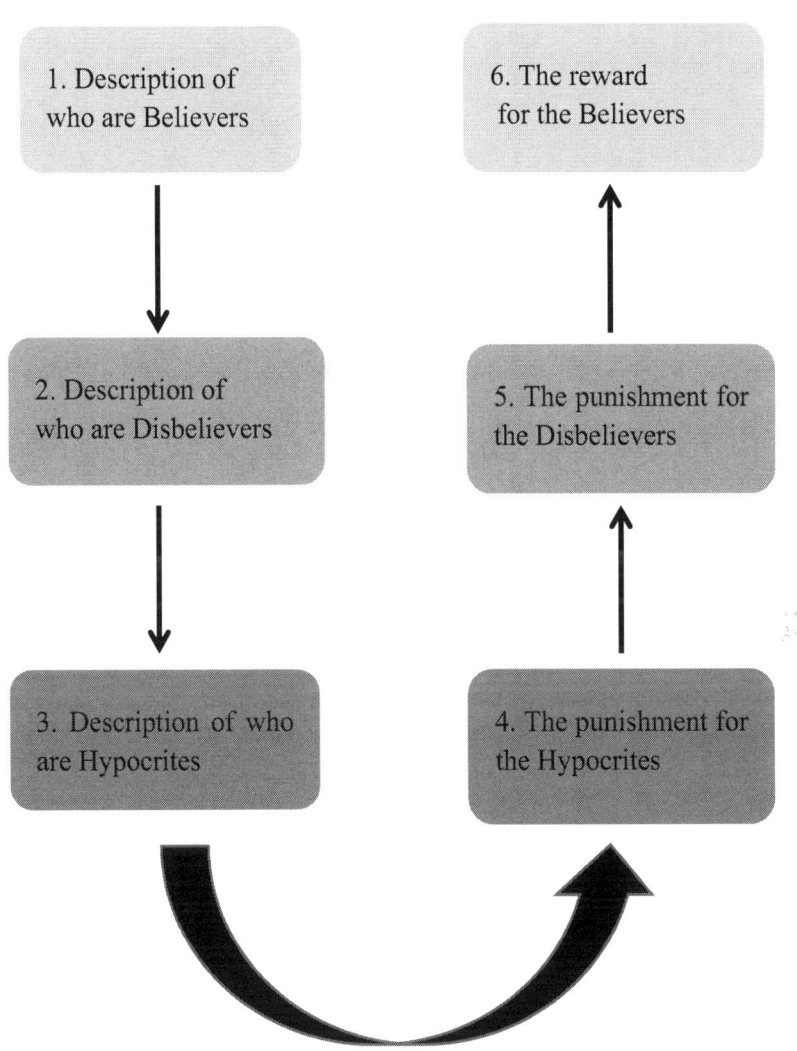

Figure 4
Example of ring structure seen within a *single* verse (The Throne verse -
Ayat ul Kursi 2: 186); note how **the right side mirrors the left**.

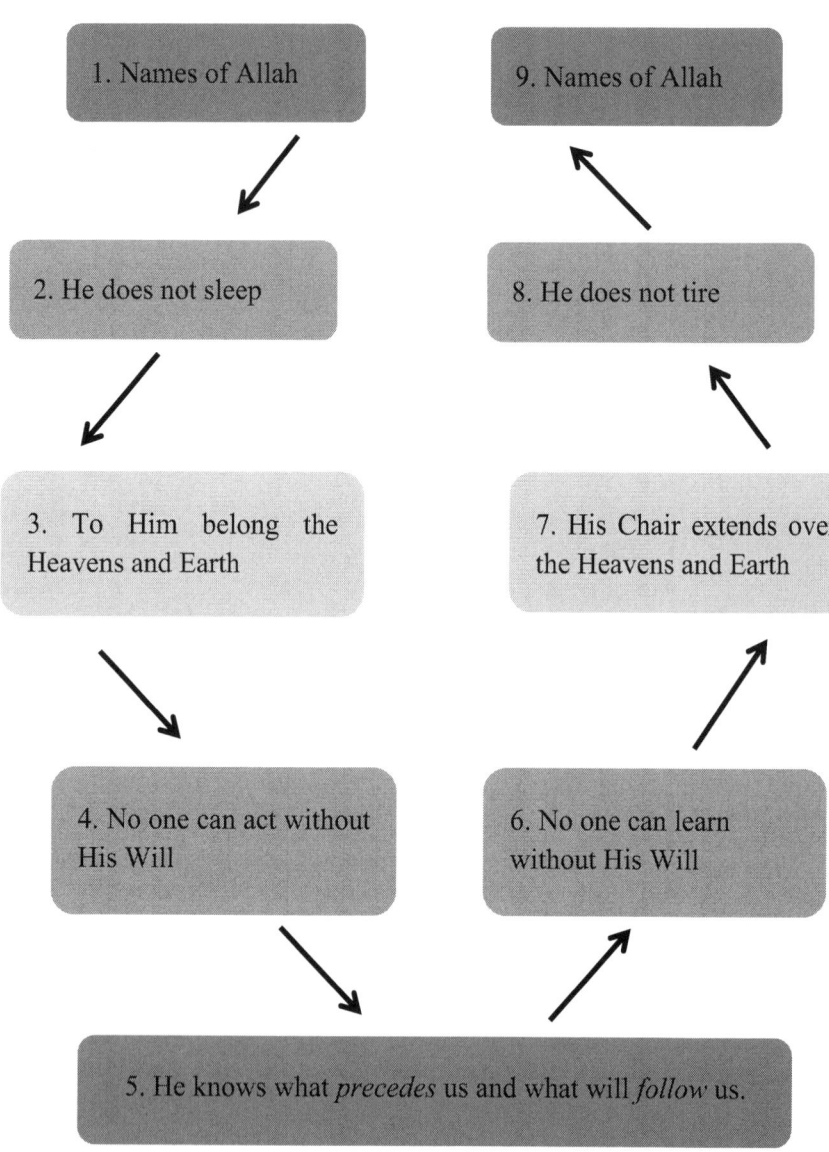

But there is more. This is just one aspect of the Quran. There are many other linguistic features that are similarly astounding. There is a feature described as dovetailing – the ending of one chapter (*surah*) links into the beginning of the next one, with **both** themes and key words. There are symmetries also seen in the rhyming patterns as well. There are pairings seen between chapters. There are astounding linguistic features to do with word choice, word order, and grammatical shifts. I will review another feature, in *Common Mistakes Made by Muslims*. We are left with no conclusion other than that the Quran is indeed a miracle, and only a Divine source can be responsible. The Prophet explained that the Quran is the Words of Allah Himself.

But there is more still. The Prophet was special out of all the prophets, and as the final Prophet he was sent not just to his people, but for all of the rest of mankind. Similarly the miracle of the Quran is also particularly significant. The Prophet explained that whilst previous prophets also had miracles, these happened in their time, so could be witnessed by the people of that time only. The Quran is unique, in that its literary miracle is there to be witnessed by all of mankind until the end of time. It is the gift of the ever-living miracle.

The miracle of the Quran is so remarkable, it not only forms a proof for Islam as the right way, but it is also in itself a proof to the existence of God.

Example of reason for revelation

Let's come back to the point about how a great deal of Quranic revelation came in response to situations or questions that arose at the time. As mentioned above, the reasons for revelation for any verses are termed *asbaab al-nuzool*. I will give one example to illustrate this.

A woman from Medina called Khawlah bin Thalabah was divorced impulsively by her husband using an extreme pronouncement of divorce called *zihaar* that was custom at the time, where the wife is declared as being 'like the back of my mother'. Though regretful after calming down, they were both left with the predicament that their relationship was now terminated. Desperate to have this declaration absolved and allow them to resume their marital relationship, Khawlah hurried to the Prophet to seek his judgement. The Prophet was helpless to reverse the situation. Despairing, Khawlah presented her case with arguments upon argument but he could not grant her dissolution of the divorce, as he was limited to what revelations and laws had been revealed to him thus far. Khawlah, realising that the matter was not in the Prophet's control but actually for Allah to decree, turned to Allah and petitioned Him directly, pleading her matter to Him. Her words had not ceased from her lips when revelation came down to the Prophet, right in front of her:

> *Allah has indeed heard (and accepted) the statement of the woman who argues with you concerning her husband and carries her complaint (in prayer) to Allah. and Allah (always) hears the arguments between both sides among you: for Allah hears and sees (all things)... {Quran 58: 1–4}*

In this verse, which is addressing the Prophet, the 'woman who argues with you' is Khawlah. The revelation went on to ban the practice of *zihaar*. and gave the solution to absolve the pronouncement – freeing a slave, or fasting 60 consecutive days, or feeding 60 needy people.

Preservation of the Quran and the Transcribed (Printed) Quran

It should be clear from the last section that the verses of the Quran were compiled and ordered simultaneously, as they were revealed to the Prophet. This is not to be confused with the process of producing the complete transcribed Quran, which is called in Arabic *mus-haf,* literally meaning 'written verses'. Physically like a book, the *mus-haf* was initially transcribed by hand, copied by hand and subsequently printed following the invention of the printing press. Numerous Muslims at the time of the Prophet had memorised the complete Quran (such people are called *huffaz,* sing. *hafiz*). Certain Companions had already compiled their own personal *mus-hafs* at the time of the Prophet. These *huffaz* along with these transcribed copies of the Quran were the means of preservation of the Quran following the passing of the Prophet.

It is important to note at this point the literary memory of the Arabs. Being able to memorise massive poems or stories, word for word, was part of Arab tradition at the time. This might seem a little odd to us living in the modern age. But one must remember that there was nothing in the desert, nothing at all. Reciting poetry and ballads were their primary form of entertainment. The vast majority were unable to read or write, but this oral tradition was extremely strong, and they therefore had developed the mental memory to match.

A simple story from that time will illustrate. Zaid ibn Harithah grew up as a servant in the household of Muhammad before he became a Prophet. His story was that whilst travelling as a boy with his mother on a convoy, he was kidnapped after a raid by bandits who subsequently sold him as a slave. He ended up being bought in a bazaar by a nephew of Khadija, the wife of the Prophet. He gifted Zaid to Khadija, who in turn, gifted him to the Prophet. Zaid's father was heartbroken but there were no newspapers or media at that time to publicise his case, nor police to investigate. So he composed some beautiful moving verses of poetry to proclaim his sorrow and how he was searching for him. This was a specifically targeted message for his lost son.

As per the customs of the time, the poetry was recited at gatherings and market places, so ended up being transmitted far and wide. People hearing this, memorised it word for word and would subsequently recite it themselves, word-perfect, elsewhere. Today we would say that the message went viral, but the transmission medium was the people themselves and their elephant-like memories.

It eventually reached Zaid who immediately recognised his father's message and his search for him. Zaid composed some verses of his own to reply his father, telling him he was living in Mecca. In similar fashion his poetry was broadcast through recitations, and reached his father's ears who, recognising the reply, made haste to Mecca to retrieve his son.

This incident emphasises just how poetry and ballads were the entertainment of the time, and how sharp the Arabs' memory was for them, being able to memorise them whole, word for word. Interestingly if you are wondering what followed, Zaid's father offered to pay for Zaid's release. Muhammad magnanimously waived the offer, instead deferring the matter to Zaid to make his own decision – he could continue to stay with him or return with his father without any need for payment. Zaid chose to stay with Muhammad, such was Muhammad's character and kindness! Imagine that! He could return home to his father and blood family for free now, but did not want to leave Muhammad's side. Remember this was before Muhammad had been bestowed Prophethood. Muhammad then adopted Zaid as his son, as was a custom at the time.[95] The father was content that he had found his lost son, who was very happy and well cared for.

A mini modern day analogy readers may relate to, would be the generation who witnessed the arrival of the mobile phone and subsequently satellite navigation. In the old days, we had committed to memory countless phone numbers, and roads and routes. Now, we barely know two phone numbers, and cannot get from A to B without the sat-nav or Google maps.

After several military battles, especially the Battle of Yamama (in present day Saudi Arabia) when 70 *huffaz* were killed, there was concern that the Quran could be wiped out if all the *huffaz* were martyred. This led to the first Caliph (ruler), Abu Bakr, embarking on the first official transcribed volume, the *mus-haf* (633-634 CE). With the spread of Islam and therefore the Quran, to wider Arab lands a subsequent issue to emerge was that different civilizations had different Arabic dialects. The pronunciation

---

[95] Adoption (treating a child as your own, thus giving them your family name, and inheritance rights) was subsequently prohibited, much later in Islam. This is different from fostering or raising an orphan, where the child retains their original family name, and does not inherit from you as a blood relative – this is highly praiseworthy.

along with the meaning was at risk of being corrupted. The third Caliph, Uthman ibn Affan, addressed this by ordering several authentic copies to be produced (five or seven) from the master copy corroborated by the senior *huffaz* of his time (c. 650-651 CE). The *mus-hafs* were standardised to maintain the Arabic of the Quraish, the form in which the Quran was originally revealed. The Prophet belonged to the Quraish who were the chief tribe of Mecca. All unauthorized *mus-hafs* were then burnt, to maintain full textual integrity and reliability. These authenticated copies were then sent out to the major cities of the Islamic world to serve as references.

Around 695 CE, the Caliph Abdul Malik ordered the vowel markers (known as diacritical markers) to be added to further make clear the vowel pronunciation to those unfamiliar with Arabic script. It is important to remember that along with these written forms of the Quran, the Quran has been preserved throughout every generation since the Prophet by countless numbers of *huffaz*.

Accountability and Judgement

Every human will die, only to be raised up again on the Day of Reckoning, where they will be held to account for all the choices made in this world. One's deeds will be weighed up on a Scale, the good on one side against the bad on the other. The Scale will be real, and for all to see. The deeds will be visible in a physical form. It is important to note that:

1. These choices were ones made out of one's own free will. Where there was coercion or force, the person is exempted from sin.

2. One's account only opens upon reaching adulthood, which in Islam is the onset of puberty.

3. For making the right choices i.e. those that please Allah, He behaves in a supremely generous and magnanimous fashion. The weighting of good deeds on the Scale are increased by multiple folds.

4. For making the wrong choices, i.e. those that showed disobedience and displeased Him, Allah acts with justice and fairness, so a single bad deed is weighted as a single bad deed.

5. Every single deed will be accounted for, including the smallest and what may have seemed entirely trivial. There will be absolutely thorough accountability. Nothing will escape the net. Allah says deeds even the weight of an atom will be brought forth.[96] This is repeated many times, for example:

> That Day... whoever does good equal to the weight of an atom shall see it. And whoever does evil equal to the weight of an atom shall see it. {Quran 99: 6-8}

6. Allah can forgive sins committed against Allah Himself, out of His Mercy, for example, missed prayers (*salat*). But Allah will not grant forgiveness to any sins committed by one person against another. Any person who has wronged another, and did not gain their forgiveness, will have to settle this injustice on the Day of Judgement. The wrongdoer will have to hand over an appropriate amount of their good deeds to the wronged person. If they are bankrupt of good deeds, then the wronged person will pass an appropriate number of their own sins to the wrongdoer. Thus, those who were victimised will get full recompense from their perpetrators on that Day.

Allah has given the formula for success:

1. To believe (i.e. be Muslim)

2. To do good deeds

We encountered this in the *How do We Know God Exists: Moral code and altruism*. For a believer, where the Scale is heavier for good deeds and culminates in Allah's Pleasure, one is rewarded with an eternal home in

---

[96] Quran 21: 47

Paradise. There are different levels of Paradise and the balance of the deeds will determine one's level. Where the Scales weigh heavier for the bad deeds, the believer is punished by confinement to Hell for a period until one's atonement is complete. This is followed by admission to Paradise, which is eternal.

For the disbeliever, there is no Paradise. The balance of the Scales for their deeds determines which level of Hell they are to be thrown into, there being different levels of Hell. It is for this reason that recognising and affirming the truth (there is only One God and Muhammad is His Messenger, which equates to being Muslim) is so critical. A Muslim even with a deluge of sin *ultimately* has the reward of Paradise. A non-believer can never attain this. This is a terrifying prospect. Unbearable punishment that will never stop. Never. Ever.

The concept of eternity washes over us. It is incomprehensible how something can go on for ever and ever, and Heaven and Hell are unfortunately clichés in modern society. This reality however is extremely important to grasp. Muhammad Ali, the legendary heavyweight boxer, tried to convey the idea whilst he was visiting Newcastle (UK) in 1977, when asked by a young boy, 'What do you plan to do after retiring from boxing?' 'Get ready to meet God', he said and expounded his answer to include the terrifying idea of burning in Hell forever.[97,98]

The most important thing is what's gonna happen when you die. Are you going to Heaven or Hell? And that's eternity! How long is eternity?? Let's imagine. Take the Sahara Desert. There's a lot of sand in the Sahara Desert, right? Then imagine that one grain of sand represents 1000 years... To give you an idea of how long eternity is, take the Sahara Desert and I told you to wait 1000 years and every 1000 years I want you to pick up a grain of sand until the desert is empty. Ok, wait 1000 years - pick up a grain, wait

[97] https://bit.ly/39odXiO
[98] https://bit.ly/33Npyad

another 1000 years before you get the next grain, keep that up until there's no more sand in the desert.

It is so important that every person sincerely searches for the truth. So much rides on getting it right – literally, an eternity. Following the ways of your family or community is not sound nor sufficient, every person gives account for themselves alone. When a person spends a lifetime without bothering to search for the true Creator of all things, and/or acknowledge Him, why are they surprised to meet a bad outcome in the life to follow?

Those who never received God's message

An important caveat is that those people who never ever received God's message and guidance are not judged as disbelievers. Allah's justice is such that He will not punish a people who never had the choice to obey or disobey His instructions, as they remained oblivious. Historically such people would be those who lived in remote habitats where no messenger ever reached them. There are no messengers now of course, as the Prophet was the final Messenger, but the idea remains that the message of Islam needs to be conveyed to people and communities for them to choose to accept or reject it. At first we might think of, for instance, native Indians living in the Amazon rainforest. However, in the modern age, there are other more surprising examples. An American or Australian living in a completely rural outback, who never ventures out of their home town, may never come to know anything of Islam. In fact their only 'knowledge' of Islam may be all the negative reports seen on television, which keeps them fearful and at bay of Islam. This serves to keep Muslims from being judgemental about non-Muslims, as only Allah knows the truth about who received the message and rejected it, and those who remained oblivious. No one knows who is destined for Paradise and who is destined for Hell – Allah alone knows.

A bit of Hellfire

There is a very important misguided belief held by many Muslims that needs to be dispelled at this point. On the basis that they will ***ultimately*** gain Paradise, many are happy to commit sins and accept that they might have to spend a 'little' time in the Hellfire to make up for that. 'A little time in the Hellfire, that's no big deal', they say, 'we will be going to Paradise in the end'. It leads some Muslims to lie, some to drink alcohol, some to cheat others, some to party and fornicate, others to generally behave with poor conduct.

Let's just think about this in earthly terms first. Imagine a destitute person, struggling to make ends meet for himself and his family. He is offered unimaginable wealth, properties, palaces, and estates that will keep his family extremely comfortable for countless generations to come. All he needs to do is agree to be slow roasted on a special spit, suspended in such a way that it will produce all the intense pain of burning but without killing him or making him pass out. Just for 24 hours. Who would accept this challenge? Very few. Those who think they need to man it up and that they will be able to handle it, will beg for release as soon as they are experiencing the flames.

But what does Allah say about the degree of torment in the Hellfire? Let's take the ***least*** level of torment. Allah describes how those standing at the entrance of Hell, whilst waiting to be thrown in, will experience a whiff of breeze from Hell as the door to Hell briefly swings open and closed. The anguish from this mere puff of air will cause them to squeal excruciatingly, 'Oh my goodness, we must be in the *worst* level of Hell!'[99] Yet they are merely standing outside Hell, they have not even entered it yet, and what they experienced was just a puff of air, not the boiling water, the flames, or the lava. That is incredibly intense.

The torment of the Hellfire is such that even a few seconds will be beyond intolerable. There is no relief from this. And the time scale will not be like earth, the time periods in the Afterlife are much, much longer. A 'little' time in Hell will be equivalent to thousands of years in earthly time. It is a

---

[99] Quran 21: 46

terrifying place, to be avoided, desperately avoided, in its entirety. In fact Allah specifically describes those with whom He is pleased as being ones who beg Him to protect them from being in the Hellfire for a long time or *even a very short time.*[100] The sense of justice can be seen here as well. Though affirming Muslim belief is the most important thing one can do, and is the ultimate determinant of Paradise, one still has to answer for one's deeds. **Paradise has to be earned**.

Bottom Line:

• Every person is accountable for their actions done out of free choice.

• On the Day of Judgement every single deed, no matter how small, will be weighed up on a Scale.

• Allah gives the formula to succeed as 'Believe **and** Do good deeds'.

• The believers' ultimate abode is Paradise, whilst for the non-believers it is Hell.

• The balance of deeds determines the level of Paradise or Hell.

• Hell is excruciating beyond comprehension, even for mere seconds.

• The believer may have to atone in the Hellfire before admission to Paradise, for sins committed, or for arrogance residing in their heart. The believer must desperately strive to avoid this.

What is the Islamic Definition of Success?

When people think of success, universally they picture tremendous wealth, fame, prestige, a great job, an amazing home, or wonderful spouse and family. These are all forms of **worldly** success. There is nothing wrong with these per se, but Islam defines success differently. *It is gaining*

---

[100] Quran 19: 65-66

Allah's good pleasure. This is our absolute goal. If we end our lives with Allah being pleased with us, then we are truly of the successful ones. The reward for achieving this goal is an eternal home in Paradise. Worldly success **may or may not** form part of this journey. A destitute pauper may be a 'failure' in worldly terms, but may have the highest station with God, perhaps due to their being sincerely grateful for what they were blessed with, little though it may seem to others; or their effort at serving their family or community, or their parents (recall the story of Owais Al Qarni, *Relationship with Parents*).

How do we achieve this goal? By worshipping Allah. We discuss this below. Let's recall that one needs to make use of the ability and opportunities Allah affords to each one of us. Excellence in our work and endeavours (see earlier) is part of obedience to Allah. Therefore worldly success may also be part of our journey through this world, though critically, it is not our end goal. As a result, one cannot abandon the world and people, turning into a hermit to engage in 24/7 ritual worship - this would not be right. We need to give account for our talents and opportunities. The world is a tool in this endeavour.

What Does It Mean to 'Worship' God?

Worshipping Allah means to:

1. Remember Him

2. Praise Him

3. Thank Him

4. Obey Him

5. Engage in ritual worship (i.e. combining all the above into prescriptive ritual forms of worship eg ritual prayer, charity, fasting etc).

Obeying Him necessitates following His guidance, the central tenet of which is to do good deeds and abstain from sin.

Everyone Will Be Tested in This World

Make no mistake, everyone will undergo trials and tests. Everyone, without exception. This therefore makes clear that the world is not an extension of Paradise, where one enjoys unfettered bliss and happiness. By definition, difficulties will come along the way. That is the purpose of being in this World. Allah talks of this many times, for example:

> *Every soul has to experience the taste of death. We test you with both hardships and blessings. In the end you will all return to Us. {Quran 21: 35}*

> *And surely We shall test you with something of fear and hunger, and loss of wealth and lives and crops; but give glad tidings to the patient ones... {Quran 2: 155}*

> *Or do you think that you will enter Paradise without such (trials) as came to those who passed away before you? They were afflicted with severe poverty and ailments and were so shaken that even the Messenger and those who believed along with him said, 'When (will come) the Help of Allah?' Yes! Certainly, the Help of Allah is near! {Quran 2: 214}*

The ways that one can be tested include:-

- Loss of family members and friends

- Loss of wealth

- Loss of health

- Loss of job

- Public humiliation – even being maligned for something false

- Lack of basic amenities – food, clean water, shelter, security, warmth, education

- Pain and anguish

- Failure – in our studies, work or relationships

- Being on the receiving end of evil

- Having desires or aspirations that can never be met

This realisation therefore puts in perspective such questions as 'why do bad things happen in the world?' Or 'why is there evil in the world?' The world cannot be a test unless difficulties do come along. However, we will explore this very question next.

Why is There Hardship and Evil in the World?

Why do some people seem to have unfathomable luxury and wealth, whilst others are starving and do not even have clean drinking water? This can be somewhat perplexing and can shake one's faith, for God is supposed to be Just and Merciful. So where is the equality in that? There are people without food to eat, a home to live in, or children who lose their parents. If God really is just and kind, why does He allow such hardship?

It is not possible to determine someone's or something's qualities without testing them. How fast a car can go, needs it to be raced on a track. Who is the strongest boy/girl in the class, needs them to have an arm wrestling competition. Who is the smartest child in the class needs a class exam. Being kind and generous to a close friend is not difficult at all; but being kind to someone we do not know shows a higher level. Being generous to someone who is malignant towards you is the ultimate level, and true kindness.

After our Creation, Allah could simply have kept us in Paradise where life is beautiful, comfortable, and free of hardship. But He sent us down to the earth for a purpose. This world is a testing ground. What is truly in our hearts will become evident in the choices we make. Every soul shall have to face some degree of trials and tribulations. It is not a question of 'might have to face', but 'will have to face'.

These hardships may occur for one or more of the following reasons:

- to test our character and faith, and serve as an opportunity to show, or increase, our patience, obedience, and gratefulness

- to remind us of Allah, and draw us back to Him and His way, and save us from heedlessness (i.e. being oblivious to Him)

- as expiation for sin i.e. Allah is erasing sins we have accrued, through the hardship

- as a punishment in this world, for a grave sin (with punishment in the Afterlife to follow unless repented for).

A believer understands that **whatever Allah does for a person, is always for the best**. When going through a difficult test, though one may struggle to comprehend this, one has to know this with certitude. He is the One with All Knowledge. We might never know what worse outcome awaited us, either in this world or the next, but for Allah changing our circumstances. In some cases, with time we may come to understand His Wisdom.

A simple example is the bright, young A-level student applying to university. He has his heart set on the Top University, but fails to get an offer. He is profoundly disappointed, and life is at rock bottom. He settles for a place at another quite reasonable university, but it simply does not have the prestige as the Top one. During his time, however, he goes on to win a deluge of prizes across the board. His CV is glittering and beyond impressive now. His career pathway after graduating, becomes fast-tracked and he reaches the pinnacle of his profession in record time. One day, he reflects back to the time of his university applications, he notes how fortunate he was, that things did not go according to his desires. At Top University, he would have been an average student, with no prizes. His career would have been mediocre. Instead, he went to a less prestigious institution, but came out loaded with distinction which catapulted his whole career. If he could turn back the clock, would he still have wanted to go to Top University?

Note the reasons above for why trials occur fall into two groups – they serve as a blessing or as a punishment. The first three are a blessing whilst the fourth is a punishment. How can someone work out which type of tribulation has befallen them? Scholars have determined that one's response to the tragedy holds the key. The one who responds with calm and patience has been bestowed a blessing. The one who responds with panic and a 'Why me?' attitude has been dealt a punishment.

At the time of writing a young white supremacist Australian has sadly massacred fifty Muslims who were congregating for Friday (Juma) prayers at two mosques in Christchurch, New Zealand.[101] The brutality and the callousness of how he live-streamed his slaughter has left the world reeling with horror. In this painful and tragic event, the grief of the families affected will be unbearable. As the acuteness of the pain lessens some poignant reflections will be apparent. The victims of this atrocity are automatically martyrs, having been killed whilst engaged in worship, and their reward is guaranteed Paradise. This will eventually be a source of comfort to the bereaved relatives.

Yet there are other astonishing events to evolve from this. Muslims have been subject of increasing Islamophobia in the current era. The horror of this act has led to an unprecedented outpouring of sympathy and empathy for Muslims from non-Muslims. Media and politicians who have been stoking Islamophobia are being challenged. Many non-Muslims are wanting to stand in solidarity and are now curious about Islam. The message of Islam will suddenly reach far greater numbers now and, by the Mercy of Allah, many will heed the call. The killer who had an agenda against Islam may turn out to have done more to propagate it than any scholar or institute of Islam.

When undergoing a trial, a person must show patience. This means not letting their emotions overwhelm them. They maintain faith, and continue to be grateful to the Almighty, because He continues to bestow countless other blessings. They continue to obey Him and strive in His way. No

---

[101] https://bit.ly/39hr31q

doubt, this may be challenging to do.

There is a lesson too for the 'bystanders' observing the person going through the test. It serves as a reminder for what they still have, and what could have befallen them. They should rush to be grateful they have been spared, and double their own efforts in obeying Allah. They should also hurry to help the troubled one, as best as they can.

Recall that Allah says that He will test each person with both good things and bad times:

> ...*We test you with* **both hardships and blessings***. In the end you will all return to Us.* *{Quran 21: 35}*

For those who are struggling to make ends meet in this world, the test is clear. They need to strive, make an honest living, maintain good character, and show gratefulness to the Almighty. For those bestowed with affluence, the test is much less obvious. We understand this apparent dichotomy by remembering each one of us is accountable for how we utilise everything Allah bestows upon us, EVERYTHING. The affluent must:

1. Show profound thanks to Him for easing their situation in this world

2. Their test is to spend their wealth (and utilise opportunities and other benefits) in the way most pleasing to Him.

That means using it in the most beneficial manner for society. Spending in charity, setting up projects to benefit the community, such as providing food and clothing to the needy, shelters and homes, job opportunities, education etc. Spending on your family and yourself is also part of your responsibilities, and you may enjoy the blessing of wealth; the Prophet explained:

> *'The arrogant, even with pride equal to an atom's weight in his heart, will not enter Jannah.' A man enquired: 'What about if a person likes fine dress and fine shoes?'*

He said: 'Allah is Beautiful and likes beauty. Arrogance means rejecting truth, and looking down on people.' {Sahih Muslim}

But luxury has to be kept to reasonable limits. Overly-luxurious and extravagant life styles may be superficially enjoyable, but will be held to account on the Day of Reckoning. The affluent need to feel a much greater sense of responsibility and show even more obedience to Allah's Commands. The need to give back, is true and necessary. As well as being a blessing, wealth is a very serious responsibility and in actual fact a very stern test. Those with wealth need to have an internal conversation as to where they draw the line between a comfortable lifestyle for themselves and their families, versus spending on others.

A story narrated by the Prophet captures how this works. Three men from the time of Moses each had afflictions. One was a leper, one bald, and one was blind. An angel in the form of a man was sent to them who asked what they wished for. The leper wanted cure of his leprosy, the bald man wanted beautiful hair, and the blind one wished for sight. The angel supplicated to Allah, Who granted their wishes. On top of that they were given wealth in the form of whatever they desired, camels, cattle, and sheep respectively. They all grew massively wealthy.

The same angel revisited them at a much later date, this time in the form of a wayfarer who had lost his wealth on his way, and mimicking each of their previous afflictions. He pleaded with each one of them for help. The leper and bald man both refused to help. When the angel probed them, that had they not also previously suffered poverty and afflictions, they lied, saying they had inherited their huge wealth. The blind man, on the other hand, was generous in help, acknowledging that Allah had restored his sight and granted him abundant wealth. 'Take whatever you need from my wealth, with no account from me', he said. The angel informed him that Allah was pleased with him, but He was angry with the other two.[102]

---

[102] Sahih Bukhari

This story illustrates that when good times come, one needs to remain thankful to Allah and be ready to help others.

We can see these tests in simple everyday scenarios. You are in your car driving down a street and you see a man hobbling along on a pair of crutches. He clearly needs to get somewhere. He does not have the aid of a car, but you do. Do you drive past him, or pull over and offer him a lift? You are galloping down the stairs at the train station, and see an elderly woman struggling up the stairs with some heavy bags. You have good health and physical strength, she does not, do you go back and offer to help her, or continue on your way? A colleague's mother dies after battling cancer, leaving him bereaved along with crippling medical and funeral expenses. You have a better financial situation, do you help out with the expenses or say, 'Well, that's life'? If you do not have the financial means, do you organise some fundraising for him, or maybe even do some extra work yourself to raise money for him?

A Muslim knows that **those who are closer to Allah are tested more**. In fact the sternest trials afflicting mankind were placed on the prophets themselves. Prophet Ibrahim (Abraham) was told to sacrifice his son, Ismail. Ismail had been born to him in his old age whilst barren of children and so was especially beloved to him. Allah was testing that Ibrahim was willing to place Allah higher than any of his worldly attachments. Ibrahim shared this command with Ismail, a pious child, who encouraged his father in his obedience to the Almighty, aware of the consequences for himself. Ibrahim complied with Allah's order. When he took the knife to his son, Allah spared him the sacrifice, replacing Ismail with a ram. (This gives rise to the ritual sacrifice that accompanies Hajj, and is celebrated on the Islamic festival of Eid ul Adha).

Similarly the Prophet Muhammad faced incredible trials. He was born an orphan with his father having died before his birth. He received the love of his mother but sadly witnessed her death when he was just six years old. Imagine the pain and anguish of a child losing his only parent at such a tender age. He went on to lose important guardian figures throughout his life, his grandfather followed by his uncle. He suffered bereavement of his first wife, Khadija, to whom he was totally devoted. They had been married for 15 years before his Prophethood was endowed. She stood firmly by him, and encouraged him when the difficult days of Prophethood began.

He had six children with Khadija, two boys and four daughters, and another son from a later wife. He witnessed the death of all of his children in his own lifetime, bar his youngest daughter, Fatima. He endured great poverty and famine to the point that at times he tied two stones to his stomach to lessen the hunger pangs. Everyone would of course wish to be on the same level as the prophets, to have that honour, that closeness to Allah, and the highest rewards in the Afterlife. *Yet who could tolerate the lives and trials they endured?* We want to enjoy the level of the prophets but we shy away from a life with that degree of testing.

Those going through hardship have additional recompense. In this world, their prayers (*duas*) are given special weight by Allah and therefore more likely to be granted. Hardship also serves as a means of expiation of sins. On the Day of Judgement, this translates into Scales that will be lighter on the side for sin. Those who have lived in poverty in this world, will find additional compensatory privileges on the Day of Reckoning – a terrifying Day of searing heat with souls sweating to the point that some will be drowning in their own sweat. That day will last 50,000 years. Each soul will be desperate to have their Account judged as soon as possible to relieve them the torment of that Day. The poor and destitute on that Day will be first in line, ahead of the affluent, who will be desperate but will have to wait their turn.

Another example of recompense is the loss of a child. This is a terribly traumatic experience in this world. Whilst this is excruciatingly painful for the parents, it is a matter of great comfort to know that as their Book of Deeds had not opened. Children have no account to answer for, and are, therefore, guaranteed Paradise. If one makes sure their own account is in order, they can be sure to be re-united with them in Paradise.

Western and modern philosophy dwells heavily on this notion of how can

God exist if there is hardship in the world. Or how can God be kind if He allows hardship in this world? Both of these arguments demonstrate shallow thinking. If God wanted us to have a life of eternal peace and enjoyment, why did He send us down on to the earth in the first place? Obviously, He could have kept us in Paradise. So by sending us to this world, we are not here to have a mortal life with unfettered comfort, followed by an immortal life of the same. Which leads us to conclude that this life is about facing downs as well as ups, and the downs are a necessity for us to display our true colours. This world is a transitory stepping stone to the place of eternal residence (the Hereafter).

God is abundantly kind, this is a fundamental in Islam. However, this is actually apparent from some simple reflection, even putting faith aside. There are highly 'successful' people of all faiths including those of no faith, where success is defined in worldly terms, such as wealth, prestige, honour, or fame. If we suppose there is one true faith, it follows that there are a great mass of people who follow wrong faiths yet they are still endowed with luxury and status. This is extreme benevolence, to continue to bestow upon people who choose not to follow the true faith or even worse, actually deny God's existence. This also illustrates another important point. This life is a test to come to know God and come to Him willingly. If one faith was clearly the winner in terms of worldly success, it would be a no-brainer as to what is the true faith. Nothing to contemplate then but also people would simply follow that faith, purely to get worldly success, and may have no sincerity in faith whatsoever.

Finally, hardships draw one back to the Creator. People tend to be heedless of God in the good times, their remembrance of Him is minimal. Yet when calamity strikes they feel desperate and turn to the Almighty whom they know is the only one able to relieve their condition. In these times their pleading to Allah is truly heartfelt and genuine, just as if someone is about to die, their calling out to God will be the most sincere of their life. A calamity is death without dying. This is what life is about, remembering Allah with true sincerity, recognising how helpless we are, and how He is All-Powerful and in control of everything; we are the needy and He is the one free from need and the Provider of everything. He is the Merciful One, and we are in need of His Mercy. When life is approaching its end and one was to contemplate just how much time had been spent during one's lifetime making that heartfelt connection with one's Lord, those lonely moments in times of hardship may be the only authentic ones. Those moments one was alone in a hospital bed being treated for cancer; the times one spent on their prayer mat begging Allah for the health of their child who was in hospital on a life support machine; the time one lost their job and was distraught at how to support their family. Periods that felt awful in this world may be what elevated one in the next world. So in actual fact, we see that in 'good times' there is a test hidden, and in the 'bad times' there is goodness hidden.

Bottom Line:

• This world is a transitory stepping stone to the real abode of the Hereafter.

• This world is not Paradise, it is specifically a place of testing.

• Those going through hardship need to show patience, good conduct, and thankfulness.

• Everyone must give account for their own abilities and opportunities.

• There is a test in what seems good, and goodness hidden in what seems bad.

• Those closest to Allah are given the more difficult tests.

• Hardships lead one to turn to Allah with a sincere heartfelt connection, recognising Allah is our Creator and is our everything, and we are His slaves – the purpose of life.

Why did God Create Those He Knows Will End Up in the Hellfire?

Allah created Man and honoured him by making him the highest of His Creation. Man is utterly dependent on Allah. Every single thing he has, has not only been provided by the Almighty, but is also being continually provided and maintained. From his eyesight, his hearing, his taste, his intellect, his emotions, his faith, to his parents, his spouse, his children, his home, his job, his income, his car, his education, his friends, his pets, his free time and hobbies, and the list goes on and on and on.

Imagine a billionaire technological genius comes across a little orphan girl in a hospital who has been struck down with a catastrophic neurological condition. Her brain is still good but she cannot feel anything nor move a single muscle. No one cares about her, and she is certain to die. He takes pity on the helpless creature. He invents a machine that can decode her thoughts. With him at the controls of this complex machine he can send her brain the sensory information, namely what can be seen, heard, felt, tasted etc. And he can activate any muscles that she wishes to use, so she is able to use her body as she likes. What a machine! Only he has the genius to be able to work this amazing machine. So, he does so, night and day. He dedicates his life to her well-being. She grows up enjoying life. He provides for her a home, so she always has warmth, shelter and security. She enjoys her own room, own clothes, own toys. His family become the girl's family, and she now has the love and companionship of an adoptive father, mother and siblings. She is spoilt for food. Trying to survive every day has been replaced with fun, play and education. As she grows up, she gets married and has a family of her own. What a joyous life.

For all this, the billionaire asks the girl for only one thing in return– that she simply thank him every day, for what he has done for her. The orphan, however, feels that she is entitled to all of this. Used to a life of luxury from the beginning, she feels she deserved everything. She owes nobody a thing. She chooses instead to slap him in the face, every single day, 'How dare he ask me to thank him!'. No thanks, just a great big slap supplemented with ongoing complaints about what she did not get. The billionaire continues to provide love, and bewildering support without fail. But, day after day, he continues to take the slap and the ungratefulness. That goes on for a week, then a month, then a year. The years roll by. As the orphan goes through adulthood, she remains fully dependent on the adoptive father, but she remains defiant and insolent.

How would we expect the compassionate genius to feel after a lifetime of this ungratefulness and defiance? Seven decades of this rotten attitude and stinking behaviour. Extreme compassion and mercy simply spat back in the face of the benevolent one. If this were playing as a movie, the viewers' blood would be boiling by the end of it. Wouldn't the audience feel great satisfaction if the insolent girl got her comeuppance and falls into a vat of boiling oil, to meet a hideous end, slow and tormenting.

So it is, that Allah has filled this world and universe with signs that point to Him and His astounding Magnificence. On top of that, He bestows infinite Mercy upon all of mankind. His Generosity is beyond limits. Every person receives great bounties well in excess of this fictional girl. Man has free-will. This is critical to grasp. This is what distinguishes man from the rest of creation, as discussed earlier in *Why Have We Been Created*. It is all down to man's choice to respond to Allah with obedience and worship, or defiance. When he spends a lifetime in defiance, disobedience and mischief, then he has earned his damnation all of his own hands.

If God Controls Everything, Why do We Need to Bother?

Allah is the Creator, Controller and Maintainer of all things. He is the Provider of everything. He is the Knower of all things. These are all part of Islamic faith. This leads some to ask 'Why do I need to do anything when Allah controls everything anyway?' The idea being we simply need to have faith, and then just sit back, Allah will make things happen. So in our work, we do not try, our success will come from Allah. In our education, we do not study, Allah will sort out our grades. People are dying from starvation, I do not need to bother, Allah will provide for them. Is this true?

It is important not to confuse belief with action. They work in parallel. One cannot replace one with the other. Recall earlier that Allah tells us to **'believe and do good deeds'** (See *Accountability and Judgement*). This equates to BELIEF *plus* ACTION. Iman is our level of faith, whilst *tawakul* is our trust in Allah. Of course it would be absurd to think that our food will land in front of us whilst we relax on our couch at home. Money will materialise in our wallet from nowhere, we just need to be strong in our belief. Claiming Allah will provide so we need not make any effort of our own, is laziness and / or misunderstanding. When we work, earn our keep and sit down to eat our food, we know that, in reality, Allah has provided for us. We made the effort, but He was our real Provider. Similarly, when we are in need, we pray and supplicate to Allah for His Help and Mercy. That is extremely important in its own right. But at the same time, we make our best efforts, with whatever means are available to us. We know that we are helpless in reality, but we do not act helpless. Given the faculties Allah has given man along with free will, man must strive to make the best decisions and strive to undertake the best actions. Islam is a religion of effort. One makes the best effort they can. The result is from Allah.

How do we know this? This can be illustrated from a few examples out of many from the Quran. The life of Moses and the struggles he faced are described at length throughout the Quran. It is well known that when he led the Israelites in fleeing Pharaoh, they reached the Red Sea with the tyrant hot on their heels. With no way forward, and a savage army behind, Moses is standing in a predicament and his people are beside themselves crying that they are sure to be killed now:

> ... *the people of Moses said: 'We are sure to be overtaken. (Moses) said: 'No, for sure, with me is my Lord! He will guide me'. Then We revealed to Moses: '**Strike** the sea with your staff'. And it was parted...* {Quran 26: 61-63}

Allah furnishes a miracle. He parts the sea to allow Moses and his people through, but as Pharaoh and his army attempt the same, He releases the mountains of water to drown them. What is to be noted is that Allah is going to deliver help in the form of a miracle but He does not tell Moses 'Not to worry, I will part the sea for you now'. He tells Moses to strike the sea *first* then He produces the miracle. The message is to make your effort, Allah delivers results. But make your effort.

In the story of Mary and the delivery of her virgin son, the Prophet Jesus, we see the same. After becoming pregnant, Mary removes herself from her community to a secluded place. During the pangs of labour, she rests under a date palm tree, where she is to be provided food and drink from Allah. She is informed of this provision:

> *Then (a voice) cried to her from below her, saying: 'Grieve not: your Lord has provided a water stream under you. And **shake** the trunk of the date palm towards you, it will drop fresh ripe dates upon you.' {Quran 19: 24-25}*

Mary is alone, with no support nor provision, but Allah will tend to her. The dates from the tree could simply have fallen from the tree, she is in labour after all. But here again Allah is making the point that despite the very challenging situation, she should still make some effort. The message is clear again – make effort, that is required from our end. Results are delivered by Allah alone.

There are countless such examples. The whole life of the Prophet himself was a grand demonstration of the importance of making committed effort. Take for instance, the time after the Muslims had established themselves in the city of Medina, the Meccan tribe of Quraish (the Prophet's own tribe) in alliance with hostile Arab and Jewish tribes, launched an attack on the city, seeking to exterminate the Muslims once and for all. The Muslims were massively outnumbered by the enemy forces. The Prophet, alerted to their imminent assault, did not sit back, content that he is the Messenger, so Allah will look after him – no need to lift a muscle. Instead, he gave careful consideration in consultation with his Companions to the best strategy for defending the city. One of the Companions, Salman Farsi, suggested digging a moat around the city to render it impassable. The Prophet himself and his Companions then toiled flat out for several days to dig the massive trench around the city to serve as an impenetrable defence. The confederate assault was thwarted successfully. No one had more faith than the Prophet, but he exhausted himself in making effort.

The fact that results are determined from Allah alone is also exemplified from another episode during the life of the Prophet. The second war the Muslims undertook as part of their battle for survival was the battle of Uhud. An army of 700 Muslims took on a 3000 strong Quraish army. Despite gross numerical inferiority, they overpowered the Quraish enemies, and were on the brink of victory. The overexuberance of the Muslims at this point led to a battalion of them, who had been stationed on a small hill charged with defence of the rear guard, abandoning their positions as they rushed forward to collect booty from the fleeing enemy. This opened up a counterattack from Khalid bin Waleed, a highly shrewd military tactician, who led the Quraish cavalry in a pincer movement from the rear now, dispersing the Muslim army and forcing their retreat. This was a defeat for the Muslims. If anyone was deserving of success at every juncture it was the Prophet of Allah. The message was loud and clear from this encounter, and was for all generations to come. Allah gives results, and that is based on His wisdom.

The Prophet summarised the need to make effort when a man asked him 'O Messenger of Allah, should I tie my camel and trust in Allah, or should I leave her untied and trust in Allah?' The Messenger of Allah, peace and blessings be upon him, said, Tie her and trust in Allah.'[103] The camel was the transport of the time and the man was inquiring to leash it up when he camped somewhere to stop it escaping, or that trust in Allah (*tawakul*) was sufficient in itself to keep the camel from absconding.

The message was clear - do not make the excuse that Allah will look after

---

[103] Sunan at-Tirmidhi

my affairs, so there is no need to tie its leash. You need both. Having faith and trust in Allah is not to be confused with laziness.

A nice modern-day example of this in practice is given by cricketer Adil Rashid the England leg spinner who was part of the cricket World Cup winning team in 2019. Initially not a very practising Muslim he noted how results generally preoccupy us: 'You have a good day, you are buzzing. If you have a bad day then you feel depressed.' Following his spiritual awakening in 2015, things changed: 'I really got into Islam and started reading up on stuff so after that, whether I had a good or a bad day, I knew Allah was in control. That really got me content, level-headed and relaxed. You still work hard but the outcome became irrelevant.'[104]

The most extreme version of this question is 'Allah already knows whether I will go to Heaven or Hell, so why do I need to bother?' Indeed *Allah does know,* ***but we do not know***. Allah knows because He knows absolutely everything in the universe including what we have done, are doing and will do. Remember Allah created time, and time does not exist for Allah. Allah is not bound by the law of time. However, that does not take away that every person has been given free will and the right to make their choices, good or bad. Allah says:

> *Each soul is responsible for its own actions; no soul will bear the burden of another. You will all return to your Lord in the end, and He will tell you the truth about your differences. {Quran 6: 164}.*

Again, we can only try to seek out the truth and therefore 'believe', and make our best efforts and thus, seek to 'do good deeds'. The opportunity to do right or wrong is the same for every individual. Man himself is the one who makes his choice and seals his own fate, good or bad.

---

[104] https://bbc.in/3dxzWHt

Bottom Line:

• Islam requires BELIEF <u>with</u> ACTION.

• Islam is a religion of effort : Effort-centric.

• Tie your camel.

• Islam is not result-centric because results are from Allah.

• Allah makes clear man has free will – he makes his own choices which seal his fate.

Ritual Obligations of Worship

The ritual obligations are classically taught as being the 'five pillars':

1. Belief in Allah as the One and only God, and that Muhammad is His (final) Messenger (*shahada*)

2. Ritual Prayer (*salat*)

3. Paying charity (*zakat*)

4. Fasting the month of Ramadan (*sawm*)

5. Performing Hajj (the major pilgrimage)

The first is a belief and a core tenet of faith. The others (2 to 5) are rituals acts, of which there are obligatory ones, incumbent on all Muslims, and there are voluntary, extra acts to gain not just additional reward but also spiritual upliftment.

The Declaration of Faith (*Shahada*)

'There is no God but Allah, and Muhammad is His (final) Messenger.'

The declaration of faith known as the *shahada* is a state of the heart, that knows with certitude that Allah is the One and Only God, and that

Muhammad is His final Messenger. The certitude is such that it is as though one *sees* this with one's own eyes; hence the Arabic word *shahada* is used, which literally means 'witnessing' – one witnesses with one's eyes. Here it is not a case of 'seeing is believing' but rather 'believing is seeing'.

Imagine a great competition where the prize is one billion pounds. A real needle has been placed into a real haystack. But there are one thousand giant haystacks. Everyone is searching, but people slowly give up after hours and hours of no joy. But you are in luck. A friend, who happens to work on the farm, tells you that they saw the needle being placed into haystack number seven, for sure, with their own eyes. Now you feel totally different. You head to haystack no.7 and you are fully confident you will certainly find that needle. Just keep going patiently. That is the effect of certitude. The certitude brings with it the conviction necessary to put attachment to this world aside, and to work hard and focus on the finish line, which is the Hereafter.

This declaration is the absolute fundamental of Islam. A person is not Muslim unless they believe this, no matter what good deeds they perform. And it is necessary to believe **both** components of this article, not only the Oneness of Allah, but also that Muhammad is His final Messenger. Why so?

A Muslim's goal in life is to show complete submission to Allah – ***Allah is our Master and we are His slaves***. Therefore how one leads their life, what is allowed for them, what is forbidden for them, what are the rules one has to follow, what are the boundaries, how should one behave – all of the answers to these come from divine Guidance, and ***that*** was revealed through Prophet Muhammad. In one's accepting that Muhammad was His final Messenger, one acknowledges that the guidance that Muhammad divulged is guidance from God and that is guidance that one is to follow.

Note also that Muhammad is Allah's final Prophet and Messenger:

> *Muhammad is not the father of (any) one of your men, but (he is)*

*the Messenger of Allah and the **last** of the prophets. Allah has full knowledge of all things. {Quran 33:40}.*

Therefore, any version of 'Islam' that claims to have a 'prophet' that succeeded Muhammad is a corruption, and not Islam.

The *shahada* and the conviction associated with it are no.1 in the 'five pillars' of worship because there is no Islam without it.

The one who finds Islam and converts, will ritualistically start with a pronouncement of this *shahada*. Note though that it is the state of heart accepting this that really determines if one is Muslim, not the ritual pronouncement. Conversion will erase all the sins of that person's past, making them like a newborn baby, born with a totally clean slate. This is a great, great gift from Allah. Some effort would clearly have been made to reach this point but it is not the end of the journey. What is the guidance of Allah, what does it ask of them? The journey continues now on a new path. Gradualism is important (see earlier), and one must not bite off more than one can chew. But there needs to be continued effort to learn more about their faith, along with its implementation and improvement in character.

Bottom Line:

• The *shahada* (article of faith) is central in belief for a Muslim.

• There is certitude in this belief.

• Both parts of the article, the Oneness of Allah, and Muhammad is His final Messenger must be accepted.

Ritual Prayer (*Salat*)

There are five obligatory daily prayers.[105] These are extremely important. Prayer within its prescribed time has been emphasised repeatedly by numerous Quranic verses and Prophetic teachings (hadiths). In fact the Prophet said that the performance or not of the obligatory prayers is what distinguishes a person as a Muslim or a disbeliever.[106] This drives home how critical the ritual prayer is.

The *salat* should be undertaken with full focus and without mistakes. The prayer is done imagining Allah is before you. There is no looking around, no fidgeting. The mind should not be thinking about the next task of the day, or whom you need to call next. There is a set prescriptive form to the prayer which is done in Arabic. One needs to memorise the minimum Arabic necessary with the correct pronunciation. One should be aware of the meaning too, as that helps enormously with focus. Those new to Islam should work towards this at a manageable pace.

There are set windows during the day when each prayer is to be offered. The higher reward is for undertaking the prayer as soon as its time begins. Why is this so? The one who prays as soon as the prayer time starts is displaying a greater degree of God-consciousness (*taqwa*). You have to keep your eye on the clock and keep God foremost on your mind throughout the day so as to get your prayer in, straightaway. It also shows a greater degree of obedience as you immediately put on hold all your worldly matters, and rush to fulfil Allah's command (recall the *sabiqoon*, the ones who rush, from *Make Use of Five before Five*). This can be trickier to do than it sounds. One is often engrossed in work or some matter, and even when seeing the time for the next prayer has commenced, is still unable to tear themselves away in order to pray.

Ablution (*wudu*) is the ritual cleansing of body parts. This is a prerequisite

---

[105] Quran 4: 130
[106] Sahih Muslim

to performing the ritual prayer. Water is used as the purifying agent to wash the hands, face, forearms and feet, along with wiping of the head. There is a spiritual component as well as a physical to these actions. Once complete, one enters into a state of purification (*wudu*), and remains in it unless broken by passing urine, stool, or wind, or having intimate relations. Passing wind is the most troublesome of these, as there is sometimes doubt if one has actually passed wind or not. This nagging doubt can be extremely troubling. Scholars addressed this matter by stating if one thinks they may have just passed wind, an accompanying sound or smell should be taken as confirmation they have. In the absence of a sound or smell, the doubt is dismissed and the ablution is intact.

Both the ablution and ritual prayer can be undertaken in a perfect manner (termed '*kaamil*' in Arabic), or an acceptable manner. Perfecting the ablution entails repeating each action thrice (except wiping the head), and rinsing the mouth and nostrils too. Perfection in prayer is to take time in recitation of the Quran at the relevant points, to have tranquillity in the prayer by bringing your focus back to Allah, maintaining the postures of standing, bowing and of prostrating on the ground. Naturally, the greater reward is for undertaking the prayer and the ablution in the best manner.

One also needs to strive for attentiveness and devotion in the prayer, called *khushoo* in Arabic. Ritual prayer should not be a ticking-the-box exercise, simply running through the motions. This is a time that one is connecting with Allah, and breaking from the humdrum routine of the day. The importance of taking time out of the day's chores is being increasingly appreciated with the explosion of 'mindfulness' techniques, books, classes and social media videos.

There is a misconception that the prayer can be skipped when one is busy and then made up later when more convenient. There is indeed the facility to make up a missed prayer (called *qadha* prayer) but this is for occasions *truly* beyond our control. For instance, a firefighter tackling a blaze where they have no relief or a surgeon operating on a patient, and the time for prayer has come and gone. There are actually very few occasions where one cannot perform prayer in its time. Even when travelling by airplane, one can find a spot with the assistance of the stewards. If one knows they will be out for the day, some careful forward planning usually helps to find the necessary time and place to get the prayer completed. For example, most airports have prayer rooms in the UK, so praying before even getting on the flight will be easier than praying on it. Even shopping malls often have prayer or mediation rooms.

In today's age, the issue is most acute in non-Islamic countries when one is out and about. There is first the inconvenience of performing the ablution prior to prayer. Those who hold that the feet must be washed in ablution (as opposed to wiping cotton socks) have to deal with the quizzical looks fellow toilet-users will throw, when raising the feet up into the sink. Worse is finding a sign or a cleaner that tells you that 'this is not the way in this country'. Next is finding a prayer room, a variable affair. If not available, there is the embarrassment of performing prayer in some corner of the shopping mall or restaurant (or wherever one may be), in view of non-Muslim public who may cast peculiar glances, or worse, may become abusive.

The embarrassment factor needs to be conquered. The fact that even during times of battle, the Prophet and his Companions still observed the due prayer shows it is absolutely not to be missed. The necessity of praying on time has to be accepted. Its importance is such that the Muslim should not just squeeze their prayers in during the course of their day, instead, the day should be built around one's prayers.

Consider this: you are going to make a trip across the USA from New York city to San Francisco in an electric car. At the time of writing there is a relative lack of electrical recharging points. You would have to plan the trip carefully ensuring that you had set a route and marked spots where you would be able to recharge the car. Otherwise the car's battery would run flat en route leaving you stranded in the middle of nowhere. The necessity of recharging would have to be built into the planning of the trip. Similarly when going out for the day, the ritual prayers should be worked out in advance – when will the prayer time come up, where will I be, what are the options for getting the prayer done?

One can help themselves by:

- Trying to stay in ablution as much as possible – so avoid the need to repeat the ablution

- Knowing the rules of ablution properly – so if in uncomfortable locations, undertake what is the minimum required

- Knowing the rules of prayer properly – for the same reason as above. Know what is the minimum required, if one needs to keep prayer as short as possible

- Consciously planning out where and when to pray, in advance of travelling, or being out and about

In addition to the obligatory, there are voluntary prayers. The most blessed of these is the night prayer (*tahajjud*), performed in the last one third of the night. One can catch this time by waking up about half an hour before the time for Fajr (the dawn prayer) begins. Allah has decreed it to be a time of great mercy and blessings. The Prophet explained:

> *Allah, Our Lord, descends to the nearest heaven to us during the last third of the night and says: 'Is there anyone to call upon Me so that I shall respond to him? Is there anyone to ask of Me so that I may grant his request? Is there anyone to seek My forgiveness so that I shall pardon him'. {Sahih Bukhari and Sahih Muslim}*

Finally, *when praying alone*, a common mistake many Muslims make during the *salat* is to keep silent and to 'recite' in their heart. The recitation during prayer must be verbalised, so the tongue and lips are moving and there is some sound, even if this be extremely quiet, down to a whisper. To pray without moving the mouth and tongue is deemed an *invalid* prayer – it has not been performed according to the prescribed way. This will be a revelation to many Muslims. So let's look at this in some more detail.

There are five obligations within the ritual prayer, that must be present to constitute a valid prayer:[107] Standing, Recitation of the Quran, *Ruku* (bowing whilst standing), Prostration (*Sajdah*), and the Final sitting. Our concern here is with Recitation of the Quran. A large number of Muslims take this to be the directive that some portion of the Quran must be included in the prayer (with great importance given to *Surah al-Fatiha*) and assume that Recitation includes reciting with the voice in your head i.e. you are 'reciting in your heart'; there is no actual movement of the mouth (tongue and lips) and there is no actual sound produced. However, Recitation, what is termed *qiraat* in Arabic, is the pronouncement to produce speech. This requires movement of the tongue and lips, as well as breath to generate the sounds, even if a bare whisper. 'Reciting in the heart' is therefore not true Recitation.

The evidences for this start with the famous saying of the Prophet (hadith): 'Pray as you have seen me praying...'[108] Now, the congregational prayers of Dhur and Asr (the daytime prayers) are quiet prayers i.e. the recitation of the leader of the prayer, the Imam, is done quietly, unlike the prayers of Fajr, Maghrib and Isha, where the Imam's recitation is done out aloud. It was evident during the Dhur prayer, and therefore a quiet prayer, that the Prophet was reciting i.e. verbalising Quran 'from the movement of his beard.'[109] If the Prophet's beard was moving, he clearly was not simply 'reciting in his heart'. For his beard to be moving he must have been mouthing the words.

Finally, scholars across the board have been unanimous in holding that there must be movement of the tongue and lips for the prayer to be valid.[110] For example, the great scholar Al-Kasaani (d. 1191) said: 'Recitation can only be done by moving the tongue to say the sounds.'[111] He points out

---

[107] Shaykh Mohammad Akram Nadwi. *Al-Fiqh Al-Islami vol 1*. Chapter 5: The Fards, Wajibs and Sunnahs of Salah
[108] Sahih Bukhari, Sahih Muslim
[109] Musnad Ahmad
[110] For those familiar with the *fiqh* schools of thought (*madhabs*), note that they do not differ on this matter.
[111] Al-Kasaani. Badaa'i' al-Sanaa'i'

that there is a difference of opinion whether an audible sound must be made. All scholars agree that even a gentle whisper is sufficient, but producing no sound is contentious, being accepted by some scholars but rejected by others. Clearly verbalising during the prayer, i.e. moving the lips and tongue, is therefore a must, with the safest option being to produce a slight sound as well.

When *praying in congregation* <u>behind</u> an imam, there are two opinions on what to do during the *standing part* of the prayer, when *Surah al-Fatiha* is to be recited. Without getting into great complexities here, the first opinion is that the follower should also recite *Fatiha* quietly, as they would if they were praying alone. The second view is that they stay silent as the Imam's recitation is held as sufficient to cover the congregation. For the *rest of the prayer* (bowing, prostration, and sitting), the follower needs to verbalise the accompanying invocations.

Why do We Pray and why is Prayer Described as a Gift?

Let's recap. Allah is crystal clear that the purpose of our creation is to worship Him:

> *And I did not create jinn and man except to worship Me.* *{Quran 51: 56}*

It is not surprising therefore that we have been prescribed ritual prayer to this end. However, when prayer is referred to as a gift, this is a little more difficult to grasp, especially for the heart that is persistently occupied with worldly things. Interrupting our daily life to pray five times a day can seem a 'chore'. How do we recognise this as a gift?

Salat as a gift

The first thing to appreciate is what would happen if we were NOT obligated to pray several times a day in a prescriptive manner. Man, being a lazy and procrastinating creature, would find himself in front of Allah on the Day of Judgement, having spent his whole life too 'busy', with just a measly handful of episodes where he bothered to engage in the worship of his Lord – *maybe* a handful. How embarrassing in a life spanning say seventy years, to have just half a dozen instances. Interestingly these measly remembrances of Allah probably would have been at the lowest times of his life (recall *Why is There Hardship and Evil in this World*).

Ritual prayer gives you the best form to please Allah in the way of worship – i.e. *Quality*. This is the best form, as Allah has prescribed the form Himself. Obligating this upon man five times a day ensures he has to focus on the purpose of his creation throughout the day, namely: to remember Him, praise Him, thank Him and obey Him. Now the maths – five times a day, 365 days a year is 1825 prayers for the year, and 109,500 for 60 years (counting from puberty at 10 years in a lifespan of 70 years) – i.e. *Quantity*.

Reward for worship

Now here is the mind blowing thing. In Allah's paradigm, failure to observe obligations is marked as sins, BUT fulfilling them is rewarded. Just compare this to man's paradigm, obligations and rules must be followed, with penalty or punishment as a consequence for failure. That's it, no reward. Just think about this. Our son goes to school. He needs to wear a tie, a jacket, white shirt, black trousers, grey socks, black shoes. Hair suitably combed. Arrive on time. He needs to line up when the whistle is blown. No talking in the line, etc, etc. There is no reward for any of these things, only penalties for disobeying.

Instead, imagine the Headteacher receiving every child in the morning and dishing out a reward, say a sweetie, for EVERY single obligation completed by the child. And doing that throughout the day, for EVERY SINGLE obligation. It quickly adds up to an absolute abundance of rewards. In such a school the children would probably lose all their teeth from tooth decay after just a few days! If he were to give one pound for each reward instead of sweetie, the children would become extremely rich very quickly. This is the Mercy and Love of the Most Merciful Lord (*Ar*

Rahmaan and *Ar Raheem*) for His slaves. The obligations have been given, to force man into good deeds and so earning His rewards. By placing obligations on him, Allah is actually helping man not to fail in his purpose.

The gift of the ritual prayer has been beautifully captured by the scholar, Al-Iskandari, in his book of aphorisms, Kitab Al Hikam:[112]

> *He (Allah) knew that (most of) His slaves are not self-motivated in seeking Him; so, He obligated for them obedience to Him. He pushed them towards Him with the chains of obligation. Your Lord is amused by a people who are pushed to Paradise in chains.*

Note the sublime imagery here. How Allah will force His slaves, through obligations including ritual prayer, driving them in chains rather like prisoners, practically against their will, into Paradise.

As a means to give thanks

The ritual prayer also serves as a beautiful and intimate way to give thanks to our Provider. Reflecting deeply on what has been provided to us, and how fortunate we truly are, instils a profound sense of gratitude to the Creator. How can one not be hugely grateful for one's health on seeing someone with a disability, or one's home when encountering a homeless person, or hot water and heating when the freezing snow blizzards are blowing outside. The gratitude should swell to the point it needs an outlet (see *Thankfulness* later). Ritual prayer gives one such means.

Appreciating the Sublime One

It also serves as the means of appreciating the All Powerful One. Reflecting on Allah's creation, from its sheer magnitude and diversity to the bewildering complexity and organisation at the most minute level coupled with His continuous control, and maintenance, leaves one

---

[112] Ibn Ata Allah Al-Iskandari, *Kitab Al Hikam*: no.195

awestruck and bedazzled. Allah is simply, unbelievably, phenomenally, incredulously amazing. If one is reflecting deeply enough, one sees the need to pray and appreciate His wonderousness. This is the same as when one enjoys a new meal for the first time that is melt-in-the-mouth good, or seeing a truly incredible performance from a magician or athlete, one cannot help but say 'That's amazing!' The need to appreciate it, which leads one to actually blurt it out, is natural. We feel compelled to say it even if we were by ourselves.

Staying connected with your Creator

Of course, as with all of Allah's commands, there will be a multitude of benefits. Praying five times a day helps to keep us connected with Allah. This protects us against sin. If we are about to commit a sin, knowing that we will be appearing before Allah shortly in prayer serves as a good deterrent. Concentrating on the prayer gives spiritual upliftment and reminds us the worries of this world are transient. The benefits are also tangible. The day seems more productive, and dilemmas seem to get sorted unexpectedly.

Note that Allah Himself is in *no need* whatsoever of our worship, nor any of our good deeds. He does not benefit, nor does His Kingdom increase in any way. Allah is free from all need, and indeed this is one of His Names, *Al-Ghani*. It should be apparent now that prayer benefits *us*, not only as an important tool to gain Allah's Pleasure, but also for our own spiritual and character development. Realising this point is a truly sobering thought, and should focus us to give ritual prayer its due time and concentration. After all, Allah does not need it, but *we* need to get something out it, it is not just ticking a box.

Finally, one also needs to pray out of fear of Allah. He is All-Powerful and the One to take account of everyone and their every single deed, no matter how big or small. There is no hiding and no possibility of phoney excuses. He is the All Knowing including what is in everyone's hearts. Incurring Allah's displeasure and wrath should be a very serious matter for a Muslim.

The prayer account

The ritual prayer is so integral to Islamic faith and its practice that the Prophet stated that, 'The first matter that the slave will be brought to account for on the Day of Judgment is the prayer.'[113] In other words, when the reckoning starts and a person's deeds are to be judged, the ritual prayer (or the lack of it) will be the very first one. Here the quantity as well as the quality will be accounted. So whilst we have already talked about how prayer is a gift, with its sheer number gaining huge reward for the believer, the one who is neglectful of their prayers, will find this same astronomical number held against them. Everyone has an account for their lifetime of ritual prayer.

A Muslim who has a period where they stop praying in life incurs a deficit in this prayer account. They need to make up for all missed prayers when they resume praying. If they stopped for one year, that makes 1825 prayers to make up, in addition to continuing with the present day obligatory prayers. Now that is a heavy burden of prayers to catch up on. It is clearly better not to fall behind at all. Don't neglect your *salat*.

Prayer in Congregation

Ritual prayer performed as a group is rewarded 27 times versus that of praying alone. A group is defined as two people or more. It can be seen again the sense of community that Islam fosters, encouraging meeting and praying together, regularly throughout the day. There is also an obligatory congregational prayer on Friday, to replace the regular midday (Dhur) prayer. This is compulsory on all adult males, and optional on women. A sermon is delivered by the imam (leader) of the mosque or a knowledgeable person followed by a shortened ritual prayer (two *rakat* instead of the usual four for Dhur – the sermon (Khutbah) effectively replacing two *rakat*). *Rakat* is the number of standings done during the

---

[113] Sunan Abu Dawood

prayer, rather like the units of the prayer.

Particular reward has been singled out for congregational prayer for the Fajr (dawn) and Isha (night) prayers. A teaching that Uthmaan ibn Affaan, an esteemed Companion and later the third Caliph (ruler), heard directly from the Prophet:

> *He who attends Isha in congregation, is as if he has performed salat for half of the night; and he who attends Isha and Fajr prayers in congregation, is as if he has performed salat for the whole night. {Sahih Muslim}*

Meaning that praying either of these in the mosque carries the reward equal to spending half the night in worship in the mosque. Attending for both in the mosque therefore carries the reward equal to praying in the mosque the entire night.

Prayer of Guidance and Prayer of Need

There are times where one is faced with a big decision in life, or a decision needs to be made but one has absolutely no idea what is the better option. For instance you are offered a job at a new company, or you are looking for a new house and have found a property. Do you go for it? Muslims recognise that despite all their due diligence and efforts, they can never know everything. And we certainly do not know the future. Only Allah is the All-Knower. So there is the prayer of guidance, known as *Salat ul Istikhara*. Here one prays a short voluntary prayer of two *rakat* (number of standings) and makes a supplication to finish, asking Allah as the All-Knower and All-Wise to make easy the better option of the two, better for this world and for the Hereafter. In our example, this would be taking the new job or not, or buying the house or not. Having done this, the matter is left to Allah, and the better path will become clear. In my own personal experience this often results in one path actually closing off completely, leaving only one option to move forwards, or one path becomes much easier of the two. So for instance, with two job offers available, one is withdrawn suddenly, leaving the other one. In *Istikhara*, one seeks guidance in binary matters, i.e. there are only two options.

Sometimes one has a particular problem or a particular need. A young man or woman is looking to get married, but failing to find a suitable spouse. Or someone has lost their job, and is desperately trying to find a new one. In this instance there is a prayer of need, called *Salat ul Haajat*. It is similar to the prayer of guidance, but one concludes a two *rakat* prayer with a supplication beseeching Allah, as the All-Powerful, to remove their burden and provide relief for their specific need.

Both of these are gifts for the Muslim, alleviating difficult decisions, or situations, and getting help from the One who has all the knowledge, power, and ability. As *tahajjud* (the night prayer) is a particularly blessed time, making these prayers at this time amplifies the supplication. It is a good tip to follow up these prayers once they have been answered with two *rakat Salat ul Shukr* (thanks), to acknowledge and thank the Almighty for His guidance and Help.

Bottom line:

• Ritual worship (*salat*) is a great gift from Allah, as it gives the means (both quality and quantity) to fulfil the purpose of our Creation, namely to worship Allah.

• Allah's paradigm of reward for obedience shows His extreme benevolence and mercy.

• The obligatory ritual prayer in its prescribed time is extremely important and must be fulfilled.

• The day should be built around the five prayers, and not vice versa.

• The highest reward for the prayer is performing it in a perfect manner, with the perfect ablution, as soon as the prayer times commences.

• Everyone has a prayer account that will be the first out of the deeds to be examined on the Day of Judgement.

• Missed prayers must be made up in one's lifetime to avoid their deficit on the Day of Judgement.

• Praying in congregation carries greater reward.

• The voluntary night prayer (*tahajjud*) is a highly blessed and rewarded prayer.

• For help with decisions or relieving a need, prayers of guidance (*istikhara*) and prayers of need (*haajat*) are great tools.

• Allah is in *NO* need of our worship; ritual prayer is of profound benefit to *us*.

• We *need* to pray to show:

– our love to Allah

– our sincere gratitude to Allah

– our amazement at Allah

– to gain Allah's Pleasure and His rewards

– out of fear of Allah.

Supplication (*Dua*)

Following each prayer, supplication is made to Allah, asking him for whatever are one's needs. This is termed *dua*, literally meaning 'to call upon'. *Dua* can be made at any time, not just after completion of prayer. This is also a form of worship. Why so? Man is showing humility and demonstrating his slavehood to the Master. We are needy, and asking the only One that is free of needs, the universal Provider, to fulfil our needs. Allah loves *dua*, and we are encouraged to make as much *dua* as possible. Allah says:

Call upon Me; I will respond to you {Quran 40: 30}

And when My servants ask you (i.e. Muhammad) concerning Me -

indeed I am near. I respond to the invocation of the supplicant when he calls upon Me. {Quran 2: 187}.

There is no intermediary between us and Allah. This verse makes clear that He is right with us. Allah always responds.

There are certain special times to make *dua*, and these are to be capitalised upon. The last one third of the night before the dawn (Fajr) prayer, called *tahajjud*, has been discussed above. The most important night of the whole year is the Night of Power (*Laylatul Qadr*) which is encountered in the month of Ramadan – see *Fasting* later. Similarly, the period just before breaking one's fast. These are special times where there is particular favour from Allah, and a greater chance of the invocations being accepted. These times are similar to when shops have their sales on, and the public flocks to pick up bargains. Allah loves to give and wants to give, so, not surprisingly, there are numerous other such times.

A special form of *dua* are those that were made by the prophets themselves. As they were people of special stature and endowed with wisdom, their invocations carry extra weight. These are called the *masnoon duas*. They are numerous and for countless situations and times of the day. For example, there is a *dua* for entering one's home, another for leaving, a *dua* upon waking up, another for going to sleep. A *dua* for putting on one's clothes, another for taking them off. A *dua* for starting to eat, and another when finished. These provide another way of being God-conscious (having *taqwa*) *all the time*, so we are remembering Allah as frequently as possible in our daily life, and constantly seeking His Good Pleasure and Mercy.

Allah is the All Compassionate and All Kind, and He wants man to show the same quality (see *Kindness*). In this vein, a Muslim can make *dua* (supplicate) to Allah for something good on behalf of somebody else. This is an act of tremendous kindness. It could be to deliver some good in this world, such as a child, a good job, good exam results, a good home. It could be to relieve them of some difficulty. Or it could be to reward them and grant them success in the Afterlife. Not only is this pleasing to Allah, but in Allah's magnanimous fashion, He ensures the supplication is also replicated for the one making the supplication. The Prophet informed us:

> *There is no Muslim servant who supplicates for his brother behind his back but that the angel says: 'And the same for you'.* *{Sahih Muslim}*

Here supplicating 'behind his back' means doing so in private. So supplicating sincerely for your fellow man is actually a tremendous act. One is demonstrating kindness (so pleasing Allah and rewarded in itself), one is begging Allah (so showing slavehood to Allah, and rewarded in itself), and one receives the same supplication if appropriate (so acquiring the requested benefit for oneself whether in this world or the next).

Why is Allah Not Responding to My *Dua* (Supplication)?

This is a very common question: 'If Allah always responds to *dua*, then why am I not seeing what I am asking for?' or 'I have made so much *dua* to Allah for this, why is He not hearing me?' It is necessary to understand how Allah responds to *dua*. Response can be in the following ways:

1. He bestows what has been asked for.

2. He bestows something else which is beneficial.

3. He prevents a calamity from striking instead.

4. He grants a favour not in this world, but in the Hereafter.

Allah is generous beyond measure (so carries the name, *Al Kareem*) and loves to bestow (*Al Wahhaab*). Allah's dominion will not diminish in the slightest even if He grants every person every single wish. So if He is not granting exactly what is being asked for, there is a reason. As Allah is All-Knowing, He knows what is beneficial for us. A particular request we make may not be good for us, perhaps even harmful; He therefore withholds this, but grants something in lieu. It may be a question of timing.

What we desire will be better for us at a future time, so we must wait. Allah does not tire of giving, and man should not tire of asking. Crucially one must not show impatience or exasperation. Our supplications should be accompanied by the proviso 'if Allah thinks it will be better for me and my family for this world and the next'.

Although Allah always responds in what is the most appropriate way, there can be occasions a person's *duas* will be shut off. A person engaged in major sins may find their supplications rejected. If one is supplicating repeatedly and feels they are not receiving their requests, they should reflect if some serious sinful behaviour is at fault. This would require repentance and ceasing that behaviour. One should also beseech for forgiveness, called *Istighfar*, for sins committed knowingly or *unknowingly*. Finally, persevere with the supplication with patience and certitude that Allah is hearing and responding in His way. The Prophet Ibrahim was blessed with his sons Ismail and Ishaq (Issac) in his old age. Prophet Yaqoob (Jacob) was re-united with his son Yusuf (Joseph) after several decades whilst everyone else had assumed that Yusuf was dead.

Constant Remembrance of Allah with Dhikr

Similar to *masnoon duas*, another way of remaining constantly God-conscious is, to repeat words or short phrases that praise Allah. This is termed *dhikr* and examples are *Subhaanallah* (Glory be to Allah), *Alhamdulillah* (All thanks and all praise is due to Allah), and *Allahu Akbar* (Allah is Great). These are found repeatedly in the Quran, and are also embedded in the ritual prayer. They can be uttered quietly, and repeated throughout the day. These three phrases are in fact recited at the conclusion of the obligatory prayer, 33, 33 and 34 times respectively, as there is great blessing in doing so. When some of the poorer Companions complained to the Prophet that the richer ones were gaining more reward as they had wealth they could spend in charity, he explained that remembering Allah after prayer with these *dhikr* would carry reward to a similar degree.

The Prophet described great rewards for remaining engaged in constant remembrance, and the use of certain phrases:

> *Whoever says, 'Subhaan Allahi wa bihamdihi,' one hundred times a day, will be forgiven all his sins even if they were as much as the foam of the sea. {Sahih Bukhari}*

> *(There are) two words which are dear to the Beneficent (Allah) and very light for the tongue (to say), but very heavy in weight on the Scales. They are: 'Subhaan Allahi wa-bi hamdihi' and 'Subhaan Allahil-Azeem'. {Sahih Bukhari}*

Subhaan Allahi wa bihamdihi means 'Glory be to Allah, and all praises and thanks go to Him'. *Subhan Allahil-Azeem* means 'Glory be to Allah, the Mighty'.

The *masnoon duas* and *dhikr* are important tools for humankind. The purpose of man's Creation is to worship Allah. The more one can engage in this throughout the day, the more they are fulfilling this.

Bottom line

- *Duas* are invocations made directly to Allah asking for one's needs.

- Allah loves *dua* as one is affirming their slavehood to Him.

- *Masnoon dua* and *dhikr* are great tools to allow one to remain engaged in the worship of Allah throughout the day.

- Allah always responds to *dua* in what He knows is the best way.

- The exception to Allah responding is engaging in major sin, which needs sincere repentance.

Charity (*Zakat*)

It is obligatory for Muslims to spend a small portion of their wealth on certain prescribed forms of charity. This is called *zakat*, and it is the third pillar of faith. The obligation falls on those who are adult (whether male or female) and have sufficient wealth. The charity amount is hardly onerous at 2.5% of one's surplus wealth. Surplus means in excess of one's living expenses and bills and is calculated on cash, stocks of gold or silver (including as jewellery), or other financial assets. The recipients of *zakat* are defined by Allah in the Quran[114] and largely pertains to those who are poor with their means failing to reach a financial threshold called *nisab*.

The Quran contains guidance on matters of importance. Where these are of very serious concern, the guiding principles are repeated, even many times. *Zakat* is mentioned 32 times in the Quran. It has been mentioned alongside ritual prayer 27 times. There can be no doubt how profoundly important it is. But consider this – when Allah describes the arrival of death to a person, who is a sinner, at that point they will beg for a few extra moments of life to try and earn some good deeds. What are these extra deeds that they will choose, these deeds need to be quick to do but massive on the Scales. Will it be doing more ritual prayer (*salat*)? More affirmation of faith (*shahada*), more *dhikr* (remembrance of Allah), or perform Hajj or Umrah? No, they will ask for the chance to give more charity:

> *My Lord, if only You would delay me for a brief term (from death) so I would give charity and be among the righteous. {Quran 63: 10}.*

At that dire time they would desperately seek the chance to spend their wealth in charity, to transfer them into the category of the righteous ones. This is the gravitas of giving in the way of charity.

The wisdom behind it is evident even from a secular viewpoint. The most

---

[114] Quran *9: 60*

poor in society need support from the more affluent for their basic needs and survival. Islam promotes redistribution of wealth, to ensure the most needy are not neglected. Recall from earlier, '*Looking After the Orphan*' – the worth of a society is based on how it takes care of its most weak members. Also recall from before, '*Everything is a Loan from Allah*', so wealth is to be spent in accordance to Allah's Laws. The amount to be paid as *zakat* is not even viewed by the Muslim as belonging to themselves, but actually as the property of the needy.

Wealth is supposed to be put to use. This could be in trade, investing in business projects or in research. It could be by giving out loans to the needy (remember from earlier '*Strict Prohibition of Usury*'). These loans are done as charities, the amount the lender receives back will be exact to the amount loaned out – not a penny more. There are stern warnings about hoarding wealth. The whole of Chapter 102 in the Quran is a severe warning to those who busy themselves hoarding wealth; it is actually named '*At-Takaathur*', meaning 'Those who compete in worldly hoarding'. These same people are given a grave scolding in another chapter (104) as well called '*Al-Humazah*', which means 'The backbiter'.

There is prioritisation in *zakat* as well. 'Charity begins at home' is true - one must first look to their family, the nearer relatives followed by more distant, to give their *zakat* before reaching out to the wider community.[115] This can be a sensitive matter. Family members may not wish to ask for financial support out of their dignity. It might not be easy to identify if a family member qualifies for *zakat* i.e. do they own less than the *nisab* (minimum) amount. If one is suspicious, subtle enquiry may be required, or a judicious assessment.

---

[115] A man cannot give zakat (obligatory charity) to his immediate family members including grandparents or grandchildren, as he is obligated for their financial upkeep anyway. For zakat, he must seek out extended family first before the community. A woman can spend zakat on her immediate family, including husband, if they qualify for it. A man can give *sadaqa* (voluntary charity) to immediate family members.

Non-obligatory charity is called *sadaqa*, and can be given to anyone regardless of faith, or financial status. It also includes close family members. There are great rewards for spending extra in charity. As per His Magnanimity, Allah makes clear that wealth spent in charity does not decrease one's wealth. On the contrary, He promises to increase it.

> *The example of those who spend their wealth in the way of Allah, is like the example of a seed (of corn); it grows seven ears, and each ear has a hundred grains. Allah gives manifold increase to whom He wills. And Allah is All-Sufficient for His creatures' needs, the All-Knower.*

> *Those who spend their wealth in the cause of Allah, and do not follow up their gifts with reminders of their generosity or with insult, their reward is with their Lord. On them shall be no fear, nor shall they grieve. {Quran 2: 261-262]*

The first verse shows that the reward of spending in charity is multiplied exponentially, whilst the following verse reinforces that the intention of spending must be sound, namely for the sake of gaining Allah's Pleasure. The donor should not ingratiate themselves with the recipient, and should maintain the dignity of the recipient, neither reminding them of their favour nor making them feel bad.

The Prophet also expounded that Allah says:

> *'Spend, O son of Adam, and I shall spend on you.' {Sahih Bukhari and Sahih Muslim}.*

Bottom Line:

- Charity is an important means of supporting the poor and needy of society.

- Giving a portion of wealth in charity is obligated on the Muslim (*zakat*).

- Giving additional voluntary amounts (*sadaqa*) is exceedingly encouraged.

• The reward of giving charity with sound intention is increased exponentially by Allah.

• Giving in charity does not decrease wealth, as Allah promises to increase it.

Fasting and Ramadan

Fasting is abstaining from all food and drink, and intimate relations, from dawn until dusk. It is compulsory upon all adults in the Islamic month of Ramadan. There are two types of exemptions. The first is the one who suffers a chronic illness, that renders them unable to fast. As there will be no recovery from their condition, they cannot make up the missed fasts at a later date. Instead, they can feed a poor person two square meals for a day in lieu of each day missed.

The second type of exempted people are those who have a temporary situation that prevents them fasting, such as those who are traveling or who have an acute illness. This group must make up the missed fasts at a subsequent date when they are no longer traveling or have recovered, respectively. This can also include pregnant women or breastfeeding mothers, if they find fasting too difficult. Women in their monthly cycle are not permitted to fast, as they are in a state of ritual impurity.

Whilst many Muslims are focussed on the food and drink element, in actual fact, fasting and Ramadan are about spiritual upliftment and character improvement. Allah says:

> *That fasting has been prescribed upon you, like peoples before you, so that you may become God-conscious and pious. (Quran 2: 183).*

With even greater care than usual, a Muslim is to uphold excellent character and abstain from sin. Lying, backbiting, anger, cheating are to be shunned meticulously. The Prophet warned that:

> *Perhaps a person's fasting will receive nothing from his fasting except hunger and thirst. {Sunan Ibn Majah}*

– implying the one who simply abstains from food and drink but engages in bad character and sins, has actually failed to get the true rewards and benefits. One should also engage in extra acts of worship, especially increased recitation and reflection of the Quran.

As with other form of ritual worship, in addition to the obligations, one can undertake extra voluntary fasts. Whilst only the fasts of Ramadan are compulsory, fasting an additional six days of the following month (Shawwaal) transforms the reward into the equivalent of fasting the whole year. These can be any six days of Shawwaal, consecutive or not.

The Prophet used to fast a great deal. Consistently he fasted Mondays and Thursdays in every week, as well as the 13th, 14th, and 15th of each Islamic month (known as the 'white days' as they correspond to the full moon). He also fasted the day of Ashura, the 10th of the Islamic month of Muharram, which commemorates the day Musa (Moses) and the Israelites were delivered from Pharaoh. This day is combined with a second fast, either the day before or day after, to be distinct from Jewish practice which is to fast only on the 10th. The first nine days of the month (Dhul Hijjah) in which the major pilgrimage, Hajj, is performed are also extremely blessed days, and it is recommended for non-pilgrims to fast these days for their reward (it is not recommended for the actual pilgrims themselves, as they need to conserve their energies for Hajj which can be quite arduous).

The fast itself commences just before dawn, and it is strongly recommended to consume something prior to this. This pre-dawn snack or meal is termed *suhoor*, and was the recommended practice of the Prophet. There are blessings in the *suhoor*, and it could be as simple as a few sips of water. The fast breaks at sunset, which is also the time of the dusk prayer, Maghrib. The meal taken at this time is called the *iftar*. Traditionally the fast is opened with dates, either fresh or dried, or with water. The time preceding the *iftar* is a blessed time, and a time when supplications (*duas*) are accepted by Allah.

The month of Ramadan is completed with the festival of Eid-ul-Fitr. A joyous occasion to celebrate the opportunity granted, and the anticipated rewards of such a blessed month. There is a congregational prayer held in the morning, once the sun is up, and before the midday prayer (Dhur). All are recommended to attend this prayer, men, women, children, the old, and the sick. There is a sermon followed by the ritual prayer.

Well in advance of Eid-ul-Fitr, a nominal compulsory charity, the *zakat-ul-fitr*, needs to be distributed or paid. This currently amounts to around £3 to £5 per family member. Those who have the minimum wealth (called *nisab*) are required to give this charity for each member of their household, whether adult or minor, male or female. Historically, this charity used to be food distributed to the poor, so that they too can have a joyous meal on the day of Eid. Hence it needs to be given well in advance of (i.e. several days before) Eid, not just before the Eid prayers. Some scholars hold that only food can be given as per the tradition, not money, whilst other scholars have concluded that giving the equivalent in money to the needy is acceptable. In the modern day, however, it is better given as money. Why? It is a common sight now, that when food is given, the poor are found trying to sell this for money instead. Worse, they sell it back to the same shop keeper you bought it from but get a lower price than you paid!

The Rewards of Fasting

Keeping oneself hungry and thirsty for the whole day is no small task. One must suppress and struggle with normal desires. One is putting aside what is not only permissible, but also one's needs during the day. Not surprisingly Allah grants tremendous rewards for obeying this obligation. The Prophet reported:

> *Allah says 'Every good deed of the son of Adam is for himself (i.e. for his own benefit) except fasting; it is for Me. And I shall reward for it (with due magnanimity).' {Sahih Bukhari, Sahih Muslim}*

It is important to recall Allah's weighting of good deeds and bad deeds (see *Accountability and Judgement*). A good deed is rewarded not as one good deed, but Allah multiplies its weighting by between ten to seven hundredfold. Here, Allah is revealing that He will multiply the deed of fasting *beyond measure*. That is for just one fast. Now imagine the reward of thirty fasts from one month of Ramadan. Suppose a person fasts 60 Ramadan months in a lifetime, that equates to 1800 lifetime Ramadan fasts. All increased in reward by a massive multiplier beyond our comprehension. The Prophet also informed us that

> *Fasting is a shield with which a servant protects himself from the Fire (i.e. Hellfire). {Sunan Ahmad}*

> *Whoever fasts during the month of Ramadan out of sincere faith, and hoping to attain Allah's rewards, then all his past sins will be forgiven. {Sahih Bukhari, Sahih Muslim}*

Another majestic reward. It is important to remember, though, 'the past sins' refers to sins committed towards Allah, not sins committed against others. For that one must seek forgiveness from the wronged person. Also, when asked by a Companion as to tell him of an action by which he may enter Paradise, the Prophet replied:

> *Take to fasting, there is nothing like it. {Sunan An-Nisai}*

There is in fact a gate of Paradise, called *Ar-Rayyaan*, which is the exclusive gate of entry for those who used to fast. The month of Ramadan is an extremely blessed month. Aside from the rewards of fasting, there is an increase in rewards for all good deeds and acts of worship.

Laylatul Qadr (the Night of Power)

This is an extremely special night amongst the last ten nights of Ramadan. Sincere worship during this night carries the mind-boggling reward of fasting for 1000 months (83 years)[116]. That equates to 30,000 fasts. This is like the 'buy one get one free' deal in the shops but here buy one get 30,000 free! This is yet another example of extreme mercy from the Almighty who has given opportunities beyond measure to allow us to increase our account of good deeds. To gain this reward, worship with sincerity and a yearning for forgiveness is required during this night, or part of it.

Now let's go back to our reward calculation from earlier. 60 Ramadans in a lifetime, in which the person gains the Night of Power each time, works out to:

60 Nights of Power = 60 x 30,000 = 1,800,000 fasts

60 Months of Ramadan fasts = 60 x 30 = 1800 fasts

6 days of Shawwal fasts to follow Ramadan = 60 x 335 = 20,100 fasts

Total fasts = 1,821,900 fasts

Reward from Allah = 1,821,900 x *Allah's multiplier for each fast*!!!

The actual night has not been revealed, but the most sound reports from the Prophet are that it is one of the nights amongst the last ten, with a likelihood of being on an odd night. The wisdom of not revealing the exact night can be understood if you consider what would transpire if it had been revealed – people would be half-hearted and disinterested in the whole of Ramadan, but would step up to cash in on that one special night. As the start of Ramadan, like all Islamic months, is based on the sighting of the

---

[116] Quran 97: 3

moon, inevitably variations arise as to the exact day that Ramadan starts between different populations. This implies an odd night for one community may be an even night for another community. The safest course of action is therefore to seek out this night in *all* the last ten nights, odd and even.

The reward of this night extends beyond the fasting. Each good deed is rewarded 30,000 times. It is therefore good to give some charity each night, to catch the reward. Giving £10 on each night, gains the reward of £300,000 on *Laylatul Qadr*.

Itikaf (Seclusion in the Mosque)

A special measure to secure this night is to confine oneself to the mosque for the last ten days. This is called *itikaf*. It was a practice of the Prophet. The days and nights are spent entirely in the mosque, and as much worship is undertaken as possible, with a focus on night time worship. This is a form of retreat and worldly matters are to be cut off completely or limited as much as possible. One is not supposed to leave the mosque.[117] The greatest reward is to follow the Prophet and spend all ten days and nights in the mosque (called *Sunnah Itikaf*). However, miniature versions are also possible. Depending on the scholarly opinion followed, the minimum could be one whole day and night, or even less, such as a few moments made with the intention of sincere worship and seclusion.

People wonder how on earth one can spend ten days and nights confined to the mosque. 'How do you spend the time? Don't you get bored?' are questions I have encountered. Interestingly the time passes remarkably quickly. If you make a plan at the outset of what you would like to accomplish, you find amazingly there is not enough time to get done what you wish. All prayers will be in congregation which is of great benefit but

---

[117] Unless some exceptional calamitous reason.

that also takes time. Then any recitation of Quran you wish to do, or memorisation, plus understanding the meaning will take up a large portion of time, as will making *duas*, as many as you can, plus making *dhikr* and *salawat* (asking for blessings on the Prophet). This is great time, there are no worldly distractions and one is simply focussed on Allah.

Bottom Line:

• Fasting is not just abstaining from food, drink and intimate relations but about spiritual and character upliftment.

• Ramadan is a highly blessed month when fasting is obligated on healthy adults.

• Allah's rewards for fasting are especially magnanimous.

• The Prophet fasted a great deal and encouraged it.

• *Laylatul Qadr* is the most blessed night of the year, hidden in the last 10 nights of Ramadan. Worship in these nights carries astronomical rewards. It is not to be missed.

• *Itikaf* is a retreat in the mosque for the last 10 days of Ramadan to try and secure this night.

Hajj (the Major Pilgrimage)

Every adult Muslim is obligated to undertake Hajj, the Major Pilgrimage, once during their lifetime. This means traveling to Mecca before the Hajj period starts. The dates of Hajj are fixed from the 8th until the 13th of the Islamic month of Dhul Hijjah. The rites of the pilgrimage are performed in Mecca and its adjacent precincts, with the plain of Arafat being most important. In fact being in Arafat on the 9th of Dhul Hijjah is the absolute requirement of Hajj. Missing this for any reason means no Hajj. The pilgrimage is undertaken in a state of consecration, called *ihram*, with men wearing two white pieces of unstitched cloth, one to cover the lower body, and other the upper body. Women's *ihram* attire is different; they wear unpatterned clothes, as their modesty necessitates that their whole body be covered.

There is immense reward for simply being within the boundaries of the Haram[118], which is the Holy precinct containing Mecca. All good deeds and acts of worship are rewarded multifold. Prayer within the Haram, the area containing the Kaba, carries the reward of 100,000 times than usual. And most significantly, an accepted Hajj leads to forgiveness of all of one's sins, but with important caveats (see below). 'Accepted' means done in the right way in the right spirit so that the Almighty gives it a tick. It can be seen yet again the mercy and kindness of Allah's paradigm. He has obligated Hajj on those able, and then rewards them in abundance for fulfilling His order.

There is a critical poignancy to Hajj. Everyone is dressed the same and doing the same thing, there is nothing to set anyone apart in this thronging multitudinous crowd. Your job, your education, the prestige you enjoy in your community or at work, your wealth, your home, your nobility, your family, servants you may have, the good things you enjoy in life – none of this matters and none of this is apparent, nor distinguishes you here. Standing and moving along in the vast sea of white-robed pilgrims emblazons upon you just how you are one insignificant being amongst millions of others. And you are all calling out to your Lord, '*Labaik Allahuma labaik*' – 'I am here, My Lord I am here'. But you see that you are one voice amongst millions of others there, and in fact an insignificant voice among the billions of the human race. Why should Allah hear you? The reality of our existence is driven home. Obedience to Allah and doing all we can to please Him are what we hope for now. Of course Allah hears every one, He is the *As-Samee* (All-Hearing) and He responds to everyone, He is the *Al-Mujeeb* (The Responder). But we cannot escape our reality: our complete and utter dependence on the Creator, and our desperate hope that we have succeeded in pleasing Him.

---

[118] This is distinct to *haram* (pronounced haraam) which means prohibited.

This also mimics to a tiny degree that setting and feeling of the Day of Judgement when all mankind will be gathered up after resurrection for accountability. No worldly privileges will avail anyone at that time. One will be a lost face in an infinite crowd of souls. Their desire to please Allah and their obedience will hopefully have culminated in a sound heart and an abundance of good deeds, which will be all that count on that Day.

Also inescapable during Hajj is just how all mankind is equal. Namely there is no superiority of any race over another. People of all nations and races are there together embarking on the same humble mission. Hajj is a strong reminder that all mankind are brothers and sisters, and is a vivid message against racism (recall *Equality amongst Makind*).

Hajj is patience

This cannot be overstated. In the modern age, there are more than two million people who descend on the city of Mecca for Hajj every year. There is enormous congestion. What would take a few seconds to do usually, takes several minutes to several hours. For example, a short walk of a few hundred metres that would take no more than half a minute, can take half an hour simply due to the congestion. Processing at the airport, normally a matter of 30 to 45 minutes, can take the whole day, quite literary. Patience is needed in abundance. One should start off with an expectation that everything will move along very slowly, and that this will be a training opportunity in developing patience. One should also expect that things will not go according to plan, an inevitability given the sheer volume of people in the same limited boundaries trying to do the same thing, in the same time period.

Perform Hajj as early in life as possible

Hajj is incumbent on all adult Muslims who have the money and adequate health. The reward of Hajj is forgiveness of all of one's sins, with the person returning with a clean slate like that of a newborn baby. Many Muslims, especially from the Subcontinent, therefore hold back on going for Hajj in the misguided belief that going late in life is better, as then all of one's lifetime of sins will be forgiven. This is a terrible mistake for several reasons.

Firstly, Hajj is mandatory. If one has the money and the health, it is incumbent to go. If a person dies before they managed to perform Hajj, though they had the opportunities and the means during their lifetime, they have failed in this obligation and will have to answer to Allah for this disobedience. Everything in this world is transient. Money can be lost, health can be lost, and opportunities may fail to come in the future (recall from before, *Make Use of Five Before Five*). Umar, the close Companion of the Prophet and the second ruler (Caliph) to succeed him said: 'Whoever is able to do Hajj but does not do Hajj, then it is all the same whether he dies as a Jew or a Christian.'[119] This hits the point home – skipping Hajj in one's lifetime when the opportunity was there is akin to being a non-Muslim.

Secondly, Hajj is a spiritually uplifting experience and should be a turning point in one's life. Improvement in worship and character should be of the fruits of one's Hajj. Hajj helps steer a person's outlook and vision. This should be capitalised upon as early as possible in life, to make sure life's trajectory is correct. Not discovered close to one's time of departure from this earth, whereupon there will be great regret as to how most of one's life was squandered.

Thirdly, Hajj is physically taxing. Performing the rites involves a lot of walking and traveling. This is of no concern when one is young and fit. But it is a completely different matter when there is even the slightest joint trouble or health issue. A slightly arthritic knee playing up can end up with the person doing Hajj in a wheelchair. Undertaking long walks on uneven terrains in blistering hot weather amongst great congestion becomes insurmountable even with a slightly dodgy toe. A blister acquired on the foot can transform the whole Hajj into an arduous affair.

---

[119] Tafseer Ibn Kathir

Finally, the sins referred to here that get forgiven are those sins committed against Allah, such as missing prayers, or fasts, ungratefulness (which will be abundant), *NOT* sins committed against fellow men. This is why people setting out for Hajj call up everyone they know beforehand and seek their forgiveness, especially those they have wronged. And it is not enough to simply ask their forgiveness. If they have wronged someone, they need to make amends in addition to asking for forgiveness. For example, if they have cheated someone out of money, they need to repay this too. Just asking for forgiveness, but not expecting to amend the wrong, simply demonstrates insincerity.

Try and correct the basics of your recitation

When undertaking Hajj, one tries to perform it in the best manner. You want to get it just right. During Hajj you will be praying extensively, reciting Quran, and making copious *dua* (supplications). Our recitation of Quran should be sound. Ideally one should have learnt the correct pronunciation of the Arabic letters (termed *makharij*) and rules of Quranic recitation (called *tajweed*). This requires studying with a sound teacher. Although many Muslims, especially those from the Indian subcontinent, have undertaken a 'complete' recitation of the Quran, usually as children, often they never learnt the correct pronunciation or recitation. It is important to rectify this in its own right as it impacts one's basics of worship such as *salat*. There are several similar letters in Arabic with subtle differences in pronunciation. There are many words where, getting the pronunciation wrong, dramatically changes the meaning. One should not have a spent a lifetime of *salat* (ritual prayer) insulting God rather than praising Him!

However, when the opportunity for Hajj arrives, these things may not have been achieved by then. As a minimum, one should learn the correct pronunciation of the Arabic letters, and the correct recitation of the ritual prayer (*salat*) which will include the crucial Quranic *surah*s (i.e. *al-Fatiha* and *al-Ikhlas*, Chapter 112). This can be done relatively quickly, even as an emergency measure, and will save one from making gross errors.

The Kaba

The large black cube-shaped building that Muslims circumambulate is called the Kaba. It is black on account of the specially made thick black cloth that shrouds it, called the Kiswah. The Kaba also gives the direction for the ritual prayer; the salat is performed with the face and body towards the Kaba, this direction being called the *qibla*. It is important to note that the Muslims do *not* worship the Kaba itself. The Kaba serves as an epicentre for prayer direction or circumambulation. Muslims often refer to it as the house of Allah, but, of course, it does not house the Almighty. The reference here is that it is a sacred building.

What is the need for the Kaba? Imagine there was no holy land, and no holy epicentre. When Muslims offer congregational prayer, how would they organise themselves? Line up and face a random direction? What about those in the holy land (called the Haram, in Mecca), where would they face? Congregational prayer is highly encouraged, but without a *qibla* it would be a chaotic affair, with different people facing different directions. Man needs direction in life, not just spiritually but also physically. The Kaba gives that physical direction. It also instils unity and forges cohesiveness amongst Muslims, creating a sense of community. Community is a powerful concept and ideal in Islam, as we shall cover at the very end of this book . In ritual prayer, Muslims line up facing the *qibla*, and move in unison led by the leader of the prayer, the imam. Where thousands pray together, this is a majestic sight to behold.

The Kaba and the holy precinct also offer a place where one can escalate their worship, or plead for help to the maximum. Those going through particularly difficult hardship, or those who simply want to gain the most reward, put their money, time and effort to traveling here. The Prophet himself used to press himself up against the wall of the Kaba and would weep as he begged for Allah's help.

Umrah – the lesser pilgrimage

This is the voluntary and supererogatory pilgrimage. Unlike Hajj, it can be performed any time of the year, and it is confined to the precinct of Mecca. It comprises donning the *ihram* (the garment and state), performing *tawaaf* (circumambulation) seven times around the Kaba, followed by the *saee* (pacing back and forth between the hills of Safa and Marwa, a total of seven times). Being in the holy precinct multiplies all good actions including prayer exponentially, as well as dramatically increasing the chances of supplications being accepted.

Bottom Line:

• Hajj, the major pilgrimage, is obligated on all adult Muslims.

• Hajj is all about patience.

• Hajj should be undertaken as early as possible in life.

• At a minimum, ensure the basics of your recitation are sound.

• Hajj is a turning point in one's life.

• Both Hajj and Umrah, the minor pilgrimage, carry great rewards.

• The Haram is the holiest and best place to beg Allah for whatever one wishes.

PART IV:
FURTHER GENERAL
PRINCIPLES

The Importance of Intention

Actions are judged by intention. {Sahih Bukhari, Sahih Muslim}

The degree of reward for a good deed and its value in the sight of Allah is influenced by the person's accompanying intention. For a deed to be accepted *fully* by Allah and *rewarded to the highest level*, the deed needs to have been done for the sake of seeking Allah's pleasure alone. Nothing more. This is true altruism.

What appears to be a good deed can be discounted, or even worse, marked as a sin, if the accompanying intention was disingenuous, had a secondary agenda or was even malevolent. Say, a person gives charity, not out of genuine help, but to be seen as a philanthropist and known as generous by society. Showing-off risks converting this into a sin for him. A celebrity turns up to a soup kitchen to help feed the homeless. Paparazzi and media turn up for what was really a photo opportunity and a publicity show, no sincere concern for the homeless. This is an unworthy deed, compared to one who turns up discretely, without any media, purely out of a sense of giving back to the less fortunate. A maths tutor coaches super bright, underprivileged children for free, knowing they will outperform the exams, his reputation will skyrocket, after which he can start charging exorbitant fees.

It is vitally important that we mind our intention when undertaking good deeds. Are we really doing this for goodness' sake, or are we doing this for our own (hidden) benefit? A good deed may indeed benefit us, secondarily, which is entirely acceptable. But our primary intention must have been altruistic. If the 'good' deed is being done for an ulterior purpose, reflection on the intent should prompt its correction, and if necessary, of the action as well.

Intention can also become corrupted with time. So what started out with genuine intentions surreptitiously morphs into something rotten. For instance, you start a soup run project in a sincere effort to help the homeless. After becoming known for this in the community, this endeavour becomes more about your reputation as a humanitarian and less about altruism. If the project has to come to an end after some years and your thoughts are, 'What will people say about me now?' rather than, 'How will these needy people get help now?' then the intention has perished. It is imperative to continuously review one's intention. It is as prone to insidious corruption, just as humility is to erosion.

Finally, by having the right intention, you change what are worldly acts that are not in themselves acts of worship, into acts of worship. For example, going to work. You go to work to earn a living. This is a necessary and permissible act, but is not an act of worship per se, such as ritual prayer. But if you make the intention that you are going to work to earn a clean living, which will put food on the table for you and your family, and it is being done to seek Allah's Pleasure, this becomes an act of worship. This is yet another tremendous mercy from the Almighty. Another example is eating. We all need to eat, the act itself has no value of worship, it is neither rewarded nor sinful. But if the intention is to eat healthily in order to be fit and active, seeking to please Allah by contributing to your family, department and society, then eating has been turned into an act of worship. This is incredibly powerful as it transforms ordinary non-worshipful life, such as sleeping, eating, drinking, work, study, play, spending time with family, etc which is the majority of one's time, into ongoing acts of worship, which is the purpose of man's creation. See Figure 5. What a great gift from Allah!

Intention is Also Rewarded in Itself

Having a sincere intention, but not having the means or opportunity, to achieve the deed, is accepted and rewarded by Allah the same as if the person had actually done the deed. This is the Mercy of the Almighty. A colleague's car breaks down, and you and some others offer him a lift home. He chooses to go with someone else, but as your concern was genuine, you receive the reward as though you had taken him home yourself. You see a mother with her toddler in a stroller getting ready to tackle some stairs at the train station. As you advance to offer her help with the stroller, someone else pips you to it. You are rewarded the same as the guy who lugged the pushchair up the steps. This even extends to giving charity. If you do not have the wealth yourself, but, on seeing someone in need, you sincerely wished you had the money to help them, you receive the same reward as though you had actually given the alms.

This is profoundly important. Firstly it is a great mercy that you can be rewarded where you actually did not manage to do the deed. Secondly, knowing that you will be rewarded for genuine intention, means you will not be fixated on being the one who delivers. This builds true team-players. If someone else can score the goal easier, you pass the ball without any hang-ups. It also builds great leaders. You are working for the true betterment of the team, not for your own glory, so you manage your team in the best way to achieve success.

Bottom Line:

• Our real intention influences the value of our deeds.

• Check, and correct your intention if necessary, before doing a deed.

• Periodically review your intention for ongoing deeds to avoid its corruption.

• Sincere intention, even without doing the action, is rewarded in of itself.

• Aligning our intention with what pleases Allah, changes ordinary worldly actions into worshipful actions.

Figure 5a: Different aspects of life

In the diagram the box represents the life of a typical young male adult who is studying at university. The different activities of his life are represented by circles of different sizes in proportion to the waking time spent on them. 'Islam' for the young man comprises just salat (ritual prayer) on a daily basis. Islam is therefore a very small component of his life.

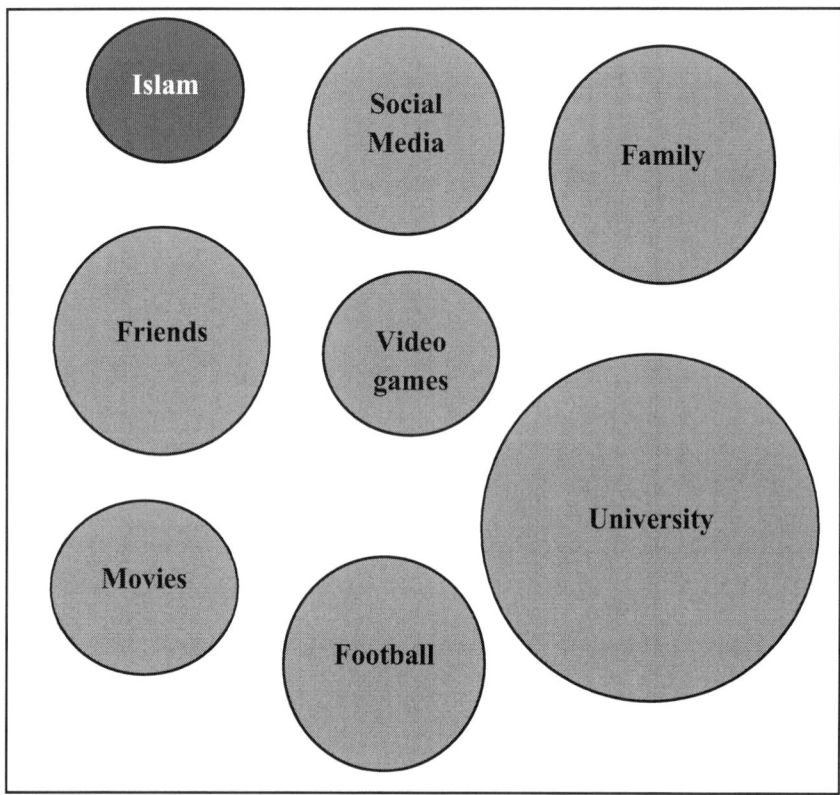

Figure 5b: Reviewing and making the right intentions

He has made an intention to undertake his activities to please Allah and follow His Command. Now, his studies, family time, time with his friends, leisure time, sports have become about making himself a better person through education, physical exercise or being of service to family or friends. The intention has now changed all of his life activities and thus his whole life into 'Islam' – worship of Allah.

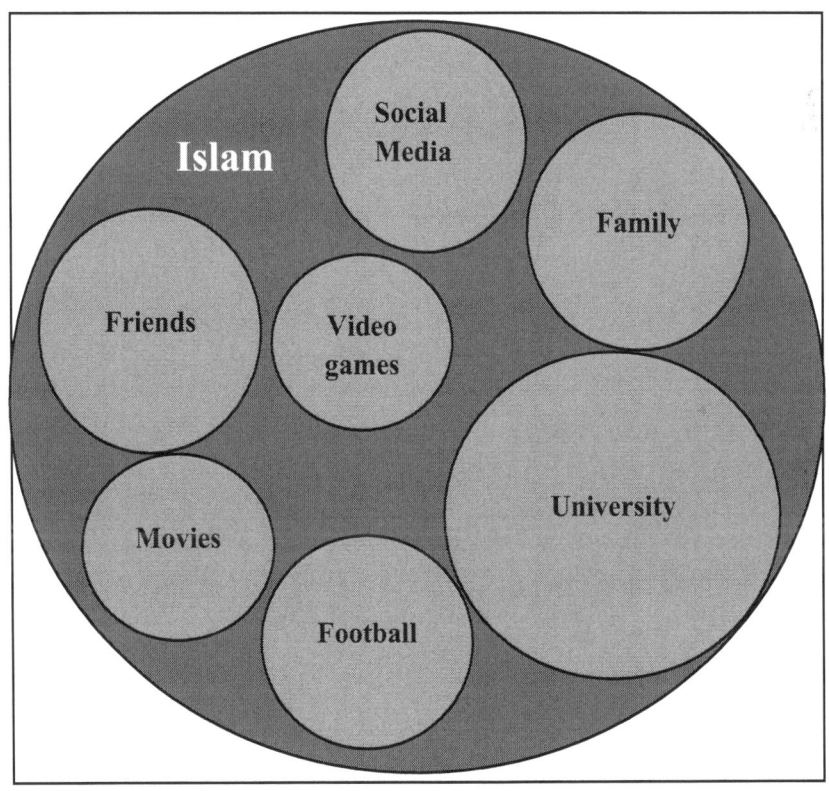

Thankfulness (*Shukr*)

Thankfulness is acknowledging that someone has done something good for you. Thanking Allah is one of the absolute cornerstones of worship. Why is this so? When one starts to try to comprehend just how much Allah does for us, deep and sincere gratitude will burgeon and lead to love for the Creator. Love for the Creator will lead to a desire to please Him and obey Him. Man unfortunately preoccupies himself with his desires. The need for a specific job, home, wife / husband, school for their child, or simply material possessions. It can be the need to be in control – a particular thing needs to be done in a particular way. When these fail to materialise, complaints and grumpiness ensue, manifest externally, internally or both. Allah actually provides for each person in extraordinary abundance, more than one can enumerate. Knowing that man loses sight of the bigger picture, obsessing with that one thing he did not get, Allah spells out:

> *And if you try to count the favours of Allah, never would you be able to count them. Truly, Allah is Most Forgiving, Most Merciful. {Quran 16: 18}*

In fact, Allah provides for us a tremendous amount we do not even think about, and we take for granted. Unfortunately, man is prone to ungratefulness, and Allah repeatedly points out in the Quran, thirteen times in fact, how 'most of mankind are ungrateful', or 'how little thanks they give'. We need to take a step back, and appreciate what we *do* have, not what we do not have. The Prophet expounded:

> *The one (among you) who wakes up secure in his place, healthy in his body and has his food for the day, it is as if the whole world were brought to him. {Sahih Bukhari}*

In other words, a person with decent health, enough food for the day, a place of residence, and living in a land of peace and security, as most do in the developed countries, is like the king of the world. Man's nature is to take everything around him for granted. Some reflection and mindfulness exercises are required to break this heedless robotic persona. In fact, Allah undertakes this for us several times:

> *Say: it is He who has created you and endowed you with hearing and seeing and hearts. Little thanks do you give.* *{Quran 67: 23}*

Just how important is our sight to us? Reflect on this. Suppose a billionaire falls blind and needs a living person to donate both his eyes to him to regain his sight. If we were offered £100,000 for our eyes would we accept that? How about one million pounds? How about one billion pounds? Is there any amount of money that we would accept to give them up? How priceless are our eyes that we would not give them up for all the money in the world – literally. We actually own something truly priceless yet do we reflect on this or give profuse thanks.

Alternatively try a simple exercise: don a blind fold for just half an hour one day and try to carry on your normal day. Without our vision, life would grind to an excruciating halt, so dependent are we on our vision. Similarly our hearing is invaluable. Yet, Allah is pointing out, we do not stop to ponder this at all, and worse we do not give thanks for this. Those who lose their sight or hearing, plunged into permanent visual or aural darkness, know exactly the magnitude of these favours from Allah.

> *Then He made his (man's) offspring from worthless fluid (i.e. semen). Then He fashioned him in due proportion and breathed into him the soul; and He gave you hearing, sight and hearts. Little is the thanks you give.* *{Quran 32: 8-9}*

Here Allah is describing the development of the fertilised egg to produce a baby which is then fashioned and shaped into a child and then adult. When your child is born it is mind boggling to contemplate how a single cell gave rise to countless cells, each of which determined what sort of cell it needed to be, and migrated to the right place to be so. Imagine the ear cells migrated to the place for the nose, so an ear is found where the nose should have been and vice versa. Cells organise to form organs perfectly, and everything ties up in sublime synchrony to produce a human being.

As your child grows it is awe inspiring how their body grows, and how the body proportions change to match. The child learns about the world around them, and gains skills, intellect and emotions. How incredible it is to watch their expressions form and change. They learn to smile, lift their eyebrows, wrinkle their nose. One day your little child goes from very basic sentences to throwing in the word 'actually' for the first time, leaving you spell bound. This should lead one to give thanks for a majestic process that is smooth, beautiful and gives rise to one's progeny.

If we step back even further we see other favours of Allah that do not even enter our minds. The fashioning of the earth itself. The earth has land that we can walk on, and a sky that serves as a canopy and protects us.[120] Most of the planets in our solar system do not afford this. The alternation of night and day[121] – who thinks about this? Yet if we had constant daylight it would be impossible to get any rest and sleep. Sunny places would, in fact, becoming baking hot infernos from the relentless heat. And where there was constant darkness, there would be freezing cold conditions and going out to earn a living would be extremely challenging. Both of these habitats would be uninhabitable. Life would only be possible at the watersheds of where these two meet.

Acknowledging Allah's favours and thanking Him is embedded into the purpose of our creation. It is also the command of Allah:

> *Therefore remember Me. I will remember you, and be grateful to Me (for My countless favours on you) and never be ungrateful to Me. {Quran 2: 152}*

> *Why should Allah punish you if you have thanked (Him) and believed in Him. And Allah is All-Appreciative and All-Knowing. {Quran 4: 147}*

The Prophet provided a glimpse of the scale of thanks we need to give. He

---

[120] Quran 2:22
[121] Quran 28:73

told his Companions that every person must give a charity for every joint in their body.[122] A charity here was not referring to financial charity per se but he explained it as being any good deed, such as saying a good word to someone, smiling at someone, or removing something harmful from the path. As we know today, there are approximately 360 joints in the human body, which equates to a lot of good deeds needed daily. And that is just for the joints in our body! Not our sight, our hearing, or health, or family, or education, or home, or wealth, or food and drink. So we need to be as profuse in our thanks as possible, because we can never be thankful enough. Recognising one's inadequacy in this regard, the prophets used to supplicate Allah to help them be as thankful as possible[123], and we can make use of these supplications ourselves (see *masnoon dua* earlier).

As with all of Allah's commands, obedience is met with magnified generosity. For being grateful, Allah actually promises to further increase the provision:

> *And (remember) when your Lord proclaimed: 'If you give thanks, I will give you more (of My blessings); but if you are thankless, verily, My punishment is indeed severe. {Quran 14: 7}*

Someone sincerely grateful for the wealth they have, will find it increases. The one truly grateful for success in their work, will find their success increases. One should be very fearful of the reverse – if Allah can give easily, He can take away easily too. Imagine a person in the prime of their life, healthy, fit, with a good home, job and family. One day there is a car accident and they find themselves paralysed from the waist down. Life changed in an instant. Or their spouse is suddenly diagnosed with incurable cancer. Or a terrible business deal leads to bankruptcy and homelessness overnight. One of the worst cases I have seen personally was a man whose wife left him, he lost his job, and was diagnosed with a very large tumour of the food pipe (oesophagus), all simultaneously. If one is unable to feel

---

[122] Sahih Bukhari, Sahih Muslim
[123] Quran 27: 19

gratitude that generates love and obedience to the Creator, then the minimum starting point is to give thanks, and strive for obedience, in fear of what could be taken away.

Being grateful is a matter of the heart, the tongue and the body. It is a state of heart, true sincere gratitude, recognising astounding generosity and compassion, bestowed without any worthiness on our part. It is also something to be verbalised, with the use of sayings (*dhikr*) such as '*Alhamdulillah*', which means 'All praise and all thanks belong to Allah'. This is repeated frequently in the Quran, and is built into the ritual prayer (see *Constant Remembrance of Allah with Dhikr*). When a Muslim is asked how they are, they say 'Good, *Alhamdulillah*'. Finally, gratefulness of the body is to obey Him, and undertake actions in accordance with what pleases Him, namely good deeds.

Thanking people for what they do for you is also not to be neglected. The Prophet taught that:

> He who does not thank people does not thank Allah. *{Sunan Abu Dawoud}*.

We must acknowledge good turns that others do for us. This fosters good relations, and good communities.

A great modern day example of gratitude is the story of the South African Paralympic swimmer, Achmat Hassiem, who won bronze medal in the 100m butterfly at the 2012 Paralympics in London, whilst also setting a new South African record. In 2006, a great white shark bit off his leg whilst he was swimming with his younger brother and some friends, off a beach in Cape Town. The shark had initially been heading for his younger brother, but upon seeing it, Achmat distracted it away by splashing, which drew the shark to himself. He survived the attack with the loss of a leg but then went on to become a Paralympic swimmer representing his country.

Most people would have viewed that shark attack as a terrible life changing event, and indeed Achmat talks of how at first he became extremely depressed. But now he is grateful: 'There are still nights where I sit down and thank God I survived the attack and have had all these experiences. People say sorry, but the rewards that have come are amazing. Losing a leg is nothing compared to losing a brother.' [124] Not only is he is acknowledging and giving thanks that his younger brother survived though it cost him his leg, he also is appreciating how that incident brought him benefits. The rewards, Achmat explained, being 'opportunities to represent my country, to change the world. It took me from being a little kid with dreams to actually being a little kid who has achieved all those dreams.'[125] His story also highlights how there is actually good in what seems bad; this is Allah's Wisdom, and how He always does good for His creation, though this can take time to appreciate. Achmat has gone on to become an environmental champion and an advocate for great white shark conservation. Imagine that, supporting the animal that chewed off his leg!

Bottom Line:

• Thankfulness to Allah is one of the key reasons man was created.

• Gratitude to Allah is acknowledging His prolific favours upon us, which leads to love for Him.

• Allah commands us to be thankful to Him.

• At a minimum, be thankful out of fear that Allah can take away things as easily as He gives.

• Being grateful is a matter of the heart, the tongue, and the body.

• The more we thank Allah, the more He gives.

• Deep reflection should lead us to feel that 'I am the luckiest person alive'.

---

[124] https://bit.ly/33SUeGX
[125] https://bit.ly/33M89ia

Taqwa (God-consciousness)

Taqwa **is a** *constant state of wanting to please Allah all the time.* **This** necessitates an ever-present awareness of Allah, seeking to do what He has commanded, and avoiding what He has prohibited. Every moment is about pleasing the Almighty. This state of heart and mind is the goal of the worshipper. We now see how many different facets of Islam gel together. Our purpose of creation is to remember Allah at all times. There is first of all the commanded five daily ritual prayers to ensure junctures throughout the day to stop and connect with Allah. There are the *masnoon duas* (supplications) for all different times of day and various acts to facilitate this remembrance in the manner of the prophets. There is *dhikr*, phrases for the remembrance and praise of Allah, which can be used at any moment, and are used throughout the day.

For every single action there is consideration if this will please Allah, and only if it will, then it is undertaken. So actions that are either obligated, recommended or permissible are undertaken. The first two are acts of worship but the permissible acts are changed into acts of worship too by ensuring correct intention (namely seeking to please Allah) and making supplications beforehand, such as *'Bismillah'* ('In the Name of Allah…'). Those actions that will displease Him are avoided – this means the discouraged ones as well as the prohibited.

In every second and in every moment, *taqwa* is about seeking Allah's Pleasure. All of creation is a reminder to them about the wonders of God, and so praise and gratefulness are foremost in the mind, and on the tips of their tongue. Appreciating the sun and how it powers the earth despite its great distance from the earth; the rain and how crucial it is to bring life to crops and vegetation; trees and plants, and how they provide the earth with oxygen; even insects and how the Creator packs amazing complexity into such tiny creatures.

Even eating and sleeping become about God. How is this so? Because of intention – when eating, one is thinking about consuming a diet that is conducive to health. This might sound odd, but one can eat either for health or for pleasure. For those brought up on standard modern diets, these are virtually disparate groups. The vast majority of people in affluent countries eat for pleasure, hence the booming health crises of obesity, type II diabetes, hypertension, heart disease, etc. I would recommend the reader to read Raymond Francis' book '*Never be sick again – health is a choice*'. The second half of his title says a lot – 'health is a choice'. You are what you eat. Our diet plays a tremendous role in our overall health. A healthy body is firstly looking after the loan of the body Allah gave, and secondly a healthy person can do more in terms of good deeds and contributing to his family and society. Also when you eat, you are grateful for what Allah has provided for you. Slowly adjusting one's eating to a healthy pattern will change one's tastebuds as well – the usual modern tasty treats become unpalatable, and helps one to keep off the preservative, toxic-ridden, processed modern diet.

Sleep is no longer a matter of 'I'm tired now, time to go to sleep'. Instead, one sleeps because they are now inefficient at achieving actions that will please Allah. One goes to sleep in order to rest and to recharge oneself ready to undertake good deeds again the next day. The same goes for entertainment and taking a break. The purpose is to recharge oneself mentally or physically. This could be doing some sport, which as well as re-invigorating oneself also aids physical fitness and health. It could be watching a drama or movie. The entertainment needs to be permissible; watching a movie with scantily clad women, or worse, scenes of gratuitous sex is not permissible. Entertainment needs to be in moderate doses, just like sleep, and food. If all day is spent watching television, or browsing social media or the internet, this is not taking a break, it is time wasting.

Those who are in the state of *taqwa* are called *mutaqoon* or *mutaqeen* (the slight difference in these terms is grammatical - *mutaqoon* refers to them in when they are subject, *mutaqeen* when they are in the object). There are numerous references to those who achieve this state in the Quran. The idea is actually beautifully captured by the imagery one Companion of the

Prophet, Ubay ibn Ka'b, gave to explain *taqwa*.[126] A man dressed in a fine shawl is about to pass through a narrow path lined by thorny bushes. He could get pricked or his fine shawl could get torn. How would he get through this and how would he handle his expensive shawl? By wrapping it tightly around himself and pulling his arms close to his body, treading extremely carefully looking out that his body and clothes are not catching on the thorns with each step. This tremendous diligence is *taqwa*. The path is the journey of life and the thorns are all the traps to catch one out. Every single step is taken with great caution and care.

Those who can excel in *taqwa* and are *mutaqoon* are clearly on the successful path, as they are actively engaged in constant remembrance and worship of Allah. It is not surprising, therefore, to find that Allah mentions this quality, and those who have this quality, more than 60 times in the Quran, frequently revealing that this is the station to aspire to, how He is pleased with the *mutaqoon* and how they are the successful ones:

> ...*Indeed, Allah loves the* **mutaqeen**. *{Quran 3: 76}*

> *Indeed, the most noble of you in the sight of Allah is* **the most righteous of you**. *{Quran 49: 13}*

Bottom Line:

- *Taqwa* is a constant state of wanting to please Allah all the time.

- Actions are undertaken only if they will please Allah.

- Actions that will displease Allah are avoided.

- Every moment is spent remembering, praising and obeying Allah.

---

[126] Tafsir Ibn Kathir

Forgiveness

Out of man's imperfect nature, it is unavoidable he will sin. Allah has therefore prescribed seeking His forgiveness. The sins are not to be confessed, on the contrary they are kept to oneself. One directly supplicates to Allah to be forgiven. The Prophet advised even he used to supplicate for forgiveness 70 times daily, and we should do the same.[127] Allah has three different names relating to His attribute of forgiving (*Al Ghufoor, Al Ghaffaar, Al 'Afuww*). He loves to forgive man. It should be noted that this forgiveness is not to do with the idea of original sin i.e. of Adam and Eve, as seen in other faiths. Adam and Eve were forgiven even before being sent down to the earth. It is due to man's constant nature to make mistakes. Allah says:

> *O son of Adam were you to come to Me with your sins reaching up to the sky, and you were to ask Me for forgiveness, then I will forgive you. {Sunan at-Tirmidhi }*

This is a great trait of Allah. And He wants to see man demonstrate this quality too. Allah says about the righteous ones:

> *... and let them pardon and overlook. Would you not like that Allah should forgive you? And Allah is Forgiving and Merciful. {Quran 24: 22}*

This particular verse was revealed after Abu Bakr, a great Companion of the Prophet, decided to cancel a charitable stipend for a destitute relative who had engaged in public slander of his daughter, Aisha, who was also one of the wives of the Prophet. The natural response for any person in Abu Bakr's shoes would have been to cancel their financial support. After all the man is committing evil and biting the hand that feeds him. But Allah is telling Abu Bakr and all of us, if you want to receive Allah's Forgiveness, then you too should be forgiving of others *regardless* of

---

[127] Bukhari. Other narrations mention 100 times a day.

whether they seek your forgiveness, or amend their behaviour. Abu Bakr not only resumed his financial assistance but in fact increased it.

As mentioned earlier, Allah can forgive sins committed against Himself, such as missing prayer(s), or not fasting. But sins man commits against his fellow man, are settled with justice *between them*, until the victim is fully recompensed. Recall from *Accountability*, the wrong doer on the Day of Judgement will have to hand over the appropriate number of their good deeds to the one wronged, and if their good deeds have run out, then they must accept an appropriate number of sins from their oppressed victim. Here again, however, the supreme value of good character is seen. The one who has been wronged, but who chooses to forgive the wrongdoer, is granted enormous rewards including Paradise itself.

This was demonstrated by the story of the Companion of the Prophet who was quite average in his ritual worship, but was given the good news that he had been granted Paradise whilst still alive. The other Companions were surprised by this honour, as nothing overtly marked him out, and sought to determine his secret. After observing him for a while, eventually they conceded they could not identify the special quality. When he was asked directly his secret, he replied the only thing he did extra was, every night before going to bed, he forgave all the people who had wronged him that day[128].

Sincere forgiveness shows generosity and magnanimity. Such is the value of forgiveness in the Eyes of Allah, that the reward is Paradise. Why is this so? It is an immensely difficult thing to forgive someone who has wronged you. You are in the right, and that person has violated your rights. But it shows great humility and character to still forgive the violator, to neither hold a grudge nor to seek recompense on the Day of Judgement. It also shows great certitude in faith and in the coming of the Day of Judgement. You are doing this for Allah's sake alone.

---

[128] Musnad Ahmad

As with all of Allah's commands and guidance, there is also a worldly advantage. Allah says:

> *And not equal are the good deed and the bad. Repel (evil) by that (deed) which is better; and thereupon the one whom between you and him is enmity (will become) as though he was a devoted friend. {Quran 41: 34}*

Forgiveness is an act of exemplary kindness. As was seen with the conduct of the Prophet, tremendous kindness in the face of great wrongdoing melted many hearts. This can transform a bitter relationship to a friendly one. It can also re-awaken righteousness and goodness in an oppressor who had buried these deep down, and be the point they switch from a path of evil to one of virtue.

The recent story of Abdul-Munim Sombat Jitmoud exemplifies this action.[129] In 2015, his son, Salahuddin, was murdered whilst delivering a pizza order in Lexington, Kentucky (USA). During the sentencing of a man complicit in his son's murder, Mr Jitmoud took the stand and addressed 24 year old Trey Relford directly, telling him that he and his family forgave him. He counselled him and gave him hope: 'Don't worry, it's over, you have a new chapter in life. A new beginning. You have to go and do righteous deeds, and you can start in the confinement. When you come out in the real world in 31 years, you'll prepare yourself to be a productive person.' Consider that it was his son that was murdered in cold blood. The joy of his wife giving birth, then tending to the baby, feeding and cuddling him, his first smile, then crawling then walking, his first words. Playing with him, hearing his stories, comforting him, then school, teaching him about Islam. Watching him grow into a man, who has hopes and dreams, and makes his way to university. His son was doing pizza deliveries to make some income for his university studies. All finished in a few seconds of evil, for a few dollars.

---

129 https://wapo.st/2WLNGs5

How does someone produce this level of mercy in their heart? Mr Jitmoud understood just how important and elevated forgiveness is, in Islam, and applied it. 'Forgiveness is the greatest act of charity in Islam' he explained. His magnanimity, mercy and sincere kindness moved the guilty man to tears as well as his family. In fact the whole courtroom was reduced to tears including the judge, who had to call a recess to regain her composure. Mr Jitmoud went on to hug the remorseful and sobbing Trey, and comfort him as well as his family. The video of Mr Jitmoud in the Kentucky courtroom went viral in 2017 and is very powerful.[130]

Bottom Line:

• Allah is Supremely Forgiving. He loves to forgive and wants us to seek His Forgiveness.

• Allah wants us to display this trait as much as possible between ourselves as well.

• One should forgive others to gain forgiveness for oneself from Allah.

• Sincere forgiveness of others is rewarded with Paradise.

Repentance (*Tawbah*)

This is a level up from forgiveness. Here one is not just asking Allah for forgiveness, but there is profound remorse at having committed the sin. One stops that sin and also vows not to undertake the sin again. This is enormous in the eyes of Allah, who promises to forgive those who make sincere repentance. It should be noted sincere repentance is the *only* way to gain forgiveness for major sins. Where others have been wronged, part of repentance is to make amends to the wrong. In addition to sincerely apologising, this could be returning what rightfully belongs to someone else. Where someone cheated somebody in a financial deal, they need to

---

[130] https://bit.ly/2WPRUzl

make good the loss. If they have stolen something, it needs to be returned. If they tarnished somebody's reputation, they need to restore it.

The path of sin is one great trap. Everyone has an inbuilt inertia to performing sin, especially those that one knows are serious. It takes a great deal of effort to overcome this resistance. A person will undertake a sinful action thinking that this will be the one and only occasion they will do it, or they regard the sinful deed as not being a big deal ('everyone does it, so it can't be a big deal really'). Having done it once, it becomes easy to do it again. Then again and again. The natural inherent barrier is broken and it then becomes a habit. The risk is that it will then open the door to other sins. As these happen and become the norm, the person has moved far, far away from what pleases Allah. The most powerful trap of all is then waiting to seize them - hopelessness. The feeling that they are so far gone that Allah will never accept them no matter what now, can lead them to persist on the wrong path or worse, abandon their faith.

Take the example of alcohol. A young Muslim has never had a drink, but at university sees everyone 'enjoying' it. His friends nudge him along ('you don't know what you are missing'), so he gives it a go once. Having done it once, he tells himself, as do his friends, it's no big deal, so he does it again. He starts to enjoy this and it becomes a norm. Hanging out with girls becomes the routine too, and maybe even trying some drugs. Soon he falls into fornication. Having done this once, he does not feel so bad doing it again, and this becomes a regular thing. Now he is into alcohol, drugs, fornication, prayer has been abandoned, and Allah is not a consideration anymore. One day he reflects just how far away he is from the straight path, and thinks 'man, I am so low now, there is no coming back. Allah will never forgive me now.' He decides to leave Islam as 'there is no point' i.e. no salvation.

One of the most crucial things to realise is that no matter how removed one is from the right path, no matter how much sin anyone is engaged in, no matter how awful their lifestyle and crimes they have committed, the door to Allah is never closed. Even for the one who leaves Islam. Turning to Allah is always possible, and the doorway to Him is repentance. A sincere feeling of regret and seeking forgiveness is what is required. *There is never a situation of no hope. Even after initiating the effort, one might slip back again*, but there is still hope. There is always hope. Make the effort again. Islam is effort-centric.

The one who makes sincere repentance even for a heinous sin finds it not only forgiven, but actually erased. That means the sin is not even registered on their account as 'Sin was committed but has been forgiven'. It is expunged from the record, as though it had never been committed at all. Allah's Names include *Al-A'fuww*, the Eraser of sin. Allah not only accepts *tawbah* (repentance), with another of His Names being *At-Tawwaab* – the One who accepts repentance, but in fact He loves repentance:

> *Do they not know that it is Allah who accepts repentance from His servants and receives charities and that it is Allah who is At-Tawwaab [the Acceptor of repentance], the Merciful? {Quran 9: 104}*

> *... Indeed, Allah **loves** those who are constantly repentant and loves those who purify themselves. {Quran 2: 222}*

But Allah's Mercy is boundless of course. It is not enough for Allah that He expunges the sin. He actually transforms the sins into good deeds! How extraordinary is that!

> *Except for those who **repent**, believe and do righteous work. **For them Allah will replace their evil deeds with good**. And ever is Allah Forgiving and Merciful. {Quran 25: 68}*

One might get confused here. Sins are being turned into good deeds - what is going on here? Does that mean one gets to 'enjoy' this life by doing all the prohibited stuff (the drink, drugs, fornication, partying, etc) but then one makes sure to follow up with 'repentance' and so ends up with them converted into good deeds? This is a complete misunderstanding. Firstly no one knows when their life will end. If they die before their 'repentance' has happened then all of this stacks up as massive sin. More importantly, superficial 'repentance', verbalising something but not truly believing in it, is not repentance. Repentance by definition has to be sincere and from the heart but to make this absolutely clear Allah states:

> *O you who have believed, repent to Allah with **sincere** repentance… {Quran 66: 8}*

A person has to look into their own heart to know if they are being sincere or not. Also, if someone else has been harmed in the sin, amends must be made and forgiveness is needed from that person as well. Recall that while Allah forgives sins committed against Himself, He does not forgive the wrong committed against someone else. For that the oppressor must gain forgiveness from his victim.

True repentance for a sin has four parts:

1. A feeling of *genuine* guilt over the sin(s) committed

2. Asking Allah for forgiveness

3. A *sincere* resolve not to make that mistake again (and therefore immediately cease committing the sin)

4. If someone has been wronged, making amends with them. This means not just asking them for forgiveness but also correcting the wrong, or the damage.

Bottom Line:

• Repentance is an incredible tool from Allah to come back to Him, no matter what sin has been committed, or what level a person has sunk to.

• Sincere repentance is rewarded with those sins erased from the account.

• Allah also rewards sincere repentance by converting the sins into good deeds.

• Be extremely guarded against committing a sin for the first time; it is easy thereafter.

- There is no such thing as hopelessness. The lifeline of *tawbah* is always available.

- If someone has been hurt by the sin, repentance includes seeking forgiveness from that person as well making amends.

Three Gems

Having discussed thankfulness and forgiveness, there are three beautiful treasures to share. The first is the mother of remembrances for thankfulness, the second is the mother of supplications for forgiveness. The third I have included as it is a great way to start any endeavour and includes praise for Allah combined with a supplication for blessings for the Prophet (*salawat*). I have given the Arabic here for those who can recite Arabic as it will lead to the most correct recitation, as well as its transliteration for those not familiar with Arabic, so that they can be utilised right away, along with the meanings.

For thanks

One of the wives of the Prophet, Juwayriyyah explained that one day she remained praying in her place the whole morning from the dawn prayer onwards.[131] The Prophet had left her place at dawn and on returning at the forenoon and finding her in the same position as when he left her, revealed that there was a short supplication that repeated three times was weightier than all the prayers for the whole morning:

سُبْحَـانَ اللهِ وَبِحَمْـدِهِ عَدَدَ خَلْـقِهِ ، وَرِضَـا نَفْسِـهِ ، وَزِنَـةَ عَرْشِـهِ ، وَمِـدَادَ كَلِمَـاتِـهِ

'Subhaan Allah wa bi hamdihi, 'adada khalqihi, wa ridaa nafsihi, wazinata

---

[131] Sahih Muslim

'arshihi, wa midaada kalimaatihi'

'Glory and praise be to Allah, as much as the number of His creation, as much as pleases Him, as much as the weight of His Throne and as much as the ink of His words.'

For forgiveness

The Prophet Muhammad (︙[132]) declared the best supplication for seeking forgiveness to be:

اللَّهُمَّ أَنْتَ رَبِّي لا إِلَهَ إِلا أَنْتَ خَلَقْتَنِي وَأَنَا عَبْدُكَ وَأَنَا عَلَى عَهْدِكَ وَوَعْدِكَمَا اسْتَطَعْتُ أَعُوذُ بِكَ مِنْ شَرِّ مَا صَنَعْتُ أَبُوءُ لَكَ بِنِعْمَتِكَ عَلَيَّ وَأَبُوءُ لَكَ بِذَنْبِي فَاغْفِرْ لِي فَإِنَّهُ لا يَغْفِرُ الذُّنُوبَ إِلا أَنْتَ

'Allahumma Anta Rabbee, laa ilaaha illa Anta, khalaqtanee wa anaa 'abduka, wa anaa 'alaa 'ahdika wa wa'dika mastata'tu, a'udhu bika min sharri ma sana'tu, abu'u laka bini'matika 'alayya, wa abu'u bidhambi faghfir lee, fa innahu laa yaghfirudh-dhunuba illaa Anta.'

'O Allah! You are my Lord. There is no true God except You. You have created me, and I am Your slave, and I hold to Your Covenant as far as I can. I seek refuge in You from the evil of what I have done. I acknowledge the favours that You have bestowed upon me, and I confess my sins. Pardon me, for none but You has the power to pardon.'

What is the value of this particular supplication? It was explained the one who supplicates this during the day with firm belief in it and dies the same day, they will be one of the dwellers of Paradise; and if anyone supplicates this during the night with firm belief in it and dies before the morning, they

---

[132] Benediction for the Prophet in Arabic

will be one of the dwellers of Paradise.[133]

For beginning something

In starting any endeavour we begin with '*Bismillaahir Rahmaanir Raheem*'. But follow this with the below which is actually a *masnoon dua* made for entering a mosque. It combines seeking Allah's blessings in the work, as well as a *salawat*:

$$\text{بِسْمِ اللهِ، وَالصَّلاةُ وَالسَّلامُ عَلى رَسولِ اللهِ، اللّهُمَّ افْتَحْ لِي أَبْوابَ رَحْمَتِك}$$

'Bismillaahi was salaatu was salaamu 'alaa rasoolillaah. Allahummaf tahlee abwaaba rahmatik.'

'In the name of Allah, and prayers and peace be upon the Messenger of Allah. O Allah, open the gates of Your mercy for me.'

The combination of seeking Allah's blessings with prayers for the Prophet is beautiful and my personal exhortation is to use this liberally. It is also to be used when starting one's *duas*, as it is part of the etiquette of *dua* to praise Allah, and seek blessings for the Prophet, before one begins their requests to Allah.

Hope and Fear

Allah has created astonishing balance throughout the universe. In the movement of the Sun and the planets, the electron orbiting the nucleus of an atom, the homeostasis of the organs in the human body. Similarly there is exquisite balance in His prescribed way of life. The believer maintains an equipoise between hope and fear. Hope that Allah is Loving and

---

[133] Sahih Bukhari

Merciful and so will accept all the good deeds a person strived for. That his shortcomings in his deeds, and his sins will receive Allah's Mercy and he will be forgiven. This *by itself alone* would lead a person to live a hedonistic and disobedient life, as accountability has been lost: 'Paradise here I come'.

On the other hand, fear of Allah holding us to account, for sins committed, and inadequacies in our good deeds drives us to try harder and perfect our character and our actions. However, we can never be perfect, and will always fall short. Fear *by itself alone* would therefore lead us to despair and hopelessness. Depression and anxiety will result, or the person may even abandon faith, and turn to hedonism: 'No matter what, I am destined for Hell anyway, so I might as well just enjoy this life.'

It is not possible to have one without the other. Imbalance of these is seen in other faiths, or wayward sects of Islam. God is pure love and everything will be alright, dispenses with justice. God is punishing and everyone is damned, leads to extreme practices. The true way is to keep both in harmony. This is exemplified in the Quran in the very first Chapter (*Surah al-Fatiha* - the Opening), Allah introduces Himself as:

The Extremely Kind and Extremely Compassionate. {Quran 1: 3}

- demonstrating His profound Love and Mercy. This gives us hope. This is followed immediately by the next verse:

Owner of the Day of Judgement. {Quran 1: 4}

- demonstrating that there is accountability, and there will be justice based on our behaviour and actions; so we have fear too. The Quran also gives similar counsels elsewhere:

Call upon Him with fear and hope. {Quran 7: 56}

The Prophet also gave such advice. On visiting a sick boy at death's door, he inquired how he was.[134] The boy replied that he was in between hoping for Allah, and fearing for his sins. The Prophet reassured him that a believer having these two qualities resulted in Allah granting him what he hoped for, and protected him from what he feared.

Whatever Allah does for anyone has good in it. Hardships befall someone but they carry benefit in them though they may not see it. Frequently the benefit will become evident with time but sometimes it will remain unclear. At the time of the tribulation a person can feel overwhelmed and helpless. A reaction of 'why me?' can also easily lead to a grudge against Allah, 'why did He do this to me?' Negative opinions can set in about Allah.

Allah tells us that He is how His slave thinks of Him.[135] A good opinion of Allah is met with good from Him, whilst a poor opinion of Allah will be reflected back on the individual on the Day of Judgement when every soul will be desperate to receive Allah's mercy. The Muslim maintains an unshakeable belief that everything Allah does is for their betterment. And therefore they keep an unshakeable positive view of Allah.

So Allah responds to a person based on how that person views Allah. This even includes on the Day of Judgement. This might seem a little strange. A little reflection is called for here. A person who has cultivated a love of Allah, which is what Allah is seeking from everyone, will have a good opinion of Allah. Conversely a person who has spent their life rebellious against Allah will have malice in their heart for the Creator. So a person's opinion of Allah is actually a reflection of their state of heart and belief. This teaching is to remind people that Allah always does what is best for them.

---

[134] Sunan at-Tirmidhi, Sunan ibn Majah
[135] Sahih Bukhari

Bottom Line:

• A believer maintains a healthy balance of hope in Allah's Mercy and fear of Allah's Justice.

• This balance mirrors the balance Allah shows in His creation.

• Always keep a good opinion of Allah. Allah always does the best for each person.

Knowledge

The Prophet said:

> *Seeking knowledge is an obligation on all Muslims. {Sunan Ibn Majah}.*

Knowledge is emphasised, Allah comments on numerous occasions about the elevated status of those with knowledge. Knowledge can be of two types:

– knowledge of Islam: interpreting the Quran (called *tafseer*), studying hadith etc

– knowledge of worldly disciplines: science, mathematics, languages, medicine, engineering; essentially everything else.

Guidance from God takes the form of knowledge. Through the knowledge He provides us we learn who He is, what our life is about, what is to follow the life of this world, and what He has told us to do. This knowledge can be divided into what is essential, and the more scholarly. The essentials are what every Muslim needs to know to fulfil their obligations in this life (known as *fard ul ayn*): conducting themselves in the manner Allah likes, as well as how to undertake the ritual acts of worship. You don't know what you don't know. Allah has set the rules for man, and man needs to make sure he has learnt what they are. It is important not to fail in one's obligations because one remained ignorant.

Learning the essentials and the obligatory is clearly vital. For example, if one does not know how to calculate zakat, then they are at risk of not fulfilling this duty. If one does not know that *salat* (the ritual prayer) must be verbalised, their prayers will be invalid. The more scholarly knowledge relates to more specialised areas such as laws of inheritance or divorce, and will be an obligation on some members of the community so that when these issues crop up, there are people who can deal with them (known as *fard ul kifayah*). Islam is a vast ocean of knowledge, and the journey for its knowledge is lifelong and continues even after learning the basics.

It is obvious why this kind of Islamic knowledge would be obligatory. It is also apparent that the other type of knowledge, namely of worldly disciplines, can benefit humanity. Medicine will serve to treat the sick and improve health; engineers will construct bridges, dams or transport vehicles; architects will design buildings, and so on. However there is another crucial aspect to worldly knowledge beyond its worldly benefits.

The heart specialist studies the heart which leads to an ability to treat the patient with heart disease. But this study ***when combined with reflection*** culminates in marvelling at the design and function of the heart. Here is an organ, the size of a large orange, that pumps blood all around the body, taking the vital oxygen and nutrients to every organ. It beats approximately 80 times a minute, roughly 5000 times an hour, 120 000 times per day, 44 million times a year, and in a life time of 80 years, amounts to 3.5 billion heart beats. The heart muscle pumps without tiring, and its four valves function perfectly to achieve this. The moment this all fails and the heart stops, life comes to an end. What manmade engine can operate without a moment's break for 80 years at a stretch? One can only marvel at the amazing construction of this organ and the beauty of the One who created it.

This aspect of reflecting was not lost on the great scientists in history. Issac Newton in his study of physics marvelled at how the Creator had designed a universe with its precision and mathematical laws.

The importance Allah gives to us reflecting on the world around us is understood from the numerous times He mentions this in the Quran. For example, Allah says:

> *Do they not see the birds held (flying) in the midst of the sky? None holds them but Allah. Verily, in this are clear proofs and signs for people who believe.* {Quran 16: 79}

> *Do you not see that ships sail through the sea by the favour of Allah that He may show you of His signs? Indeed in that are signs for everyone patient and grateful.* {Quran 31: 31}

Reflecting on the Quran itself is also extremely important, what is termed *tadabbur* in Arabic:

> *(This is) a blessed Book which We have revealed to you, (O Muhammad), that they might **reflect upon its verses** and that those of understanding would be reminded.* {Quran 38: 39}

Note the examples Allah gives in the Quran are those readily visible and plain for all to see. At the time of the Prophet science barely existed. But with the advent of science and its prolific advancements we are able to *see* beyond the limits of our eyesight. Each discovery should prompt us to ponder on it; each bit of knowledge we gain should prompt us to reflect.

By studying creation, all worldly knowledge combined with reflection leads to an increased appreciation of Allah. The word '*ayat*' is used repeatedly in the Quran, 382 times in fact. This word is translated most conveniently to mean verse of the Quran or a sign, but it actually carries a much broader meaning. The heavens (i.e. universe), the earth, the bee, the birds held aloft in the sky, the camel, the ships and how they float on water, the rain from the sky, the sun and the moon in their defined orbits - Allah refers to all of these as *ayat* in the Quran. The Prophet Musa (Moses) is also referred to as *ayat*.

The word *ayat* actually means a pointer in creation that points to the Creator. All of creation is in fact an *ayat*, an evidence of Allah. Hence, studying *anything* in this world, and reflecting on it, will point to the

Creator, and His amazing and wondrous abilities.

A person's quest for knowledge both Islamic and worldly will be part of the journey of life. It should continue from cradle to grave. In fact one can see that this has been built into Islam; men are obligated to attend the Friday communal prayers where they are required to listen to the imam, who will deliver some points of Islamic learning. People should endeavour to continue their Islamic education in some shape or form, whether via formal means, such as through classes or teachers, or less formally, by attending talks, or reading reliable and credible authors. This has become a great deal easier now with the internet, allowing access to scholars through online courses or even teaching sessions directly with scholars (this is not the same as 'Google scholar', see below). One should try to learn as much as possible about everything they possibly can. Be hungry for knowledge.

Returning to Islamic knowledge, it should be noted that gaining Islamic knowledge needs teachers. Books are not adequate in themselves. Concepts need to be explained and discussed to understand them properly, something a book cannot do. Teachers also need to be sound and genuine. The context to the Quran and therefore its interpretation, comes through explanations of the Prophet (hadith) and his life history. The collections of hadith, such as Sahih Bukhari or Sahih Muslim, also have a context themselves and require explanation. A lay reader can undertake a solo reading of either the Quran or the books of hadith, but needs to understand that although this may be an enlightening and beneficial experience, it will be superficial and one is at risk of misinterpreting or confusing themselves.

Authentic knowledge is transmitted from person to person via a chain. Even the revelation of the Quran had transmission from Allah to the Prophet via the angel Jibreel (Gabriel). So what marks out an authentic scholar? They should have:

– a thorough knowledge of the sacred texts (Quran and hadith)

– a thorough knowledge of their contexts

– their knowledge should have an unbroken chain of teachers back to the Prophet himself

– an understanding of the reality of the world we live in, so the knowledge can be applied appropriately and judiciously

The first three criteria above determine authentic knowledge and, crucially, validate a scholar as being authentic (see later, *Common mistake Muslims make*). The fourth criteria determines their proficiency.

Many readers may wonder why there needs to be a lineage for the teacher. Let us consider this. Someone in need of a heart operation would never agree to surgery from a self-proclaimed heart surgeon who had taught himself from books alone, no matter how much of prodigious genius he may seem. You would want to see his credentials including where did he train i.e. who has he learnt from. A genuine surgeon would have obtained his knowledge and skill from his mentor surgeons who learnt from their teachers, who learnt from their teachers – a chain of knowledge. Sound knowledge of any teacher or professional always has a lineage to it, though we do not usually reflect on this.

Furthermore, Islamic knowledge (Quran and hadith) is ***sacred*** knowledge. The original teacher was the Prophet, who explained revelation exactly as it was meant to be interpreted, and he demonstrated it through his own character. This was passed directly to the Companions and then on to the next generation and so on. This is how it has been transmitted through the generations up until today, to authentic scholars and teachers. Divine revelation was not provided as just a book that anyone can pick up and read. It needed explanation, application and demonstration by a teacher (see *The Prophet as the Best Role Model*), which was essential, not optional. 'Scholars' who have no connection to an authentic lineage of teachers, such as orientalists (non-Muslim academics) or new age reformists, cannot be relied upon to explain revelation, as they never gained it from the original source, through a sound lineage, in the right manner.

The internet has been transformative in making knowledge accessible to the remotest corners of the world. It can be used to great benefit in gaining Islamic knowledge. One can now study with erudite scholars either through authentic institutions and courses, or directly using video or teleconferencing platforms. One needs to be discerning and check the credentials of the teachers and institutions. Beware of 'Google scholar' however: browsing the internet, watching YouTube videos and reading Facebook posts, etc to find rulings on what is permissible and what is prohibited, an exercise fraught with danger. Credible teachers are needed, who can teach and respond to questions students pose them and who can clarify concepts and issues. Isolated videos can be taken out of context. Dishonest 'scholars' can corrupt susceptible minds pulling Quranic verses or hadiths completely out of context. There can be no doubt that this has been one means of brainwashing swathes of disaffected Muslim youth into extremism and radical violence.

The Quran was revealed in the Arabic language. There is a reason for this, as with everything relating to the Quran. The language is deep and rich, profoundly so. It has a dazzling ability to convey incredible meaning and imagery. The Arabic of the Quran also has a profound ability to move people emotionally. Amazingly, this includes non-Muslims who do not speak Arabic, who have found themselves weeping though they do not understand what is being recited. I personally know of such a case where a non-Muslim then went on to convert to Islam. Studying the Quran and reflecting is an unending journey, a vast ocean without a bottom, and leads to profound appreciation of Allah.

For those born in the West, this is a difficult language. The letters are totally alien; reading it, writing it and trying to understand it seem monumentally tricky. However, as with everything in life, commitment and resolve is required. If one gained the promotion of a lifetime but to a foreign country and was required to learn the new language, one would do so. Those who have married a spouse from a different country who speaks a different language will learn their spouse's language. A similar approach is needed with Arabic. Perseverance will eventually pay off, especially if the intention is there to gain Allah's Pleasure.

Being able to recite the Quran and to do so correctly, brings tremendous satisfaction. Being able to understand it, is a game-changer, taking the relationship with the Quran to a different level altogether. Looked at in reverse, imagine standing before Allah on the Day of Judgement, and Allah asking how in a lifetime of 80 years, one could not find the time to learn the language He provided His Guidance in? Was one really too busy to understand the most important thing in their lives? One should try as best as possible. We can only make effort, Allah provides the results. Our effort is all we are accountable for.

Bottom Line:

• Gaining knowledge is obligatory for everyone.

• Knowledge of the essentials of Islam is a must for Muslims.

• Islamic knowledge needs to be learnt from authentic teachers.

• Worldly knowledge combined with reflection leads to a greater appreciation of Allah.

• The whole of creation is a pointer to Allah, what is termed '*ayat*'.

• We should try to learn as much as possible about everything.

• We should do our best to learn Arabic, reading, writing and understanding. It's tricky, but just try. Start the journey.

Speculation

In the course of theological understanding and debate, as well as the understanding of scientific developments in the scheme of Islam, many issues are thrown up and discussed extensively. Sometimes these issues lead to polarisation of views and schisms can result. It is very important to put these in context. One example is whether Allah has hands. He talks about His Hands:

*(Allah) said, 'O Iblees, what prevented you from prostrating to that which I created with **My Hands**?' {Quran: 38: 75}.*

This verse relates to the story of Adam's creation, whom Allah states was created out of His own Hands, and how Iblees (Satan) refused to bow down. Yet Allah tells also us He is nothing like His creation:

*(He is) Creator of the heavens and the earth. He has made for you from yourselves, mates, and among the cattle, mates; He multiplies you thereby. **There is nothing like Him**, and He is the All-Hearing, the All-Seeing. {Quran 42: 11}*

In other words, what we think of as hands cannot apply to Allah, as He is totally unlike His creation. Much scholarly debate took place to reconcile these seemingly opposite views. The conclusion reached was that Allah does have Hands as He clearly tells us so, but they are not like anything we will be familiar with from His creation.

Let's explain this further with an example. Suppose we were living 3,000 years ago. Imagine, God's prophet of that time prophesises that, in the future, man will fly. How would we have understood that? Undoubtedly, there would have been tremendous speculation as to how this would be possible. Maybe man will finally figure out how to make flapping wings like birds? Maybe there will be giant birds in the future, that man will tame like a horse, allowing him to take to the skies? Maybe he will make some kind of giant sail that harnesses the wind, rather than the sail of boat, or a kite? Despite all the speculation, no one could possibly have envisioned a great steel 'ship' (fuselage) with giant steel protrusions (wings), powered by immensely noisy, vibrating machines (engines), fuelled by a black liquid extracted deep from the earth (oil) – the airplane. This would have been completely beyond the level of the people of that time. The only sensible conclusion we could have reached is that man will fly one day, but it is not within our realms of knowledge to know how.

Another case in point is the 'mysterious letters' seen at the beginning of some *surahs* (chapters). For instance *Alif Laam Meem* is the opening verse for chapter two (*Surah al-Baqara*: The Cow). The English equivalent would be a chapter starting with 'A – L – M'. There are 14 such combinations used at the opening of 29 *surahs* in the Quran. These letters are known as the *huroof muqatta-aat* (the disconnected letters). Again much scholarly work has gone into trying to decipher their meaning, with volumes of books having been written. The reality remains, however, that despite all the speculation no-one truly knows their meaning.

Similarly speculative matters are: are there other life forms in the universe i.e. aliens? When is the Dajjal,[136] end of days or Day of Judgement coming? What happens exactly on the Day of Judgement? Whilst the key principles and some details have been given for the Day of Judgement, the actual sequence and course of events is not known at all.

Ultimately however it is important to recognise what issues are speculation and what are core pragmatic issues that are actually directly relevant to us. For example knowing that we must pray, why we pray and how to pray are of clear importance to each Muslim. Knowing the meaning of these disconnected letters may be of interest and of intellectual curiosity but it does not change our practices in any way. In other words, speculative matters are not of concern to us and we must make sure that remains so.

Our purpose has to be to fulfil our obligations and please Allah, and one needs to be single minded in the pursuit of beneficial knowledge and good deeds. Getting bogged down with speculative matters is a distraction and misdirected time and energy.

Allah gives a directive on this in the Quran. In the story of the young men of the cave in *Surah al-Kahf* (Chapter 18: The Cave), Allah talks of a few youngsters who were true believers but whose town had fallen into idol worship. Worried they would be forced to renounce their faith or be killed, they sought refuge in an isolated cave away from their people to protect

---

[136] A one-eyed creature prophesised to come close to the end of time that will cause terrible tribulations in the world.

their faith. When they lay down to rest, accompanied by their dog, Allah put them to sleep for a few hundred years. About this narration, people subsequently speculated as to the actual number of these young men. Allah continues in *Surah al-Kahf*:

> *(Some) will say: They were three, their dog the fourth, and (some) say: Five, their dog the sixth, guessing at random; and (some) say: Seven, and their dog the eighth. Say (O Muhammad): 'My Lord knows best their number; it is but a few that know (their real number).'* **Do not enter, therefore, enter into controversies concerning them**, *except on a matter that is clear, nor consult any of them about (the affair of) the Sleepers. {Quran 18: 22}*

So Allah relates that out of the generations to follow, people speculated on the number of these young men as 3, 5 or 7. The reality of the case was known by a few handful of people i.e. most likely those who encountered them after they awoke. Allah obviously knows the number, but He deliberately chooses *not* to answer this question and settle this matter for us. He is making clear that this is not an issue for us to dwell on, and to drive home the point He adds: 'Do not enter, therefore, into controversies concerning them'. It does not impact us, it is speculation and we should not be caught up in this, nor any other speculations.

The Prophet also advised:

> *Part of perfecting one's Islam is to leave that which does not concern him. {Sunan at-Tirmidhi}.*

This refers not only to leaving other people to their business (i.e. do not poke your nose into other people's business), but also in matters of religion, be bothered only with that which affects one directly. Matters of speculation are left alone.

Bottom Line:

• Matters of speculation may be intriguing but must be recognised as not of practical importance - i.e. 'it doesn't matter'.

• The things that please Allah is what Muslims concerns themselves with.

Allah's Rules: Control of Desires

Some of Allah's Commands serve to uphold justice, equality and fairness. For example, the prohibition of murder or stealing. However there is another principle that should have become apparent by now, but is worth defining clearly as to how Allah's rules work. Natural desires have been embedded into each person. These are for enjoyment *to a set limit*, and beyond that they must be reined in. Allah defines the boundaries through His Rules. The primary purpose is that it serves as a test of submission to Allah. However alongside this test is the worldly benefit.

We have seen this principle at work throughout this book. The female *hijab* and *jilbab* (head and body covering) is to curb a woman's in-built desire to beautify herself and be appreciated. Along with control of her vanity, the benefit is to remind herself of modesty, and reduce her appeal to men of the community, therefore reducing the risk of sparking inappropriate liaisons. Men love to look at women, but they have been told to control this, again for the same benefit.

People love to chat. Cordial relations with family, friends, neighbours and all is a central tenet of Islam. Yet conversation must keep away from back-biting which is the natural tendency. The need to have a dig at some annoying person has to be controlled. The benefit is stronger communities, as a positive view is maintained about everyone. Life is far more pleasant when one is not the subject of vain talk.

Society loves to indulge in alcohol. Those who have consumed alcohol prior to converting to Islam, often comment that giving up alcohol was the hardest part. Alcohol has been prohibited. The one who resists it, receives a reward from Allah, the one who indulges receives a sin. The rule is again about control of desires. What is the worldly benefit of this rule? Alcohol leads to intoxication. Once a person has lost their senses, humiliating themselves or insulting others, through their speech or behaviour, become all too easy, with the worst outcome being they could get hurt themselves or might hurt someone else. Abstaining from alcohol protects a person from causing 'euphoric' chaos.

Charity is obligated through *zakat*, with voluntary charity (*sadaqa*) being heavily encouraged. The natural desire to hoard wealth and spend it exclusively on oneself to extravagance has to be curbed. What is the worldly benefit? Some redistribution of wealth insures that the most needy in society are being supported. However, the benefit goes beyond this. Imagine a person in your community, for instance, has hit hard times, perhaps they have lost their business. You provide your *zakat* to this individual. It provides much needed desperate financial assistance. Whilst you are curbing your desire and fulfilling Allah's command, the recipient will be truly grateful. They will have a strongly positive opinion about you and this strengthens communities. If you find yourself in need of help in the future, they will likely rush to aid you if they can.

Bottom Line:

• Allah's Commands are a test of submission: control naturally-ingrained desires.

• With this test there will be wisdom and worldly benefit.

Is the Sunnah Necessary? The Quran-only Movement

In the very beginning we discussed the importance of the Sunnah, the teachings and saying of the Prophet, and how these also constitute revelation, alongside the Quran (*The Prophet as the Best Role Model and the Spirit of Islam*). Around the turn of the 20th century, a group of Muslims subject to colonial rule, from the Indian subcontinent and from Egypt, challenged the need for the Sunnah. This group criticised hadiths on two issues: some hadith they found troublesome in light of modern i.e. Western values. Secondly, they raised doubts about the authenticity of hadiths due to the perceived deficiencies in their preservation. At the time of the Prophet and for many years after, some people fabricated sayings from the Prophet for personal or political gain giving rise to hadith forgeries. The 'Quran-only' movement proposed a methodology to abandon the *whole* hadith literature and to rely solely on the Quran for all guidance. That means interpreting the Quran completely through the verses of the Quran itself.

This position is untenable and belies shallow thinking under the guise of intellectual analysis. The illogical position ends up full of paradoxes. Emad Hamdeh's excellent article summarises some of the problems and illogicality of dismissing the hadith literature.[137]

1. All literature is only interpretable through a context. As one reads a novel, the author sets the scene and characters, and the story unfolds with the reader understanding the context laid. Without the context the actual sentences are meaningless.

In the Quran there are many verses that stand alone and can be interpreted in themselves, where they talk of attributes of Allah. For example, Allah is extremely kind and compassionate (*Rahmaan* and *Raheem*). Or Allah is

---

[137] https://bit.ly/2UPzdJo

extremely forgiving (*Ghafoor*), or has complete control over everything (*Qadeer*). However, a great many verses actually require a context that does not come from the Quran itself. The context to these comes from the situation at the time, which was thereafter relayed through the history of the Prophet (Seerah), or through the explanation given by the Prophet himself, therefore recorded as hadith. The example has already been given above of Khawlah bin Thalabah and her seeking salvation of her marriage after her husband unintendedly issued her divorce (*zihaar*) in a fit of anger, where Allah provides revelation through Quranic verses to resolve this (*Is the Quran a Miracle*).

2. The Quran is in classical Arabic. As time has passed since revelation, Arabic lexicons have recorded the meaning of archaic Arabic. However, as Emad Hamdeh points out, even the use of Arabic dictionaries to derive the interpretation of the Quran is a paradox. The same dictionaries have been preserved in similar manner to hadith. Those involved in the preservation of the language also transmitted hadiths. To dismiss hadith as of questionable authenticity would require dismissing Arabic lexicons and therefore leaving the Quran's verses uninterpretable. In the example given above of Khawlah, the word *zihaar* is used in the Quran's Arabic to indicate divorce; the use of this word in such a way was specific and unique to the Quran. *Zihaar* in normal usage means to provide assistance, but using such a meaning in understanding that particular verse renders the verse uninterpretable.

3. There are numerous matters that the Quran discusses but no details are given. For example, ritual prayer (*salat*) is a matter of great importance to Muslims, and mentioned countless times in the Quran. Yet, how the prayer is actually to be performed, at what times of the day, their length – all the specifics about them are not found in the Quran. All these answers come from the Prophet himself in the form of hadiths.

4. Allah makes clear in the Quran that there is also divine revelation other than the Quran itself:

> *He (i.e. the Prophet) does not speak out of his own desires.*

It is no less than Revelation revealed to him. {Quran 53: 3-4}

*Certainly did Allah confer (great) favour upon the believers when He sent among them a Messenger from themselves, reciting to them His verses and purifying them and teaching them the Book and **wisdom**, although beforehand they had been in manifest error. {Quran 3: 164}*

'The Book' here refers to the Quran whilst 'wisdom' refers to the teachings of the Prophet and his living example i.e. the Sunnah. Furthermore there are numerous occasions the command is given 'Obey Allah and obey His Messenger.'[138]

We did not send any Messenger but for him to be obeyed by the permission of Allah. {Al-Qur'an 4: 63}

Allah sent many messengers throughout history but only a few were accompanied by a Book. What the messengers taught through their teachings and actions was the divine revelation i.e. revelation clearly existed that was not in the form of a holy Book. As the Quran is for all of mankind until the end of time, these verses cannot be restricted just to the time of the Prophet. Obeying the Messenger, after he has passed away, is therefore a reference to follow his teachings i.e. his Sunnah, preserved as hadiths.

5. Allah also makes clear in the Quran that He guarantees the preservation of His Revelations, namely the Quran and the Sunnah. Recall from earlier *Are Other Religions also Acceptable*:

Indeed, it is We who sent down the Quran and We will assuredly guard it (from corruption). {Quran 15: 9}

The guarantee of preservation must include the Sunnah, as the Quran is not interpretable without it. The Arabs were renowned for their

---

[138] For example: Quran - 24:54, 8:20, 3:132, 4:63, 4:68, 4:79, 59:7

exceptional literary memory as we noted earlier. However preservation of both the Quran and hadith was not only through memory and oral transmission but also through written recordings, subsequently compiled as books. The records made by individuals were known as *sahifas* (literally meaning 'page'), such as of the Companion Abdullah ibn Amr ibn al-As, who was given specific permission from the Prophet to write down his sayings and teachings. Subsequent compilations of hadith were known as Sunan's or Musnad's, and culminated in the Sahih works.

6. The body of hadith literature has been intensively and extensively studied with extreme forensic analysis. There have been vast numbers of scholars through the generations starting at the time of the Prophet himself who dedicated their whole lives to collate, preserve and transmit the teachings of the Prophet. Their commitment cannot be overestimated. This was a time before communications, printing and where travel was arduous. Neither can their enthusiasm to learn the teachings of the Prophet be imagined. The Prophet was a phenomenon, a miracle in himself. The early generations that followed him would have been inspired by the stories about him, fresh in society about a man who had lived just before them. To learn and collate the hadiths required journeying right across the Islamic lands to live and study with countless different people who had knowledge of many, or even just a few, hadiths. The issue of hadith forgery was tackled with incredibly impressive scientific protocol. It is beyond the scope of this book to give in-depth details of this massive field of scholarship, but I will try to give a glimpse.

For each hadith, the actual saying of the Prophet, i.e. the content, called *matn* in Arabic, had to be accompanied by its chain of transmitters, namely who had heard it from who, going all the way back to the Prophet himself. This chain of transmitters is called the *isnad*. The quality of the *isnad* of each hadith was graded to indicate the degree of certainty about it. Hadith scholars analysed each hadith to determine who comprised this chain. Were the so-called transmitters real people? Where did they live and were they known to have actually met each other, so that a relay of information could have occurred? A hadith in which two consecutive transmitters did not even live at the same time is clearly fake. Similarly if they never happened to be in the same place during their lifetimes implies they could never have met, so again the hadith would be dismissed as fake. Each transmitter in the chain had to be known as an upright individual.

For purposes of simplicity, a hadith that had an unbroken confirmed chain of reliable accepted narrators throughout the whole chain from Prophet until the time of hadith compilation was graded s*ahih* (sound and authentic). A hadith that was otherwise sound but where there was doubt about one particular narrator in the chain was graded *hasan* (good). A hadith where there was a break in the continuity of the chain was classified as *daif* (weak). One in which its chain contained a person identified as known liar, or where there was clear evidence as to its fabrication, was *mawdoo* (fake).

Hadith scholars actually wrote great compendiums detailing the biographies of hadith transmitters to aid their studies. Hadith forgeries themselves, having been identified, were compiled into books to document them as fakes for other scholars and the wider public, in order for people to beware of them. A tremendous amount of cross referencing was done to determine a particular hadith was authentic.

So the quality of the *isnad* determined if the hadith was then graded as:

- *Sahih* (sound and authentic)

- *Hasan* (good)

- *Daif* (weak).

- *Mawdoo* (fabricated)

This grading is therefore about **narrator chain** *quality*. In addition, a hadith was also classed depending on the number of lines of transmission it had (i.e. **narrator chain** *quantity*) – namely, how many different people in a particular generation reported the same hadith:

- *Mutawaatir* - extensive number of narrators in *each* generation (exact number required to achieve this was unspecified – but enough to be certain forgery was impossible)

– *Ahaad* – those not *mutawaatir* i.e. the rest, subdivided into:

- *Mashoor*: 3 narrators minimum in each generation (but not enough to reach *mutawaatir*)

- *Azeez*: 2 narrators minimum in each generation

- *Ghareeb*: narrator chain where one or more generation(s) have only one transmitter

The most extensively reported *mutawaatir* hadith interestingly warns future generations about the gravity of fabricating hadith:

> *Whoever intentionally attributes a lie as being from me (i.e. Prophet Muhammad), should prepare his seat in the Fire. {Sahih Bukhari}*

This hadith comprised 74 narrators as its minimum, which was that of the first generation (i.e. the Companions).

Finally it is important to note from where the Quran-only movement emerged. Islamic scholars throughout history never doubted the importance and necessity of the Sunnah and the place of hadith. The compilation of hadith was necessary, as the Companions and subsequent generations of hadith scholars, passed away. The answer to hadith forgeries was to establish the science of hadith study to distinguish the authentic from the fabricated. The forensic analyses undertaken by legions of hadith scholars actually underpins the modern referencing system that is seen today from journalism to science to law, and serves as the basis for confirming authenticity. These human endeavours form part of Allah's guarantee as to the preservation of His final Revelation.

Hadith compilations that collated only *sahih* (i.e. authentic and sound) hadiths culminated in six great works, known after their compiling authors: [139]

1. Sahih Buhkhari

2. Sahih Muslim

3. Sunan Ibn Majah

4. Sunan at-Tirmidhi

5. Sunan an-Nasai

6. Sunan Abu Dawood

Of these, Sahih Bukhari and Sahih Muslim are held in the highest esteem. Both together contain several thousand hadiths; however, the other collections contain additional *sahih* hadiths that had been missed by Imam Bukhari or Imam Muslim. It is a mistake by some Muslims who take the view that only a hadith present in Sahih Bukhari or Sahih Muslim can be accepted as authentic, and hadiths in other compilations can be dismissed as not meeting the bar of *sahih*. These six works are extensive yet there are still other *sahih* hadiths outside of these works as well, for example, in the Musnad of Imam Ahmad.

The movement to dismiss the whole body of hadith literature emerged from orientalists i.e. non-Muslim westerner academics, or Muslims affected by such western thought. These non-Muslim academics do not accept Islam and therefore do not utilise the Lenses of Islam (discussed at the beginning). They approach with scepticism at best, where everything is open to question and requires 'proof', or an ulterior agenda at worst.[140]

---

[139] Known collectively as *al-Sihah al-Sittah*, which translates as 'The Authentic Six'

[140] Ignaz Goldziher (1850-1921) a famous Hungarian Jewish orientalist was mesmerised by Islam yet chose to support his Jewish faith and dismantle Islam in this endeavour, by his own admission. He recorded in his journal which was later published in German as *Tagebuch*: '...I truly entered into the spirit of Islam to

For the orientalist the Quran is not the Word of God, but a literary text to be studied like any other piece of literature. As well as lacking a sound intention, as discussed earlier in *Knowledge*, they do not have a lineage extending to authentic teachers, and so are very unlikely to have a proper and reliable understanding of the revelations. Muslims under colonial rule fell under the influence of western thinking and some felt the need to make Islam robust against oriental criticism. Concerned that hadith were a weak link, they misguidedly and erroneously jettisoned the whole of hadith literature. This was a profound mistake. What they failed to appreciate was that the monumental work of droves of hadith scholars has been the historical pinnacle of the modern referencing system. No discipline, religious, scientific or otherwise has ever matched this. Their lack of knowledge led to their lack of belief in the basics of Islamic faith.

Bottom Line:

• Hadith (the sayings and teachings of the Prophet) are a part of divine Revelation.

• Hadith are essential to explaining the Quran in meaning.

• Hadith preservation and the process of sifting through them to determine authenticity was a collective colossal endeavour of legions of life-long dedicated scholars.

• Allah guaranteed the preservation of His faith which includes hadith as well as the Quran.

---

such an extent that ultimately I became inwardly convinced that I myself was a Muslim, and judiciously discovered that this was the only religion which, even in its doctrinal and official formulation, can satisfy philosophic minds. **My ideal was to elevate Judaism to a similar rational level.**'

Violence and Jihad in Islam

What does Islam say about violence?

There are several myths relating to Islam and violence, such as:

- Islam forces conversion to Islam through violence, if necessary

- Infidels must be put to death

- Islam is a religion of violence

I have left this very hot topical question until last, as it should be abundantly apparent from this book that Islam promotes peace and mercy, along with a profound community-spirit and unity.

Allah makes clear that He is in NO need of our worship what so ever. He is free of all need. We are the needy. We need to worship Him because not only does He deserve to be worshipped but it is for our very own benefit. As explained earlier, Allah created us, to give us the chance to come to Him willingly and lovingly. Forcing people to become Muslims through coercion and violence quite blatantly defeats that objective, demonstrating the paradox of such fallacies and propaganda.

Allah explicitly states, on numerous occasions, that there is no compulsion in religion[141]. We are all free to choose to believe or not. The right to freedom of religion is firmly enshrined in Islam. People of other faiths are not only free to practise their faiths, but are also to be afforded protection if they face any threats. Allah says in the Quran:

> *... Had it not been for God's repelling some people through the might of the others, the monasteries, churches, synagogues, and mosques in which God is very often worshipped would have been utterly destroyed... {Quran 22: 40}*

---

[141] E.g. Quran 2: 256; 10: 99; 18: 29

Life is sanctified in Islam and this principle carries the highest priority in determining applicability of the rules. When one faces a serious threat to personal safety, Islam gives full permission to self-defence. One may protect themselves, their family or property. The use of violence, however, is reserved as the last resort.

Bottom Line:

• There is absolutely no compulsion in religion.

• Islam spreads peace and mercy.

• Issues are to be resolved as much as possible through kindness and compassion.

• There is a right to self-defence, if there is a genuine threat.

• Islam affords protection to people of all faiths.

What is Jihad and Martyrdom?

Jihad literally means to struggle in the cause of Allah. This can relate to our daily struggles, with doing the right thing, and avoiding actions that will disobey Allah. For instance, avoiding back-biting when others in the office are engaged in gossip; controlling your anger when someone has wronged you; being patient with, and obeying our parents when they insist on something though you are certain that is not a sound course of action.

Jihad also means to fight in the way of Allah, part of which is a military connotation. Through the media it is this military aspect that non-Muslims are familiar with. Martyrdom is death whilst one is engaged in fighting for the cause of Allah. It is highly praised and rewarded, as one has sacrificed everything, including one's life, for the sake of Allah. Its reward is instant Paradise along with even loftier rewards than for the non-martyr. The martyr, known as *shaheed* in Arabic, is forgiven all their sins (other than debt), as well as the punishment of the grave. In fact martyrdom is also a status granted to some whose death is not related to war. For instance those who are killed whilst protecting their family, property or wealth, for their faith, or for speaking up against an unjust rule. Or those whose death is a result of drowning; being burnt to death from fire, abdominal disease, tuberculosis, plague, pleurisy or abscess; childbirth or its aftermath; or collapse of a building.[142]

But what exactly is 'to fight in the way of Allah'? Military jihad serves as means of self-defence for the state. Islam promotes right to life, right to safety and right to livelihood and resources such as water. Where these are threatened, the Muslim state can utilise military means for its protection. Who can call for jihad? The head of a Muslim state is the one to do so, *for these purposes only*. There is no blind following in Islam and those called upon to fight must evaluate the purported cause. Recall from earlier, *Encouraging Good and Forbidding Evil*, every Muslim must stand up for justice and against corruption. If the cause for military action is sound and necessary, then Muslims participate. If the cause has an ulterior and unjust motive, Muslims must not embark on a military campaign of oppression but must hold their leaders to account instead. Note, **jihad is not attacking non-Muslim people, or conquering non-Muslim lands, to spread Islam**. As discussed above, there is no compulsion in religion. It is also not indiscriminate killing of non-Muslims because they are non-believers – which is simply murder. Whilst, historically, there have been Islamic rulers who have busied themselves conquering foreign lands, this was not based on Islam.

Whilst Islam seeks to avoid conflict as much as possible, it has very clear rules on war when it is necessary. **The killing of non-combatants and innocent civilians, such as women, children and the elderly, is *strictly* prohibited, and killing them is murder.**

---

[142] Sunan at-Tirmidhi, Sahih Bukhari, Sunan Abu Dawud, Sunan Nasai

Recall from earlier that the murder of a single person, the Quran tells us, is equivalent to the murder of all mankind.[143] So grave is the crime of murder.

In one of the battles at the time of the Prophet one of the Companions fought bravely and suffered extensive injuries. Unable to bear the pain he finally took an arrow from his quiver and ended his life by stabbing himself in the chest. The Prophet condemned this action and told his Companions that the man would be punished for this in the Hellfire.[144] **Suicide is clearly prohibited in Islam, and that includes suicide in battle.**

One cannot kill oneself deliberately whilst seeking to take out the enemy. There is a difference in undertaking a profoundly bold mission in which one is *likely* to be killed, versus one in which the person *will* kill themselves and use their death to take as many of the enemy as possible with them. In the first scenario, the soldier is not looking to die, though this may be highly probable – he is targeting the enemy, not himself; this is permissible in the scheme of war. In the latter case, the soldier will kill himself, and he is targeting himself along with the enemy; this is categorically not allowed. Not being clear on this, sadly, has allowed manipulative perverse groomers to prey on impressionable, disaffected and vulnerable Muslims, and inculcate the notion that suicide bombing is permissible and a great way to achieve martyrdom and Paradise. Nothing could be further from the truth.

The degree to which Islam promotes peaceful resolution can be seen from a crisis that occurred at the time of the Prophet. Six years after building a Muslim community in the city of Medina the Prophet set out with 1400 Companions to undertake pilgrimage (umrah) to the city of Mecca, the home of his native tribe, the Quraish, who were ardent enemies of Islam at the time. The Quraish had always granted open access to all for

---

[143] Quran 5: 32
[144] Sahih Bukhari

pilgrimage to the Kaba, and their reputation and standing throughout Arabia was built upon this. Upon learning of the Prophet's plans, the Quraish were unable to contain their animosity and sent a delegation to intercept the Prophet at a place on the outskirts of Mecca, called Al-Hudaibiyah, warning him not to proceed on.

The Prophet had embarked peacefully, and without military arms. The Quraish delegation made clear they would not allow him to pass. A tense situation built up. The Prophet was not to be put off his peaceful pilgrimage. A series of Quraish parties were sent to evaluate the situation, and confirmed his intentions were indeed peaceful. They could not, however, persuade their Quraish leaders to give way. At this juncture, the Prophet could have chosen to launch a military offensive to take the city of Mecca once and for all. The Muslim state was sufficiently large and powerful that the Quraish could not have resisted, and indeed the Quraish leaders were truly fearful that he was going to adopt this course.

Worried about the possibility of war, as well as their reputation in Arabia from the stand-off, the Quraish sent a delegation to put forward their terms for settlement. Their conditions seemed particularly one-sided and unreasonable. A truce of ten years would be upheld, but the Muslims were to return on this occasion without making the pilgrimage. Instead permission was given for the pilgrimage to take place the following year. During the course of the truce, any person choosing to leave the Muslims in Medina and return to Mecca would be entitled to do so, but any person from Mecca wishing to join the Muslims in Medina, would be returned to Mecca against their will.

The Muslims were mortified at the terms offered, feeling them to be a humiliation. The Prophet, however accepted the Quraish's terms in their entirety without negotiation. Very unusually the Companions made their displeasure apparent to the Prophet, so troubled were they by this treaty. However, Allah was very pleased with this course of action, and shortly after called it a grand victory in Quranic revelation, in Chapter 48 called 'The Conquest' (*Surah al-Fatth*). Violence had been averted, a peaceful resolution had been achieved, a long truce had been agreed and persecution for the Muslims had finally came to an end.

The Prophet always strived to the maximum to avoid violence and war. There are numerous such examples from his lifetime. War was strictly reserved to the need of self-preservation. The Prophet did not undertake any war other than for purposes of self defence of the Muslims. It should be readily evident therefore that in modern times, in reports of crazed 'Islamic jihadis' shooting scores of civilians in clubs or shopping malls, or blowing themselves up on crowded trains, these criminals are not actually engaged in jihad at all. They are perpetrating crimes not only against humanity and the state, but also against Islam and God Himself. Murder and suicide are grave sins, and routes to the Hellfire, not Martyrdom.

A Quranic verse that is copiously misquoted by those with anti-Islamic agendas of portraying Islam as a religion of violence is: '*Kill them wherever you find them*'. Again the context of the verse is critical here. First note the location of this verse within the text (i.e. **the textual context**):

> *And fight in the way of Allah **with those who fight with you**, and **do not exceed the limits**, surely Allah does not love those who exceed the limits. {Quran 2: 190}*

> *And **kill them wherever you find them**, and drive them out from whence they drove you out, and persecution is worse than killing, and **do not fight** with them at the Sacred Mosque **until they fight with you** in it, but if they do fight you, then slay them; such is the reward for the unbelievers. {Quran 2: 191}*

> *And if they cease, then indeed, Allah is Forgiving and Merciful. {Quran 2: 192}*

> *And fight with them until there is no persecution, and religion should be only for Allah, but **if they desist**, then there should be **no hostility** except against the oppressors. {Quran 2: 193}*

> *(Fighting in) the sacred month is for (aggression committed in) the*

sacred month, and for (all) violations is legal retribution. So whoever has assaulted you, then assault him in the same way that he has assaulted you. And fear Allah and know that Allah is with those who fear Him. {Quran 2: 194}

The first verse of this passage makes evident that fighting has been authorised for *self defence* ('*And fight... with those who fight you*') whilst stressing that this is to be done with clear limits and rules ('*... do not exceed the limits*'). The rules for engagement have already been mentioned above, that non-combatants, the weak and innocent are not to be harmed. This injunction also included the prohibition on mutilating any combatant. Once the right to fight for self defence has been ordained, Allah then gives the Muslims a rousing battle cry – '*kill them wherever you find them*' – in other words, be brave and be fierce. If fighting is a necessity, then be courageous. Before any battle, the army General delivers a motivating inspirational talk to pump up the troops, to fight to the death.[145] This is Allah's pep talk to the Muslims. If the light is green, destroy the enemy. This is followed immediately by a reminder *twice* more that if the enemy ceases hostilities then to stop fighting – violence is no longer permitted. It is apparent that the passage relates very clearly to the right to self defence. The verses do not authorise in any way unconditional violence against non-Muslims.

Now let's examine the **historical context** of these verses. We go back to the story of Al-Hudaibiyah. One year on from the treaty of Al-Hudaibiyah, as per the treaty's terms, the Muslims could return to Mecca and undertake the pilgrimage (umrah) that they had been forced to abandon the previous year. As the time was approaching to re-embark on the umrah, there was apprehension that the tribe of Quraish would fail to honour the treaty, preferring to go to battle this time to prevent their pilgrimage. Furthermore, the timing of the pilgrimage fell within one of the four holy months when fighting was traditionally prohibited. What is more, fighting was completely forbidden in the holy precinct of Mecca all year round, as

---

[145] https://bit.ly/3bA9UBK

was fighting whilst in a state of consecration (*ihram*). With these verses, (2: 190–194) Allah was removing all the apprehensions the Muslims would have been harbouring: fighting in the holy months, fighting in the holy land, fighting in a state of consecration, all approved in the matter of self defence.[146]

Allah also makes clear the magnitude of the evil that the Quraish had undertaken against the Muslims, as to why armed response was justified if necessary. The persecution referred to in '*Persecution is worse than killing*' was the indescribable torture that they used to inflict on the Muslims on account of their faith.[147] The torment of torture can cause a person's heart to lose faith.[148] This is an outcome worse than death. A Muslim dying with faith is destined for Paradise; what is more, one that has been killed on account of his faith dies as a martyr with the great rewards that go with it. However, a Muslim that is tortured and survives, but then loses their Islamic faith, becomes an unbeliever, and if they subsequently die in that state, they lose their Paradise. Hence this is an outcome worse than death. The Quraish were therefore committing heinous crimes seeking not just to destroy a Muslim's worldly life but their Afterlife too.

For further reading, I would recommend Dr Nazir Khan's excellent article summarising misquoted Quranic verses in relation to the misrepresentation of violence in Islam.[149] Nouman Ali Khan and Sharif Randhawa's *Divine Speech* also has an excellent Appendix summarising jihad and the related Quranic verses (see *Further Reading*).

Incidentally, the umrah was performed without any trouble from the

---

[146] al-Wahidi, al-Samarqandi, al-Tabari

[147] al-Tabari

[148] This refers to a genuine loss of faith in God, for example as the person feels 'why did God do this to me'. It is not referring to one whose faith is secure in his heart but verbalises renouncement of his faith in order to make the torturers stop their torture; in this case the person is still Muslim.

[149] https://bit.ly/2Uq5urn

Quraish. The Muslims did not, therefore, require resorting to arms. In fact, soon after, the Quraish violated the peace treaty, resulting in the Prophet and a 10,000 Muslim army marching to conquer Mecca. Despite the atrocities committed by the Quraish, this was done in a bloodless fashion, indicating again the degree to which Islam promotes peace.

Bottom Line:

• Military jihad is combat strictly for self defence of the state.

• Military jihad has stringent rules for military engagement.

• Quranic verses make clear that military combat is for self defence, not a licence for killing non-Muslims.

• Suicide is prohibited, even in battle.

• The killing of non-Muslims, whether men, women, or children, simply because they are non-believers, is indiscriminate murder.

Common Mistakes Made by Muslims

Clearly evident by now is that Islam is a complete way of life, governing both matters of daily living as well as ritual worship. There are a number of common mistakes made by Muslims which I will outline here. There is a fair degree of overlap between some of these, and some Muslims may fall prey to several of them. Unfortunately non-Muslims may also perpetrate these, knowingly where they have anti-Islamic agendas, or unknowingly where they may be studying the faith.

1. Thinking Islam is just the 'five pillars'

When asking children 'What is Islam' it has been incredibly frustrating to hear the answer 'the five pillars.'[150] For a lot of children and unfortunately adults too, Islam equates entirely to the ritual worship aspects of the faith – the 'five pillars'. The whole aspect of moral conduct and upstanding behaviour, as being Islam is completely lost. Islam consists of two big halves, belief and behaviour – recall that Allah instructs us to 'Believe AND do good deeds' (see *If God Controls Everything Why do I Need to Bother*). *Both* of these are necessary, one cannot dispense with either arm if trying to be a successful Muslim. Recall in the *Introduction* that I highlighted this precise issue, and in trying to emphasise that behaviour gets neglected, I chose to cover the aspects of moral conduct before belief. Being Honest, Humble, Helpful, Modest and Kind (the H₃MK) are as much Islam as the ritual forms of worship. Following the very first article of faith, the *shahada* (the testimony of faith), also obligate striving for the highest levels of moral conduct.

2. Having the wrong intention

In deciding whether a certain lifestyle or choice is permissible, many

---

[150] Shahadah (testimony of faith), salat (ritual prayer), zakat (obligatory charity), fasting the month of Ramadan, Hajj (obligatory pilgrimage).

Muslims will approach the sources of knowledge, namely the Quran, the hadith literature, or scholars, claiming to seek guidance. However, the intention is disingenuous, and the purpose is to find validation for what they have already decided to pursue. This is a rubber stamping exercise and not really seeking guidance at all. It is accomplished by some of the mechanisms described below. To gain guidance one needs to approach with humility and the desire to find the truth, the real truth on any matter. That quest may lead to the discovery that we are wrong, and need to give up or correct some action of ours. This has to be accepted and one needs to strive towards implementing that. Using the sources of guidance to 'prove' a point is a total fallacy and a dangerous exercise, bearing in mind that to make permissible what Allah has prohibited, or vice versa, thereby changing the commands of God, is a very serious transgression. Most scholars classify this as *shirk*, namely disbelieving in Islam.

Examples include the movement of so-called progressive Muslims engaged in a gay lifestyle who have declared that reinterpreting the Quran demonstrates that Islam allows homosexuality (see *Homosexuality and Islam*). Another example is women who do not wish to take the *hijab* and cover their head, put forward their fallacious evidence as the Quran does not give the command 'Cover your head'.

3. Taking Quranic verses or Prophetic narrations (hadith) out of context

Words do not carry meaning unless in sentences, and sentences do not carry meaning unless placed in context. Recall that the verses of the Quran are not ordered like a book, in which the flow of the book from beginning onwards dictates the context.

Each verse of the Quran has two contexts:

1. A textual context – namely the verses before it and after it

2. A historical context - the associated incident during the life of the Prophet that led to the verse being revealed

The Quran has the extraordinary ability to speak out to the reader themselves. The verses contain multiple depths of meaning. Many verses will stand by themselves as absolute statements, for example describing that Allah is All-Forgiving and All-Knowing, or that very few of mankind are thankful. These statements are valid even in isolation. Taking them in context, though, will add far greater understanding.

A typical example are the Quranic verses authorising fighting for self defence being ripped from their context to portray Islam as a violent religion, or alternatively to misguide and groom impressionable Muslims into extremism, as discussed in detail in the previous section. Another example is the principle of encouraging good and discouraging what is evil, covered earlier. This is a classic instance of taking a literal view of the verse of Quran, with its interpretation and application out of context of the complete framework of Islam. The result is a belligerent self righteous approach that antagonises and alienates others, many of whom will unfortunately be pushed away from Islam.

Non-Muslims pursuing anti-Islamic and Islamophobic agendas are particularly guilty of pulling verses out of context.

4. Inadequate knowledge

'A little knowledge is a dangerous thing'. When it comes to deriving permissibility on a matter, it is *essential* to review not only *all* relevant Quranic verses, along with their historical context, but also the explanations and supporting guidance found in the hadith literature, which has its own context. The evidences must then be evaluated in their entirety to come to decision on whether the matter is allowed or prohibited.

Using an isolated Quranic verse or a hadith to reach a conclusion is a dangerous exercise.

The example of the prohibition of alcohol serves to illustrate, as covered in detail earlier (see *Abstain from Alcohol, Intoxicants and Gambling*). Four Quranic verses were revealed, separated by many years. The rationale for this method was gradualism, and to allow people to adjust to the idea and lessen the use of alcohol until a complete prohibition was decreed. The last verse finally outlawed it completely. The principle of abrogation applied. Casual reading of the earlier verses may lead one to conclude that alcohol is permitted in Islam as the reader may not realise a final verse banned it ultimately and strictly. A lack of knowledge will lead to an incorrect conclusion.

Those who reject hadith are also guilty of this mistake. As covered earlier, the hadith literature has been compiled with forensic analysis by legions of scrupulous scholars for whom this was their whole life mission. The scientific endeavour they undertook has been the pinnacle of human achievement. The ignorance of this whole process underlies the belief of those who dismiss hadiths.

5. Treating the Quran as a lexicon of law

The Quran is often treated like a legal compendium. People seek answers to a specific scenario and when they fail to find that exact situation referred to in the Quran, claim that the issue is not covered, and therefore there is no relevant ruling. For instance, women sometimes ask 'Where does it say in the Quran that the head needs to be covered' or 'Where in the Quran does Allah tell women to wear a *hijab*'? They look for the exact command 'cover your hair', or for the specific word '*hijab*'. The commands to do this are indeed given in the Quran[151] (see earlier in *Modesty*) but not using these specific phrases.

The word '*hijab*', though not used in the Quran as a covering, was subsequently adopted by Islamic scholars to describe the required woman's ensemble.

Another example is the prohibition of alcohol and intoxicants. Some people pick out the word '*khamr*' as what has been prohibited *specifically*.

---

[151] Quran 24: 31; 33: 59

Khamr is an alcoholic drink fermented from grapes, namely wine. Those who think the Quran is a legal lexicon surmise that the prohibition is specific to wine only and that all other alcoholic beverages are permissible, such as beer, ale, spirits etc. In fact according to this inference, drugs such as heroin and cocaine would also be permitted, though in reality they are completely prohibited in Islam.

The Quran comprises 6,236 verses that were revealed as guidance for all mankind for all the rest of time. It is simple logic that such a book cannot serve as a lexicon of law, giving precise specific rulings on every possible situation. This would not have been possible for even the time of the Prophet, let alone for the countless generations and years to follow him. If this was the case, then we would have the paradox that the Quran should stipulate rulings on situations and technologies that do not exist now, but are to come in the future. The Book provides a framework of principles and guidance that are applicable for all time. They have to be applied to the times and circumstances of people.

The Quran talks of *khamr* utilising it as an example of intoxicants, and the prohibition is meant to be extrapolated for *all* intoxicants, not just *khamr* (i.e. wine) itself. Note how we discussed earlier the Quran uses amazing imagery from the words used and the verse constructions composed. The root word that underlies both *khamr* (alcohol) and *khimaar* (*hijab*) is the verb *Kha-Ma-Ra* which means to cover or veil something. With regards to women, the word is being used exactly to emphasise covering their heads along with their chests, whilst with intoxicants, the mind becomes veiled, namely befuddled. To interpret *khamr* as wine only is to utilise a foolhardy legalistic, and literalist approach to Quran, and/or to have a disingenuous motive. Furthermore, the Sunnah expounded clearly that *khamr* referred to all intoxicants.

6. Relying on English translations of the Quran

Translations have the inherent difficulty of trying to convey meaning from one language to another in a concise, corresponding manner. 'Lost in translation'! – this adage is true. It is impossible to portray the subtleties of meaning of specific words. Let us take an example. Allah tells us repeatedly about how He has bestowed a multitude of favours upon each and every person, and commands us to be grateful to Him (see *Thankfulness*):

> *And He gives you of all that you ask Him; and if you count Allah's*
> ***bounties***, *you will not be able to number them; most surely man is*
> *very unjust, very ungrateful. {Quran 14: 34}*

Prophet Ibrahim (Abraham) was not just a Prophet but a select Prophet with the highest station with Allah. As such he was a truly grateful slave, and his level of gratitude will be one of the highest of any human. Allah notes that he is one of the thankful ones and comments about his gratefulness in the Quran:

> *He (Ibrahim) was thankful to God for His **bounties**. God chose him*
> *and guided him to the right path. {Quran 16: 121}*

In both cases here the translations use the same word: 'bounties', yet the meaning is quite different. In English grammar there is only the plural but Arabic has a plural, implying more than two, and a super-plural indicating a massive amount. The Arabic word Allah uses for bounties in the first verse referring to His favours is '*nimat*'; a super-plural, conveying an abundance that simply cannot be measured. Ibrahim was a man who will rank as one of the most grateful of all humankind and Allah acknowledges him as such. But the Arabic word used in the second verse is '*unoma*'. This is a plural, not super-plural, indicating despite Ibrahim's elevated status and special rank with Allah, even he could thank Allah for only a handful of favours (plural), no way near the amount that Allah bestowed (super-plural). If that is what Ibrahim could achieve, what about the rest of mankind! This beauty of the Arabic language and the subtlety in meaning is clearly lost in translation.

I would again direct the reader to Nouman Ali Khan's *Divine Speech* for more detailed coverage of how the Arabic language has been used in astonishing fashion in the Quran (see *Further Reading*).

Any translation will also fail to capture the historical context of the revelation which is essential to grasp the true meaning of the verses. Explanations of the verses from the Prophet himself (hadith) will also not be present in a translation. It can be seen that translations are very limited in conveying just the bare basic meaning.

7. Exclusivity of the truth

The feeling that one knows the truth and that that is the exclusive way is a dangerous mindset. Usually this stems from a lack of knowledge leading to an unfortunate rigidity in views and intolerance to the ways of others. Knowledgeable scholars can also fall prey to this through arrogance. The consequences are a harsh attitude with others, disagreement and argumentation. Whilst Islam promotes tolerance and harmony in the community, sadly this approach can cause Muslims to create schisms in society and break with other Muslims over what can be trivial matters, labelling them as '*kuffaar*' (unbelievers), a very serious accusation. The most severe consequence is extremism and radicalisation, with the use of violence. Astonishingly such mindsets were encountered even in the time of Prophet Muhammad. How extraordinary, that the Prophet, sent to teach people Islam, was challenged by some who thought they knew Islam better! These people were known as the Khawarij.

Being born into a Muslim family does not automatically endow one with Islam. Knowledge of Islam has to be gained. Being Arab does not make one a scholar by right either, on account of their mother tongue being Arabic. The Arabic of the Quran is not colloquial, with many words found in the Quran specific to the Quran, and not found in common usage.

8. Undertaking ritual prayers (*salat*) without verbalising it (reciting in the heart)

This was mentioned earlier in *Ritual Prayer* (*Salat*), but it is important to make this point again as so many Muslims do not realise this. The *salat* must be verbalised even if very softly. The mouth and tongue must be moving. *Salat* done silently, i.e. 'in the heart' only, is not valid a prayer.

It is also worth reminding again that the Arabic pronunciation should be correct for recitation. There is a real risk of changing the intended meaning, by mispronouncing a particular letter or vowel, resulting in a horrendous alteration of meaning. For example, when addressing Allah, a single change of vowel will change 'I asked for forgiveness' into 'You asked for forgiveness!!' Non-Arab speakers need to learn the correct pronunciation of the Arabic letters. Indian subcontinent Muslims particularly do not appreciate this, under a false sense of security due to the similarity of their native Urdu script to Arabic. Native Arab speakers, on the other hand, often fail to realise that recitation of the Quran is not like normal speech, but it has rules of recitation known as *tajweed*.

Community

It should be quite apparent by now that this value runs deep in Islam. Islam is not just about the individual, it is also about building strong functional communities. This can be seen in the obligations and recommendations made about character, and the rights of others.

A Muslim has obligations to look after and serve their parents, their spouse, their children, their neighbours. They are to continue to maintain family ties, even with those who seek to sever them. They are to uphold the highest character and conduct with others, yet not to judge anyone else. Orphans are protected and raised. Ritual prayer in congregation is strongly recommended and receives extra reward, promoting regular social interactions. Charity is mandatory to help the needy in society, and voluntary supererogatory charity carries great additional reward. Modesty in dress and behaviour is mandated to guard against fornication and adultery. These latter vices along with others such as alcohol, intoxicants, gambling, and usury are prohibited in large part for how they ultimately destroy communities.

On the spiritual side, the backbone of the ritual prayer comprises a prayer at its start, aptly named 'The Opening' (Chapter 1 - *Surah al-Fatiha*). The second half of this *surah* supplicates Allah for guidance and help:

*You alone **we** worship and You alone **we** ask for help.*

*Guide **us** to the straight path*

The path of those upon whom You have bestowed Your favours

Not the one of those who earned Your wrath, or those who are lost. *{Quran 1: 4-7}*

Note the wording of this prayer is 'We', not 'I'. We supplicate not just for ourselves, but also for our brethren. This is mirrored by the conclusion of the ritual prayer (*salat*), where one recites the same supplication as was made by Prophet Ibrahim (Abraham), asking Allah for forgiveness for oneself, one's parents, and *all the Believers until the Day of Judgement*.[152]

Islam is about 'We' not 'I'.

---

[152] Quran 14:41

Conclusions

We have come to the end of our exploration of the basic concepts of Islam. I would like to thank the dear reader, and I hope you enjoyed the book. The concepts in Islam are beautiful and seamlessly interwoven. I have tried to unpick them bit by bit for the reader, and, after giving the basics, build on them, and slot them back together. This book has been about collating basic and essential principles of Islam, simplifying them, and translating them to practical application. I hope this will accelerate the journey of Islam for young Muslims looking to increase their knowledge, as well as aid parents and teachers in teaching Islam to little children.

As a word of caution, readers should not try to derive legal rulings based on this book. The field of *fiqh* (legal rulings) is extensive and detailed. Anyone who has found themselves in a predicament, needing advice, should consult reliable scholars or imams.

I would reiterate a few points I made in the *Introduction*. I have not presented an exclusive interpretation of Islam. A difference of opinion is part of Islam, and other knowledgeable Muslims may have different and valid views. I am not a scholar, but a student of knowledge. I apologise for any shortcomings on my part. Moving forwards, I would encourage the reader to continue their journey of knowledge with authentic teachers and institutes.

Figure 6: Summary flow diagram of some basic concepts

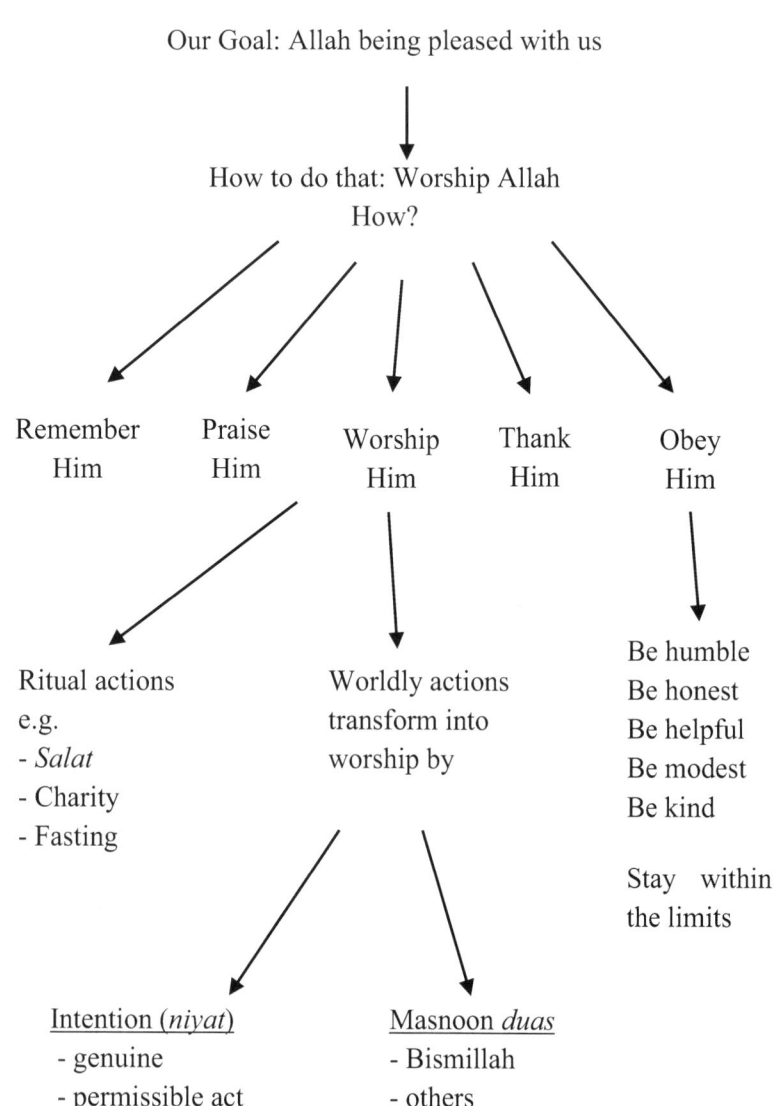

Our Goal: Allah being pleased with us

How to do that: Worship Allah
How?

Remember Him   Praise Him   Worship Him   Thank Him   Obey Him

Ritual actions
e.g.
- *Salat*
- Charity
- Fasting

Worldly actions
transform into
worship by

Be humble
Be honest
Be helpful
Be modest
Be kind

Stay within the limits

Intention (*niyat*)
- genuine
- permissible act

Masnoon *duas*
- Bismillah
- others

Further Reading

Tenets of belief

Aqeedah Tahawiyyah (The Creed of Imam Abu Ja'far At-Tahawi)

Although a very short work (more of a pamphlet), it summarises core beliefs of Islam. It can be found online, for example:

https://bit.ly/2V0kvPx

The text is best understood by studying with a teacher to understand the implications and nuances. There are commentaries on his work too, that try to convey the depth of meaning.

Philosophical discussion and Islamic theism

Hamza Andreas Tzortzis. *The Divine Reality – God, Islam and the mirage of Atheism* (San Clemente: FB Publishing 2018)

A superb coverage of arguments for the existence of God, Islam's perspective and a compelling clinical deconstruction of atheistic arguments.

The miracle of the Quran

Nouman Ali Khan & Sharif Randhawa. *Divine Speech: Exploring the Quran as Literature* (Euless,Texas: Bayyinah 2016)

Simply outstanding coverage of some of the astonishing features of the Quran that show emphatically how only God could have produced it. It builds on some of the work of Raymond Farrin, but covers more linguistic features. Very easy to read. This is a must read for Muslims.

Raymond Farrin. *Structure and Qur'anic Interpretation: A Study of Symmetry and Coherence in Islam's Holy Text* (Ashland, Oregon: White Cloud Press 2014)

Scholarly work, but easily readable. Demonstrates the incredible ring symmetries seen in the Quran's structure.

How-to-do Books

Mohammad Akram Nadwi:

Al-Fiqh Al-Islami: According to the Hanafi Madhab volume 1: Rites of Purification, Prayers and Funerals (London: Angelwing, 2007).

Al-Fiqh Al-Islami: According to the Hanafi Madhab volume 2: Rites of Zakat, Fasting and Hajj (London: Angelwing, 2012).

Both excellent works detailing how to undertake the basic rituals such as ablution (*wudu*), ritual prayer (*salat*) etc. with their evidences, according to the Hanafi schools of *fiqh* (legal thought).

Character of the Prophet Muhammad

Imam Abdallah Sirajuddin al-Husayni. *Our Master Muhammad ﷺ The Messenger of Allah. His sublime character and exalted attributes.* Translated by Khalid Williams (Rotterdam: Sunni Publications. 2016).

Written in two volumes, a beautiful and very comprehensive portrait of the sublime character of the Prophet Muhammad, with supporting evidences.

DNA and information

Stephen Meyer. *Signature in the Cell: DNA and the evidence for Intelligent Design.* (USA: Harper Collins, 2009).

Thorough scientific exploration of DNA linking to the concept of information. Very well written and easy to read, even for non-scientific people. The complexity and information content of DNA lead to no conclusion other than there must be God.

Health

Raymond Francis. *Never be Sick again: Health is a choice* (Health Communications Inc 2002).

A radical and thoughtful approach to health and wellbeing. A must read for understanding what being healthy really is and the lifestyle choices that need to be made.

Online resources

Bayyinah Institute

https://bayyinahtv.com/

An outstanding online resource led by Nouman Ali Khan. Superbly organised, erudite with relevant contemporary application of Islam. Courses range from learning Arabic to Quran studies (*tafseer*) and other thematic courses.

Al Salam Institute: https://alsalam.ac.uk/

Cambridge Islamic College: https://www.cambridgeislamiccollege.org/

Both of these teaching institutes are led by Shaykh Akram Nadwi. Both are superbly organised, with extensive and scholarly coverage of Islamic disciplines across the board from learning Arabic, to Quran studies (*tafseer*) to hadith to *fiqh*, etc. Both are superb resources.

Utrujj

https://www.utrujj.org/

Led by Shaykh Haythim Tamim, an outstanding resource, providing balanced insightful application of Islam for the modern age, and a very useful section for children on giving Muslim assemblies at school.

Yaqeen Institute of Research

https://yaqeeninstitute.org/

An excellent online resource that gives scholarly analyses of contemporary issues.

Printed in Great Britain
by Amazon